INSECT
Emporium

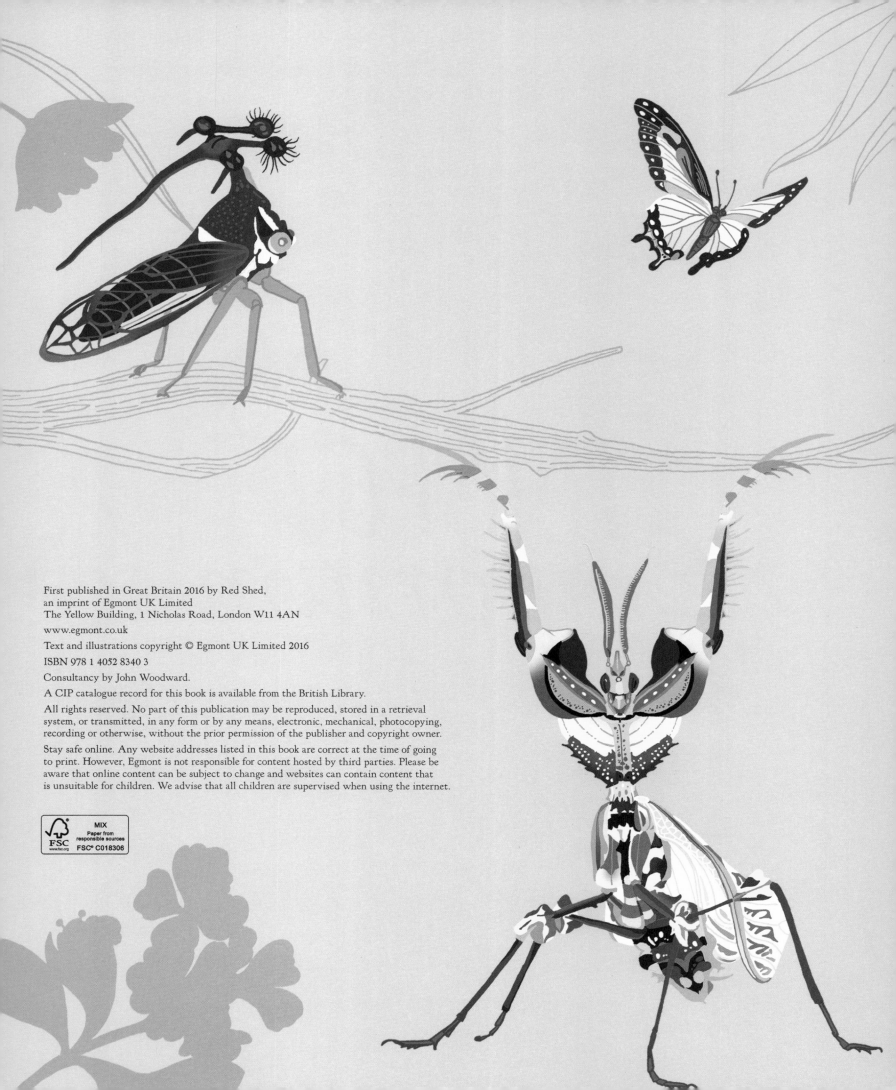

First published in Great Britain 2016 by Red Shed,
an imprint of Egmont UK Limited
The Yellow Building, 1 Nicholas Road, London W11 4AN
www.egmont.co.uk

Text and illustrations copyright © Egmont UK Limited 2016

ISBN 978 1 4052 8340 3

Consultancy by John Woodward.

A CIP catalogue record for this book is available from the British Library.

MIX
Paper from
responsible sources
FSC® C018306

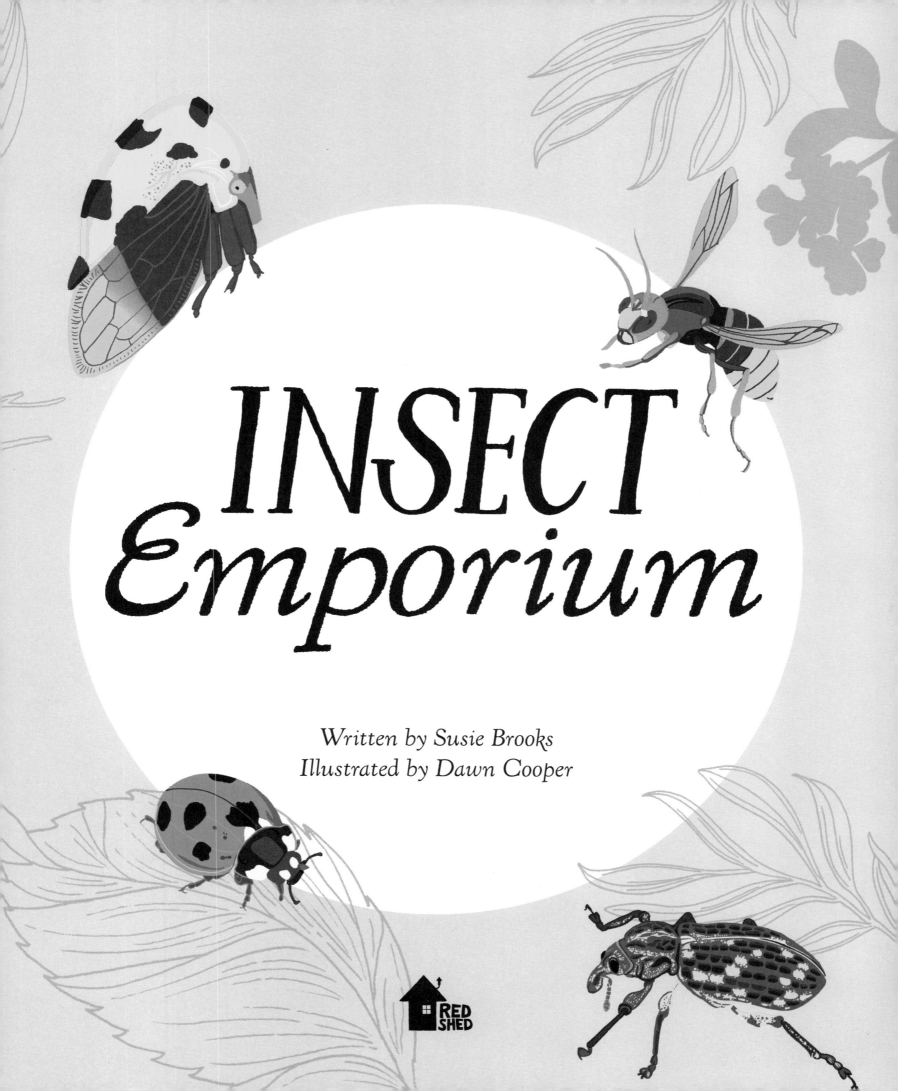

INSECT
Emporium

Written by Susie Brooks
Illustrated by Dawn Cooper

RED SHED

Contents

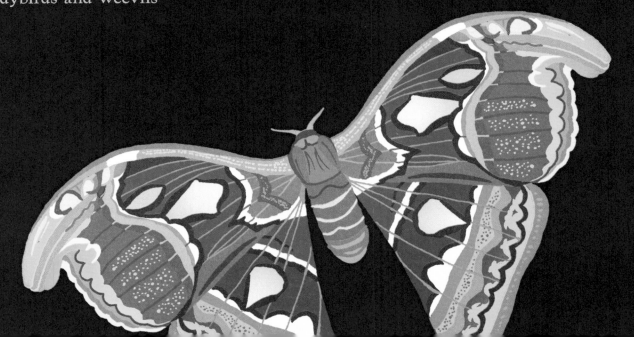

Welcome to the Emporium

Insects roam our planet, often unseen yet they are the most successful creatures alive. They have conquered every continent, outnumbered other animals and survived for 400 million years. For every human there may be 200 million insects.

Head and eyes

Insects see through domed compound eyes, with up to tens of thousands of receptors that detect light. Although their eyes can't capture detail or things far away, they can see motion and shapes in all directions.

Thorax

Legs and wings attach to the thorax, which often contains powerful flight muscles.

Legs

Three pairs of jointed legs enable the insect to walk. Many insects have hearing organs on their 'knees'.

About 73% of all animal species are insects.

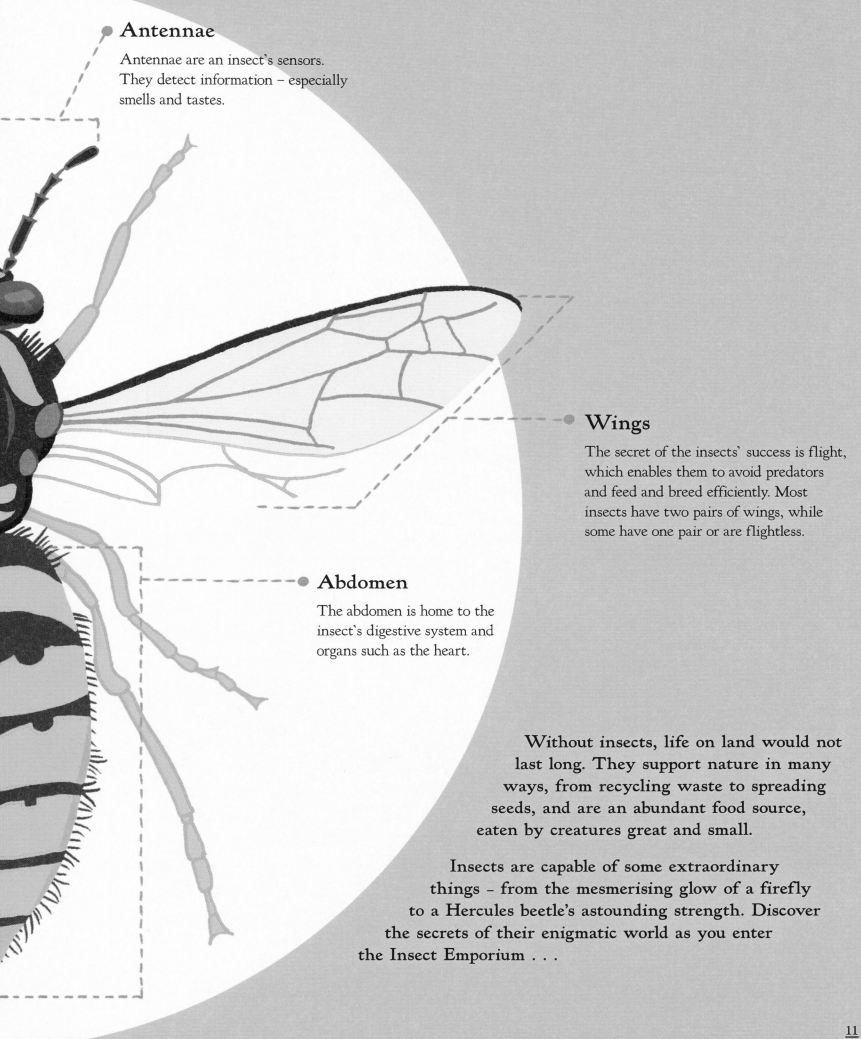

Antennae

Antennae are an insect's sensors. They detect information – especially smells and tastes.

Wings

The secret of the insects' success is flight, which enables them to avoid predators and feed and breed efficiently. Most insects have two pairs of wings, while some have one pair or are flightless.

Abdomen

The abdomen is home to the insect's digestive system and organs such as the heart.

Without insects, life on land would not last long. They support nature in many ways, from recycling waste to spreading seeds, and are an abundant food source, eaten by creatures great and small.

Insects are capable of some extraordinary things – from the mesmerising glow of a firefly to a Hercules beetle's astounding strength. Discover the secrets of their enigmatic world as you enter the Insect Emporium . . .

Life cycles

Contained within a rigid exoskeleton,
insects must shed their skin as they
grow. Many change form entirely in
a fascinating series of life stages.

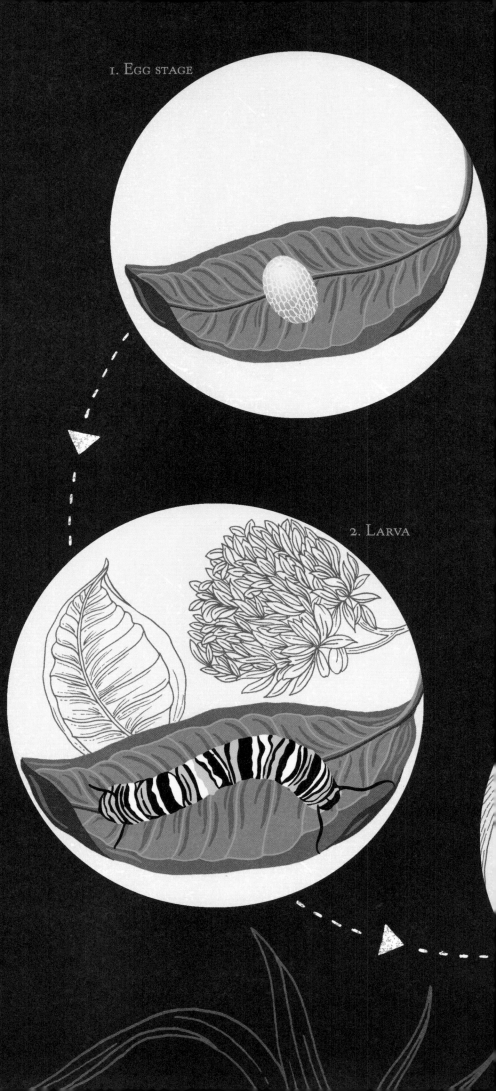

2. Larva

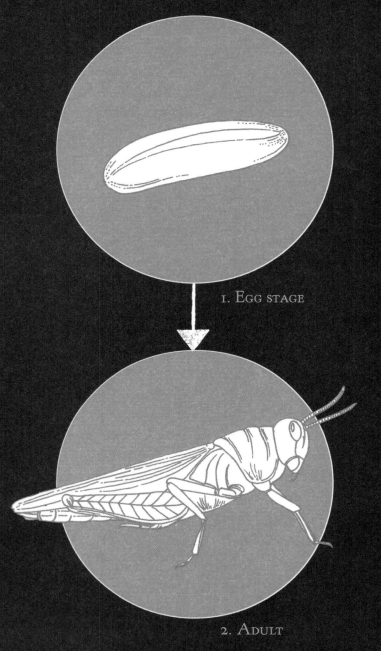

1. Egg stage

2. Adult

Simple metamorphosis

For some insects, such as grasshoppers, life is simple.
They hatch from an egg as a miniature version of
the adult and then moult repeatedly as they grow.

Complete metamorphosis

The young, or larvae, of many insects seem like distinct creatures in themselves. They eat and grow, then mysteriously shape-shift inside a shell-like pupa, rebuilding themselves into a dramatic new form.

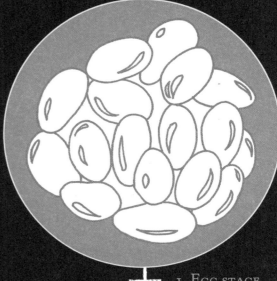

1. EGG STAGE

4. ADULT

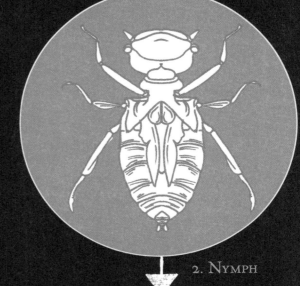

2. NYMPH

3. ADULT

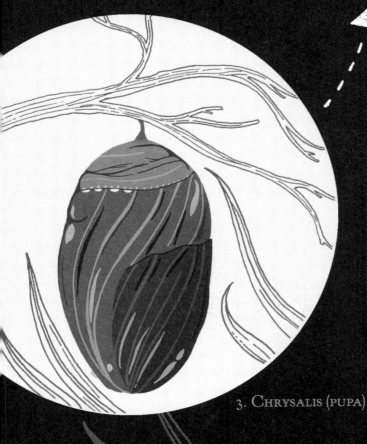

3. CHRYSALIS (PUPA)

Incomplete metamorphosis

Insects such as dragonflies begin life under water as wingless nymphs and then moult many times as they grow, until they finally emerge out of the water as elegant airborne adults.

From caterpillar to butterfly

TAILED EMPEROR CATERPILLAR
Polyura sempronius

TAILED EMPEROR BUTTERFLY
Polyura sempronius

METALMARK CATERPILLAR
Calephelis virginiensis

METALMARK BUTTERFLY
Calephelis virginiensis

QUEEN ALEXANDRA'S
BIRDWING CATERPILLAR
Ornithoptera alexandrae

ASIAN SWALLOWTAIL CATERPILLAR
Papilio xuthus

ASIAN SWALLOWTAIL BUTTERFLY
Papilio xuthus

GLASSWINGED BUTTERFLY
Greta oto

GLASSWINGED CATERPILLAR
Greta oto

QUEEN ALEXANDRA'S
BIRDWING BUTTERFLY
Ornithoptera alexandrae

From caterpillar to moth

ATLAS CATERPILLAR
Attacus atlas

ATLAS MOTH
Attacus atlas

GLASS JEWEL CATERPILLAR
Acraga coa

GLASS JEWEL MOTH
Acraga coa

ARCTIC WOOLLY BEAR MOTH
Gynaephora groenlandica

ARCTIC WOOLLY BEAR CATERPILLAR
Gynaephora groenlandica

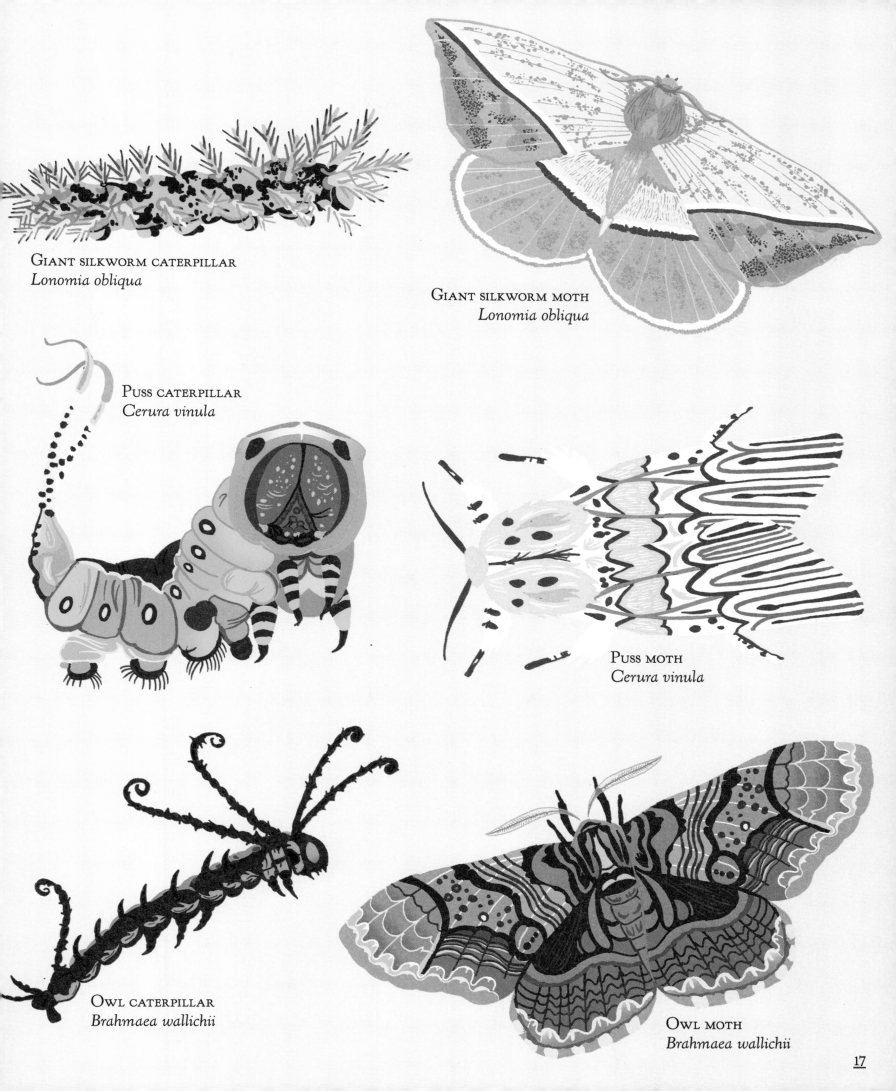

GIANT SILKWORM CATERPILLAR
Lonomia obliqua

GIANT SILKWORM MOTH
Lonomia obliqua

PUSS CATERPILLAR
Cerura vinula

PUSS MOTH
Cerura vinula

OWL CATERPILLAR
Brahmaea wallichii

OWL MOTH
Brahmaea wallichii

Dragonflies

Swooping deftly on mighty wings, a dragonfly sights its prey. Quick as a flash, this powerful hunter thrusts its six legs into a basket shape and snatches its victim in mid-air.

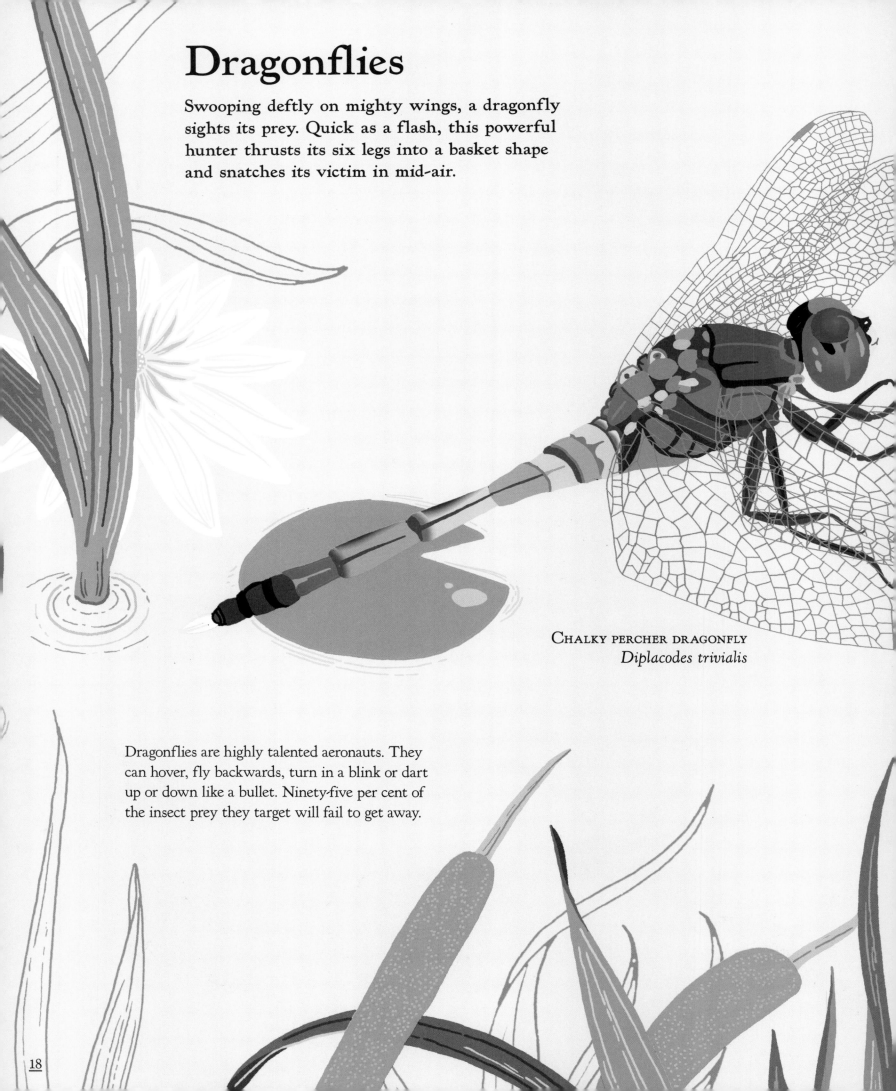

CHALKY PERCHER DRAGONFLY
Diplacodes trivialis

Dragonflies are highly talented aeronauts. They can hover, fly backwards, turn in a blink or dart up or down like a bullet. Ninety-five per cent of the insect prey they target will fail to get away.

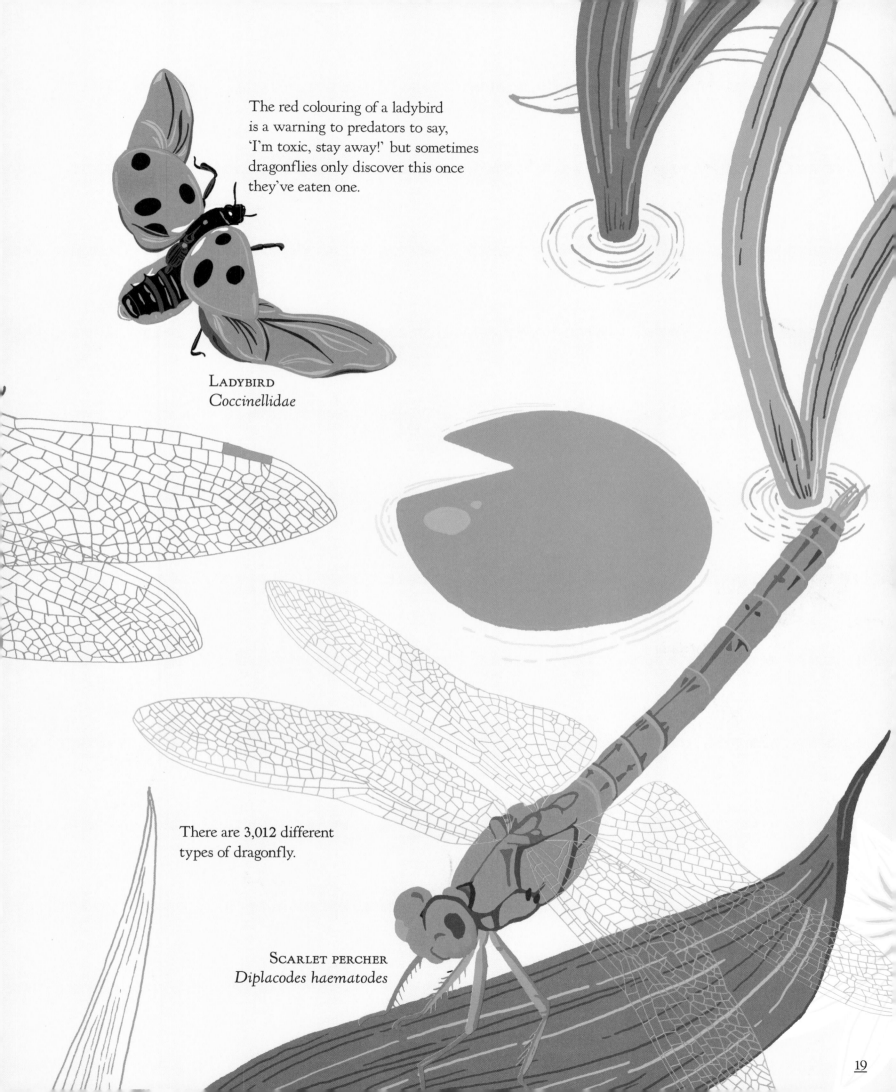

The red colouring of a ladybird is a warning to predators to say, 'I'm toxic, stay away!' but sometimes dragonflies only discover this once they've eaten one.

LADYBIRD
Coccinellidae

There are 3,012 different types of dragonfly.

SCARLET PERCHER
Diplacodes haematodes

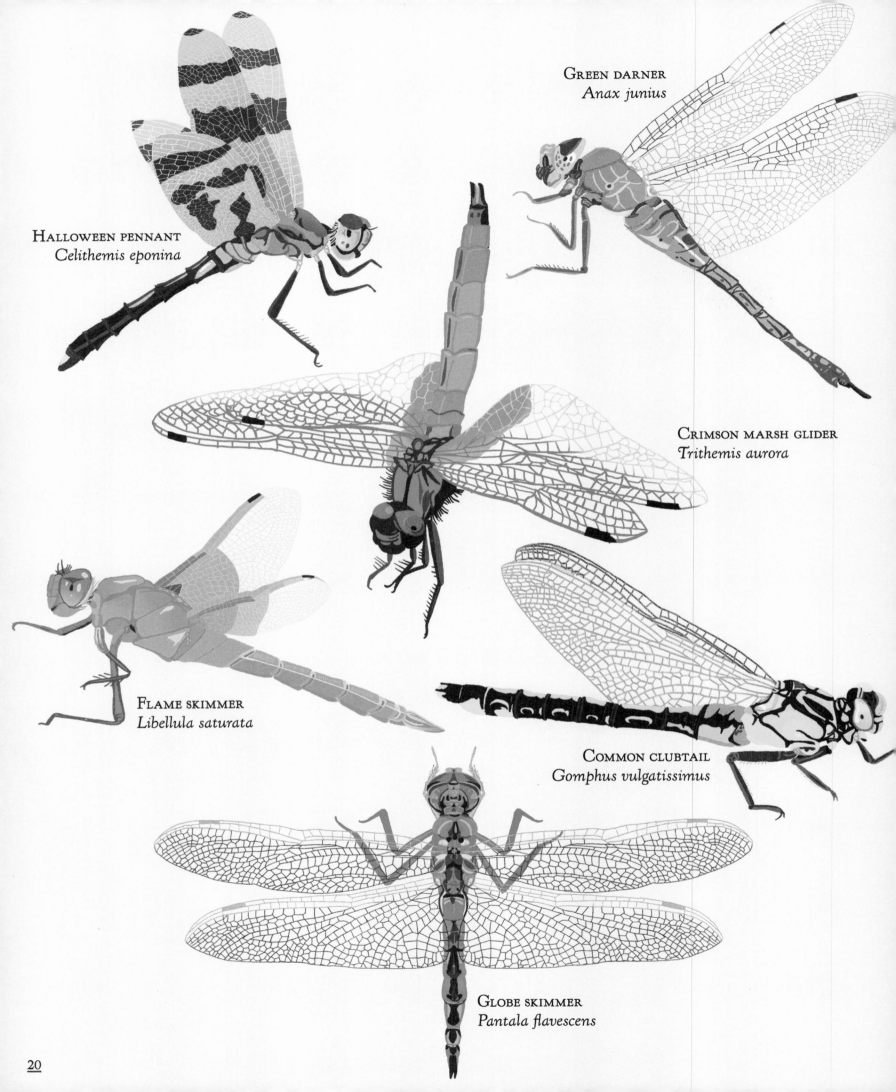

HALLOWEEN PENNANT
Celithemis eponina

GREEN DARNER
Anax junius

CRIMSON MARSH GLIDER
Trithemis aurora

FLAME SKIMMER
Libellula saturata

COMMON CLUBTAIL
Gomphus vulgatissimus

GLOBE SKIMMER
Pantala flavescens

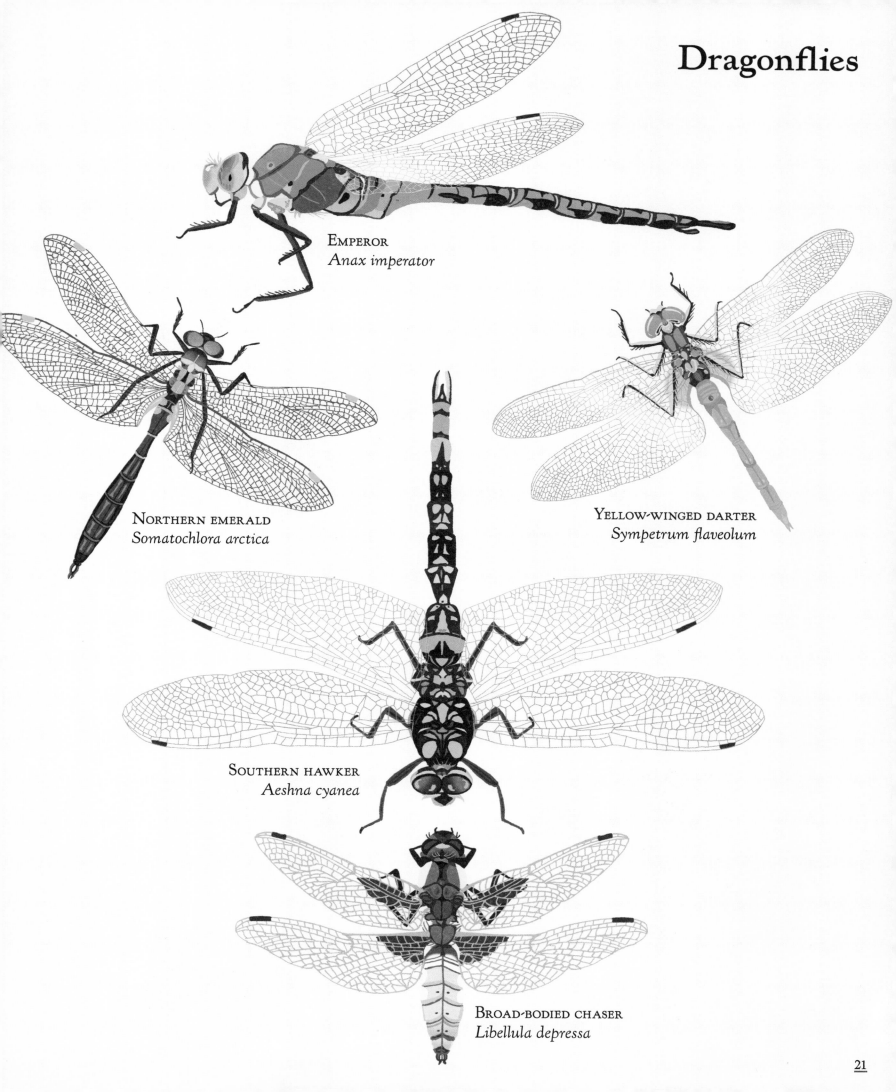

Dragonflies

EMPEROR
Anax imperator

NORTHERN EMERALD
Somatochlora arctica

YELLOW-WINGED DARTER
Sympetrum flaveolum

SOUTHERN HAWKER
Aeshna cyanea

BROAD-BODIED CHASER
Libellula depressa

Honeybees and wasps

The lightning-fast beat of delicate wings fills the air with a buzzing sound. A swarm of honeybees sets to work, busily building a nest. The bees live in harmony, but if danger threatens . . . their secret weapon is a painful sting.

HONEYBEE DRONE
(ALL MALES)

A single queen bee rules the honeybee nest. Nursed and fed by an army of female worker bees, she lays up to 2,000 eggs a day. Stingless male drone bees have one purpose in life – to mate with a queen; then they die.

HONEYBEE
Apis mellifera
WORKER (ALL FEMALES)

QUEEN BEE

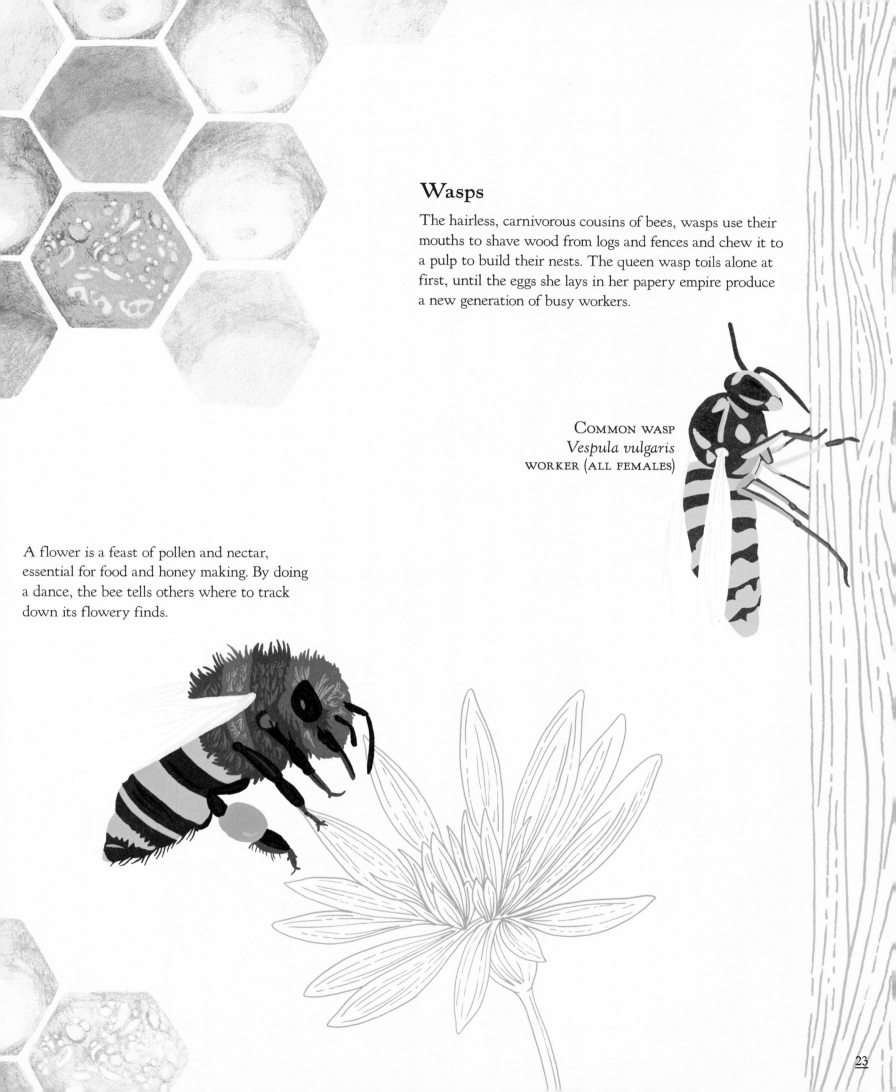

Wasps

The hairless, carnivorous cousins of bees, wasps use their mouths to shave wood from logs and fences and chew it to a pulp to build their nests. The queen wasp toils alone at first, until the eggs she lays in her papery empire produce a new generation of busy workers.

COMMON WASP
Vespula vulgaris
WORKER (ALL FEMALES)

A flower is a feast of pollen and nectar, essential for food and honey making. By doing a dance, the bee tells others where to track down its flowery finds.

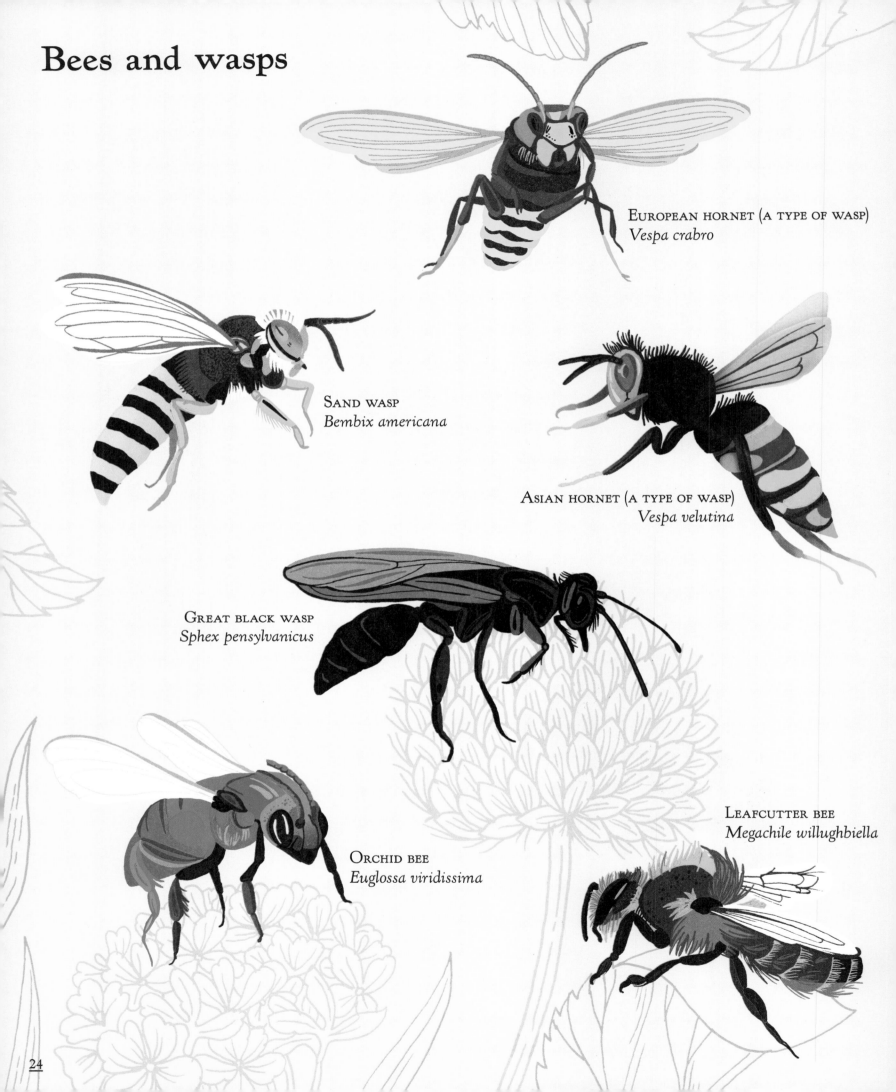

Bees and wasps

EUROPEAN HORNET (A TYPE OF WASP)
Vespa crabro

SAND WASP
Bembix americana

ASIAN HORNET (A TYPE OF WASP)
Vespa velutina

GREAT BLACK WASP
Sphex pensylvanicus

LEAFCUTTER BEE
Megachile willughbiella

ORCHID BEE
Euglossa viridissima

RED MASON BEE (MALE)
Osmia bicornis

RED MASON BEE (FEMALE)
Osmia bicornis

BUFF-TAILED BUMBLEBEE (QUEEN)
Bombus terrestris

BUFF-TAILED BUMBLEBEE
(WORKER)
Bombus terrestris

CALIFORNIA CARPENTER BEE
Xylocopa californica

BLUE-BANDED BEE
Amegilla cingulata

TAWNY MINING BEE
Andrena fulva

25

COMMON HOUSEFLY
Musca domestica

MARMALADE HOVERFLY
Episyrphus balteatus

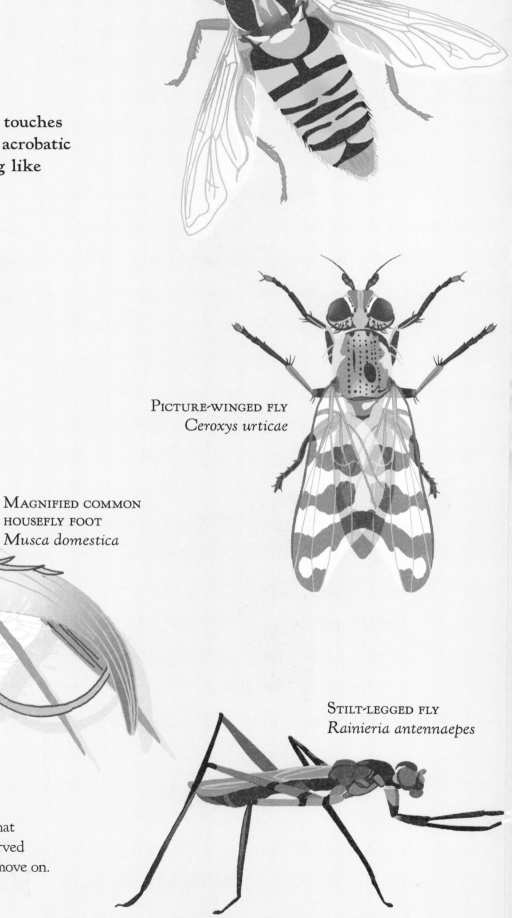

PICTURE-WINGED FLY
Ceroxys urticae

STILT-LEGGED FLY
Rainieria antennaepes

Flies

A simple swift somersault and a housefly touches down – upside down on the ceiling! This acrobatic insect clings with its feet and creeps along like a death-defying superhero.

MAGNIFIED COMMON
HOUSEFLY FOOT
Musca domestica

A fly's foot gets its grip from a sticky fluid that oozes from tiny hairs. A twitch from two curved claws is all it takes for the fly to unglue and move on.

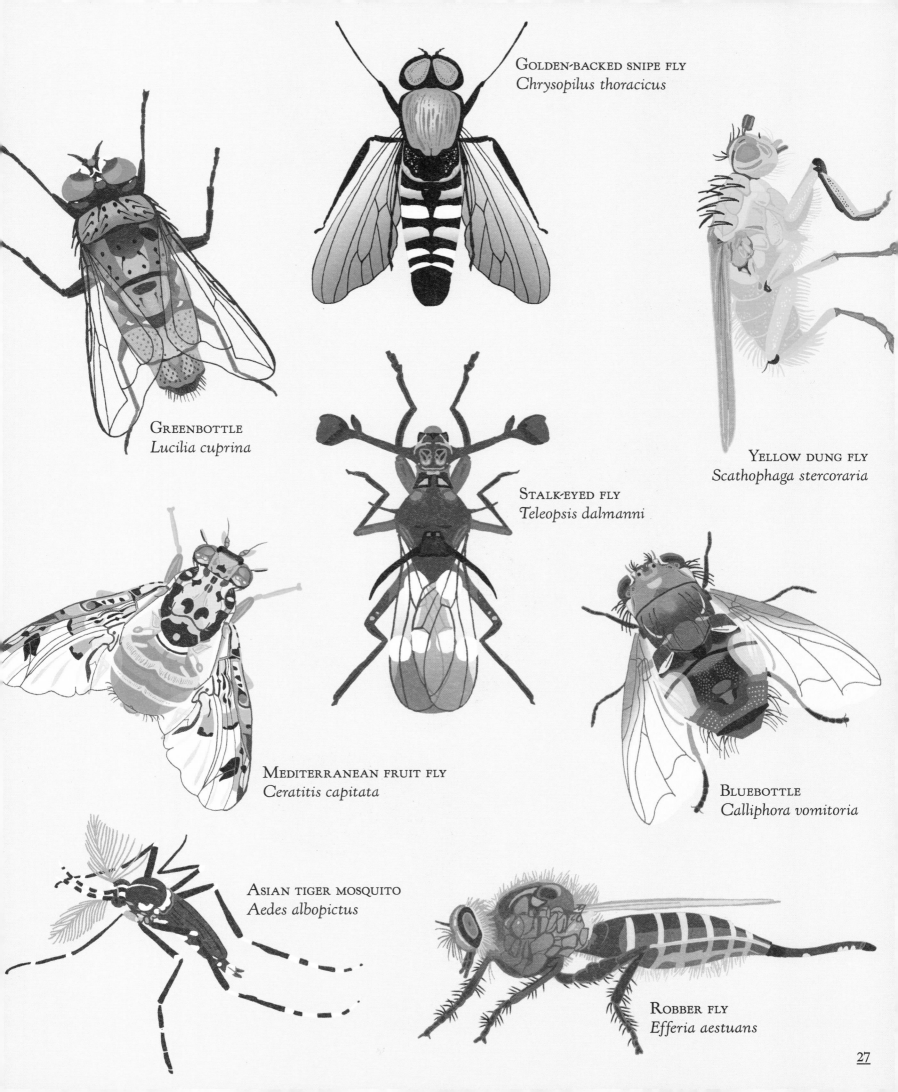

GOLDEN-BACKED SNIPE FLY
Chrysopilus thoracicus

GREENBOTTLE
Lucilia cuprina

YELLOW DUNG FLY
Scathophaga stercoraria

STALK-EYED FLY
Teleopsis dalmanni

MEDITERRANEAN FRUIT FLY
Ceratitis capitata

BLUEBOTTLE
Calliphora vomitoria

ASIAN TIGER MOSQUITO
Aedes albopictus

ROBBER FLY
Efferia aestuans

27

ANTLION
Palpares libelluloides

DOBSONFLY
Protohermes grandis

THREAD-WINGED ANTLION
Nemoptera bipennis

SILKY LACEWING
Psychopsis insolens

PIED LACEWING
Porismus strigatus

SNAKEFLY
Dichrostigma flavipes

DUSTY LACEWING
Coniopteryx species

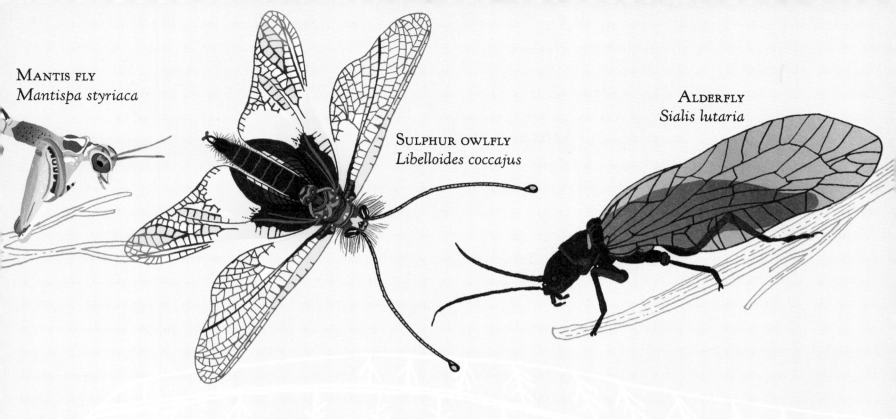

MANTIS FLY
Mantispa styriaca

SULPHUR OWLFLY
Libelloides coccajus

ALDERFLY
Sialis lutaria

Net-winged insects

More decorative than dynamic, net-winged insects
flit about on gossamer wings. They are feeble fliers
and usually emerge by night when the cloak of
darkness shields them from predators.

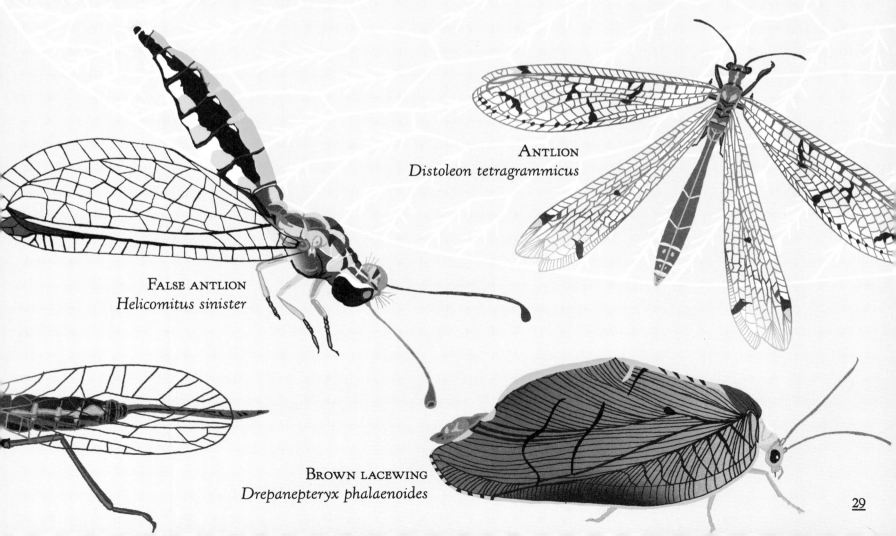

ANTLION
Distoleon tetragrammicus

FALSE ANTLION
Helicomitus sinister

BROWN LACEWING
Drepanepteryx phalaenoides

29

EUROPEAN GLOW-WORM
Lampyris noctiluca

Fireflies and glow-worms

Twinkling like stars in the dead of night, flashing in perfect unison . . . fireflies and glow-worms decorate their world with magical patterns of light. Every glint and glimmer is a secret code, known only by others of the same species.

FIREFLY
Photuris versicolor

Fireflies and glow-worms are beetles with
a difference – their own, natural light
source. This special, sparkling chemistry
helps them to attract a mate.

The railroad worm can glow both red
and green. It is thought that this light
show confuses predators or scares
them into staying away.

BIG DIPPER FIREFLY
Photinus pyralis

Darting and diving in a J-shaped
path, the big dipper firefly lights
the sky like a fairground ride!

RAILROAD WORM (FEMALE)
Phengodes plumosa

Hercules beetles aren't natural fliers, but their sturdy wings can propel them through the air. Often the glimmer of a light at night is the magnet that they'll head towards.

Hercules beetles
Dynastes hercules

Thrusting his horns like a pair of savage pincers, a male Hercules beetle storms into battle. He seizes his opponent in a full-body hold, sweeping him into the air before tossing him to the ground.

The aim of this impressive combat is to earn the winner a female mate. Incredibly, the Hercules beetle can lift 85 times its own weight. Other types of rhinoceros beetle have different-shaped horns for fighting their rivals.

Beetles

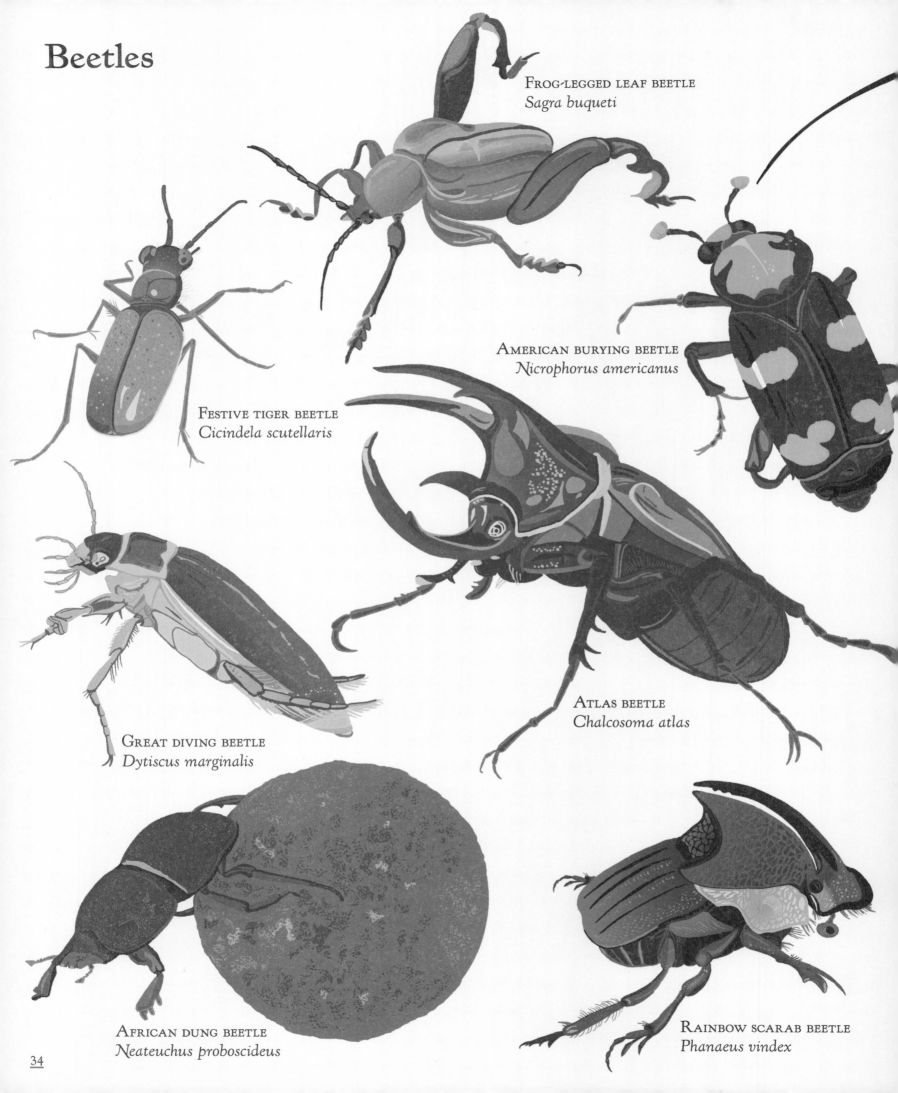

Frog-legged leaf beetle
Sagra buqueti

American burying beetle
Nicrophorus americanus

Festive tiger beetle
Cicindela scutellaris

Great diving beetle
Dytiscus marginalis

Atlas beetle
Chalcosoma atlas

African dung beetle
Neateuchus proboscideus

Rainbow scarab beetle
Phanaeus vindex

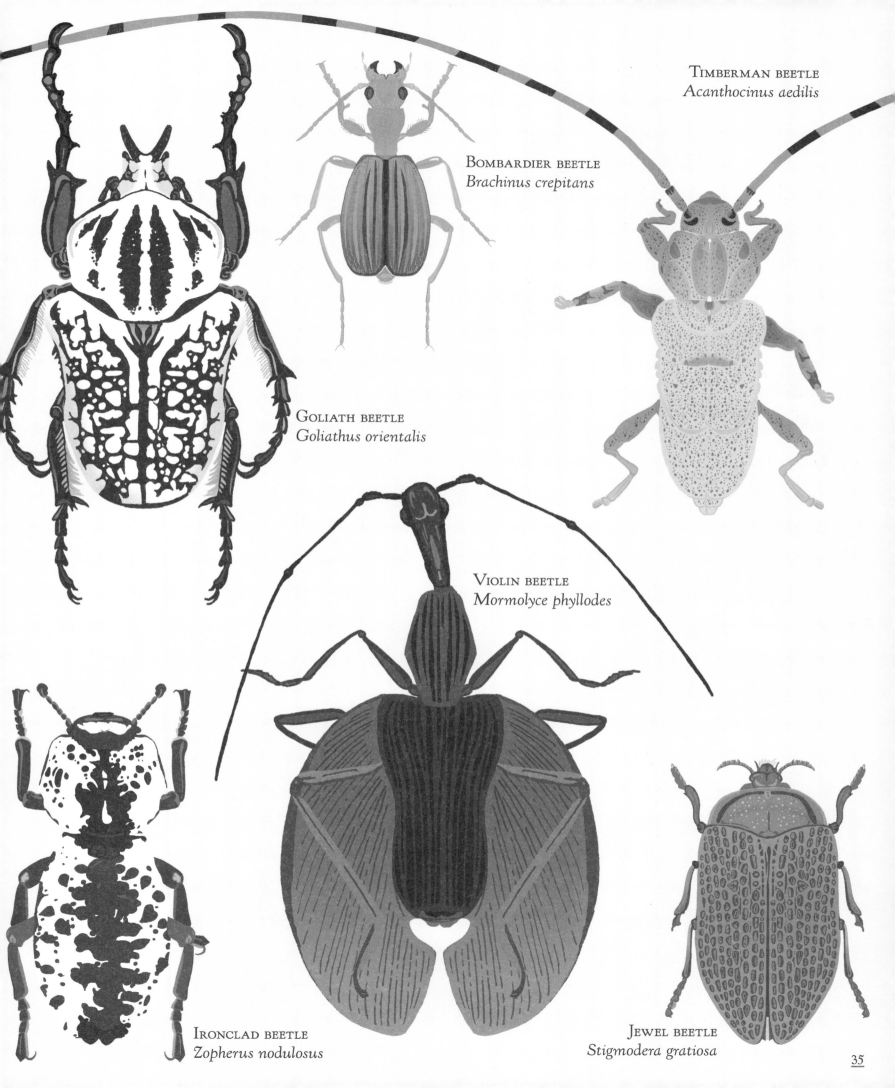

GOLIATH BEETLE
Goliathus orientalis

BOMBARDIER BEETLE
Brachinus crepitans

TIMBERMAN BEETLE
Acanthocinus aedilis

VIOLIN BEETLE
Mormolyce phyllodes

IRONCLAD BEETLE
Zopherus nodulosus

JEWEL BEETLE
Stigmodera gratiosa

35

Ladybirds

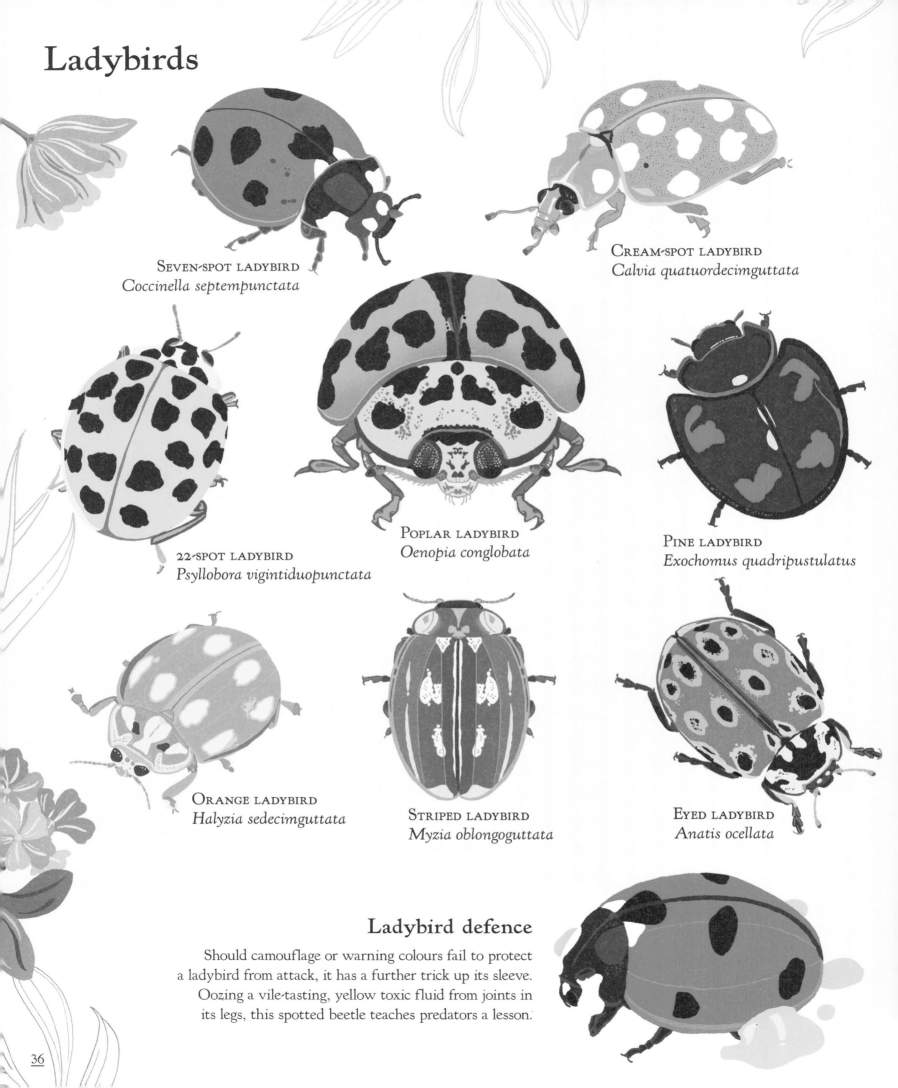

SEVEN-SPOT LADYBIRD
Coccinella septempunctata

CREAM-SPOT LADYBIRD
Calvia quatuordecimguttata

22-SPOT LADYBIRD
Psyllobora vigintiduopunctata

POPLAR LADYBIRD
Oenopia conglobata

PINE LADYBIRD
Exochomus quadripustulatus

ORANGE LADYBIRD
Halyzia sedecimguttata

STRIPED LADYBIRD
Myzia oblongoguttata

EYED LADYBIRD
Anatis ocellata

Ladybird defence

Should camouflage or warning colours fail to protect
a ladybird from attack, it has a further trick up its sleeve.
Oozing a vile-tasting, yellow toxic fluid from joints in
its legs, this spotted beetle teaches predators a lesson.

Figwort weevil
Cionus hortulanus

Bennett's painted weevil
Eupholus bennetti

Leaf weevil
Eupholus schoenherri

Weevils

Weevils are a vast and diverse group of beetles, usually recognised by their snouts. Tiny in size, they can be gigantic pests when invading crops or grain stores for food.

Cocklebur weevil
Rhodobaenus quinquepunctatus

Palmetto weevil
Rhynchophorus cruentatus

Nut weevil
Curculio nucum

Large pine weevil
Hylobius abietis

Bearded weevil
Lixus barbiger

Treehoppers

They seem like miniature aliens from a far-off planet, secretly invading Earth. Treehoppers are insects with a wide range of guises, all tailored to trick predators into thinking they're something they're not.

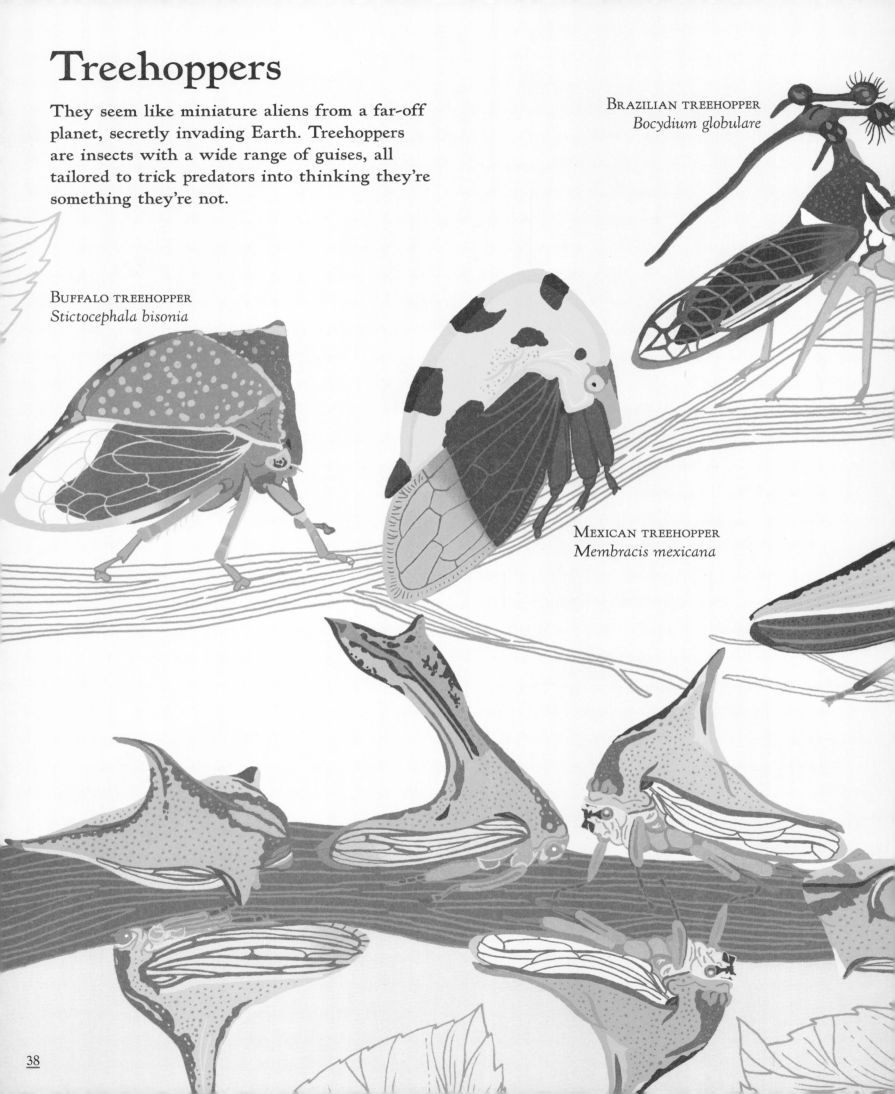

BRAZILIAN TREEHOPPER
Bocydium globulare

BUFFALO TREEHOPPER
Stictocephala bisonia

MEXICAN TREEHOPPER
Membracis mexicana

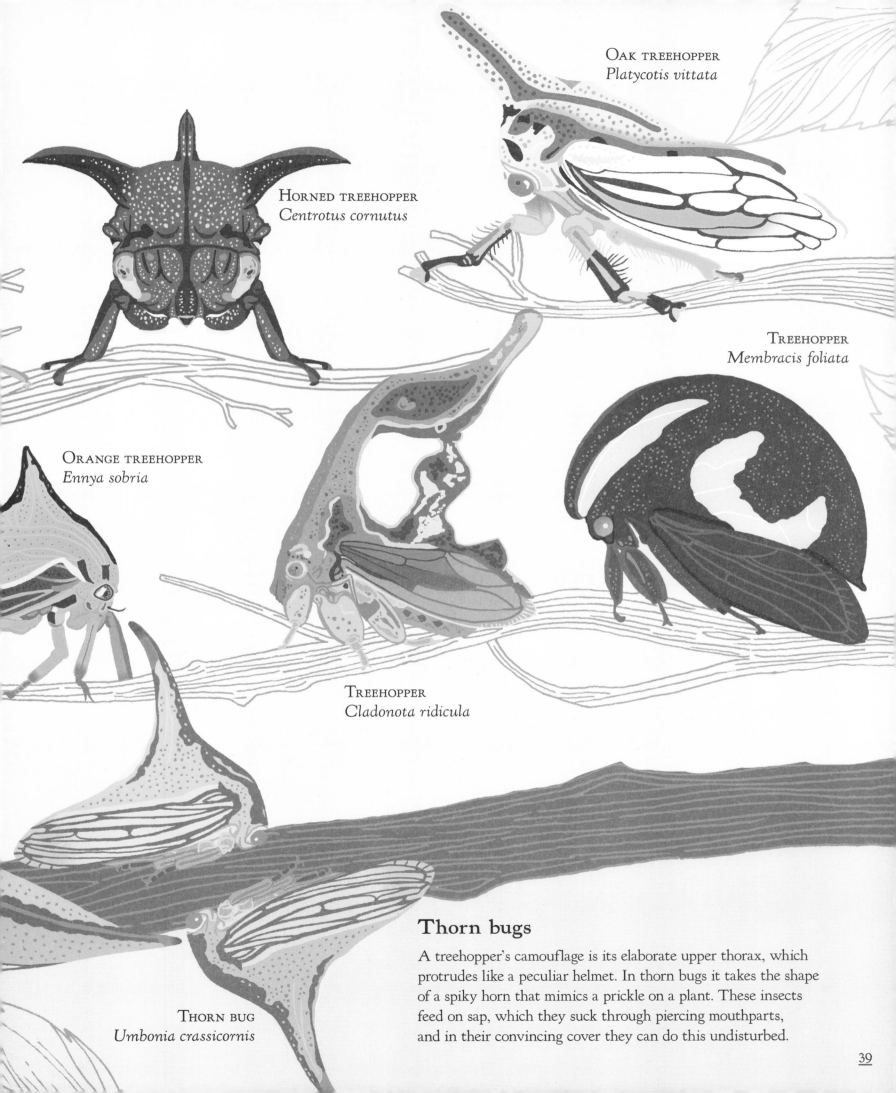

Oak treehopper
Platycotis vittata

Horned treehopper
Centrotus cornutus

Treehopper
Membracis foliata

Orange treehopper
Ennya sobria

Treehopper
Cladonota ridicula

Thorn bug
Umbonia crassicornis

Thorn bugs

A treehopper's camouflage is its elaborate upper thorax, which protrudes like a peculiar helmet. In thorn bugs it takes the shape of a spiky horn that mimics a prickle on a plant. These insects feed on sap, which they suck through piercing mouthparts, and in their convincing cover they can do this undisturbed.

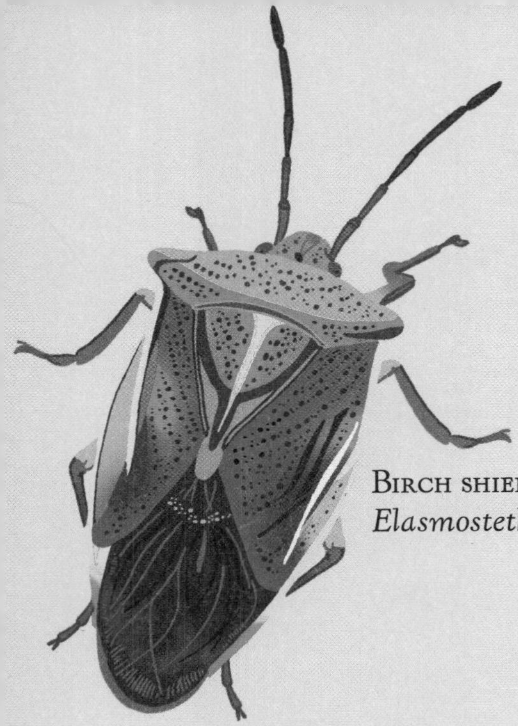

BIRCH SHIELD BUG
Elasmostethus interstinctus

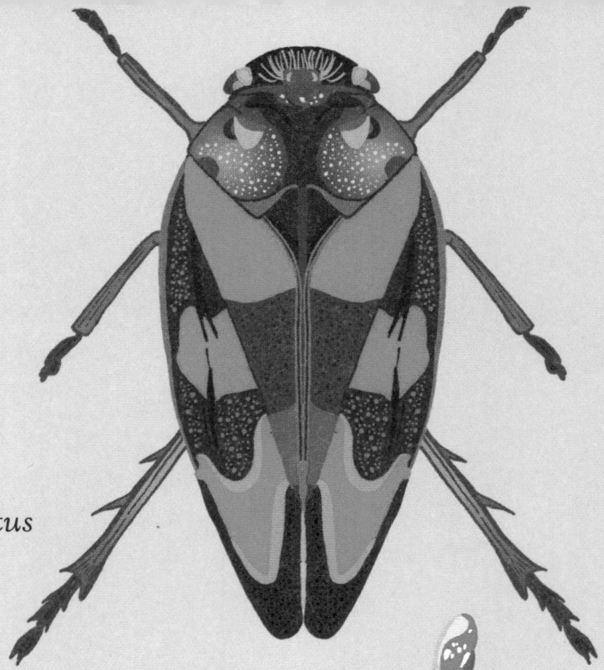

BLACK-AND-RED FROGHOPPER
Cercopis vulnerata

PINK POTATO APHID
Macrosiphum euphorbiae

True bugs

Some glide, some dive, others skate, leap or hop.
True bugs (order: Hemiptera) are incredibly diverse,
linked mainly by beak-like mouthparts and often
half-leathery wings. There are more than 80,000
species among them.

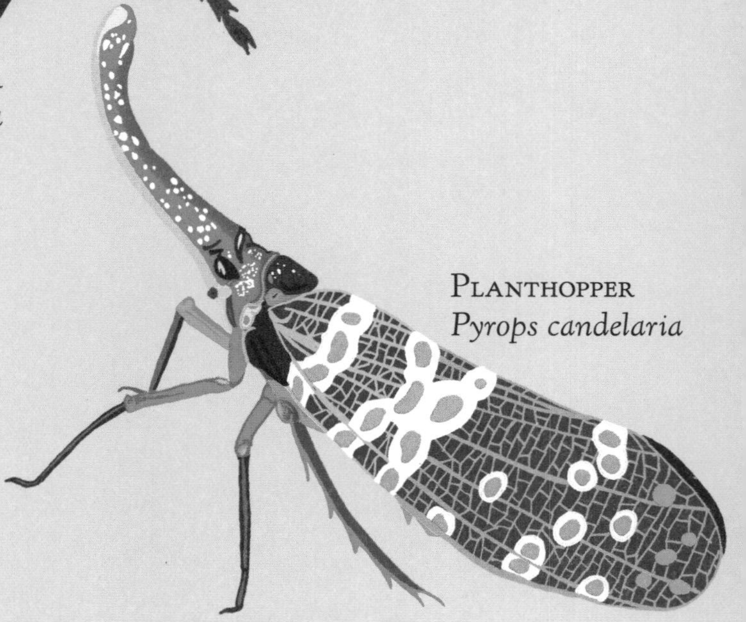

PLANTHOPPER
Pyrops candelaria

PEANUT-HEAD BUG
Fulgora laternaria

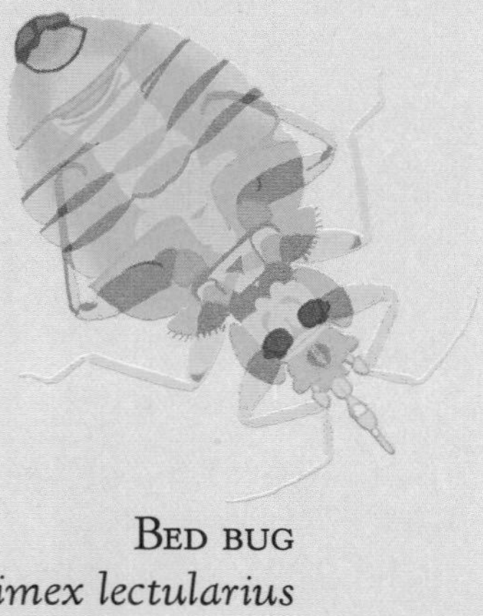

BED BUG
Cimex lectularius

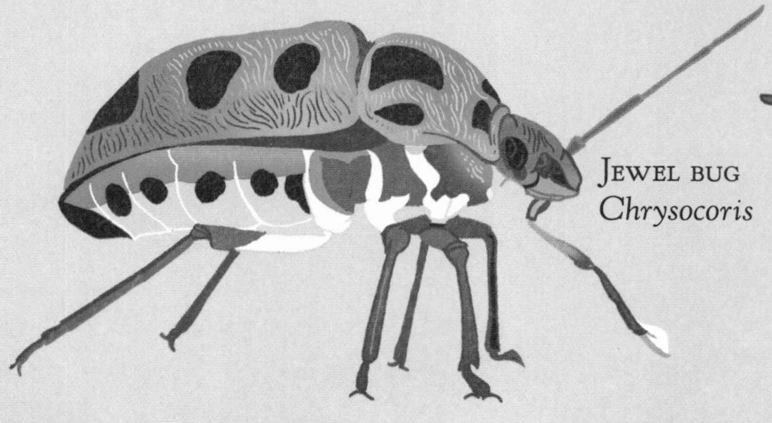

JEWEL BUG
Chrysocoris

STINK BUG
Banasa dimiata

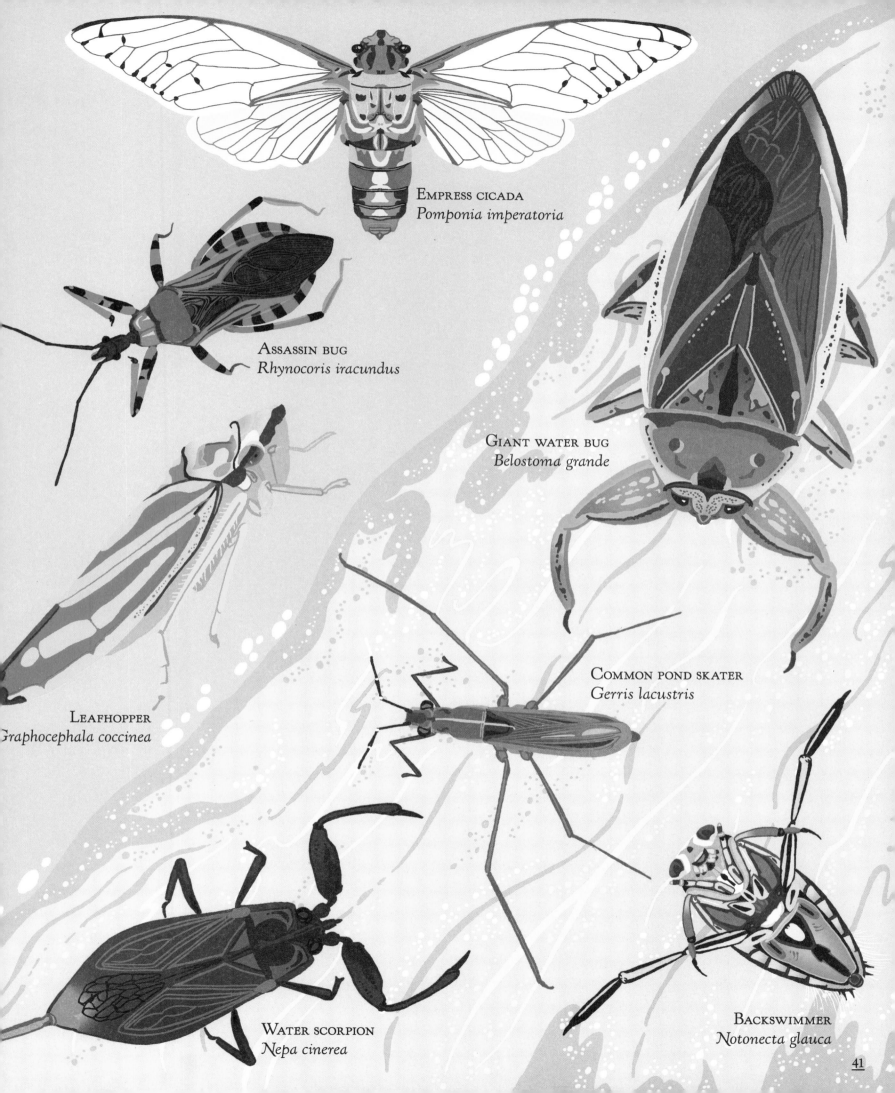

EMPRESS CICADA
Pomponia imperatoria

ASSASSIN BUG
Rhynocoris iracundus

GIANT WATER BUG
Belostoma grande

LEAFHOPPER
Graphocephala coccinea

COMMON POND SKATER
Gerris lacustris

WATER SCORPION
Nepa cinerea

BACKSWIMMER
Notonecta glauca

Termites and ants

They tunnel like miners through timber and turf, working in vast colonies. Ants and termites are social insects, born to serve specific roles within their group.

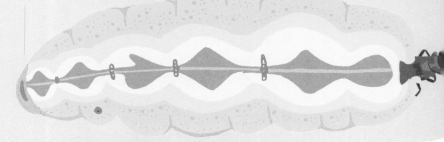

GIANT NORTHERN TERMITE QUEEN
Mastotermes darwiniensis

Giant northern
termite worker

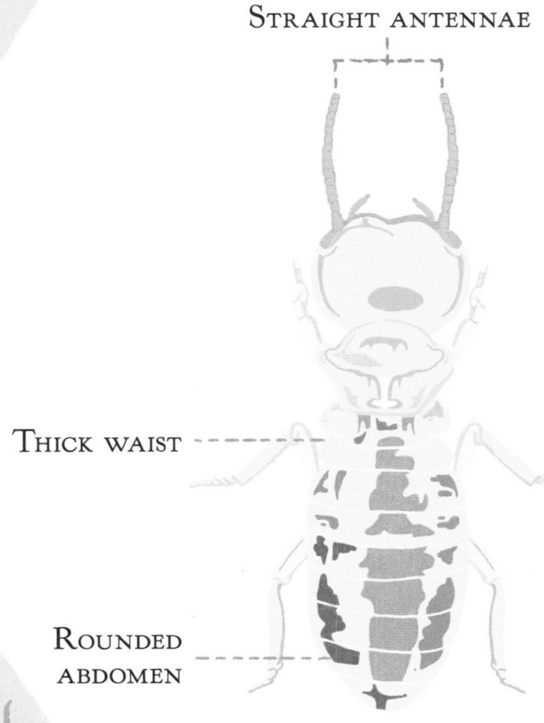

STRAIGHT ANTENNAE

THICK WAIST

ROUNDED
ABDOMEN

GIANT NORTHERN
TERMITE SOLDIER

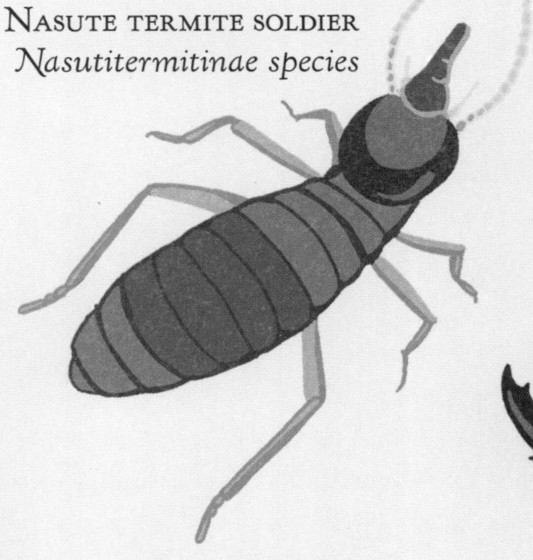

NASUTE TERMITE SOLDIER
Nasutitermitinae species

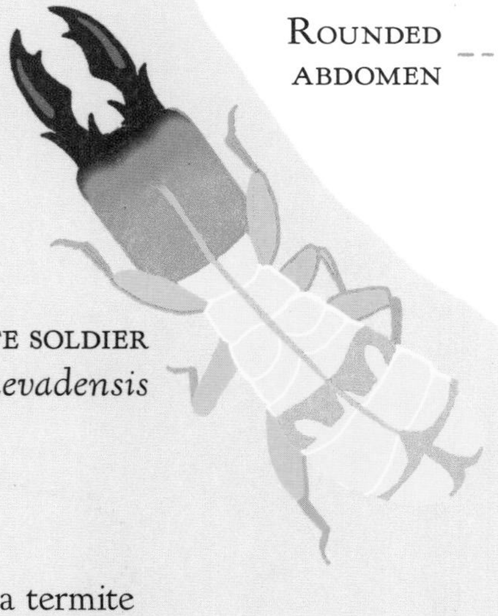

DAMPWOOD TERMITE SOLDIER
Zootermopsis nevadensis

Termite nests

Towering 5m high or more, a termite mound is the ultimate joint effort. This air-conditioned nest of soil, saliva and dung is built by workers, guarded by soldiers and ruled by an egg-laying queen.

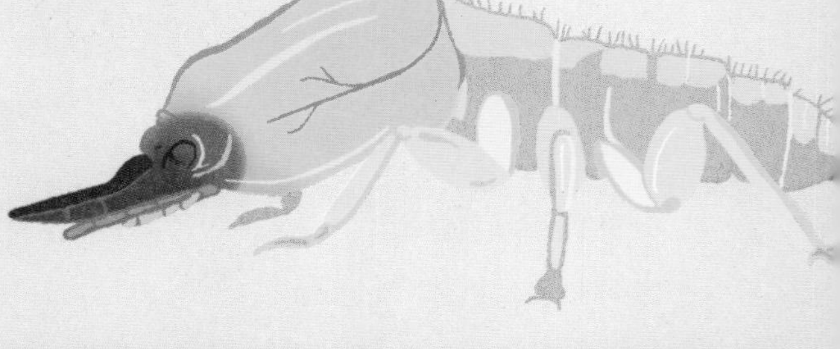

WESTERN SUBTERRANEAN
TERMITE SOLDIER
Reticulitermes hesperus

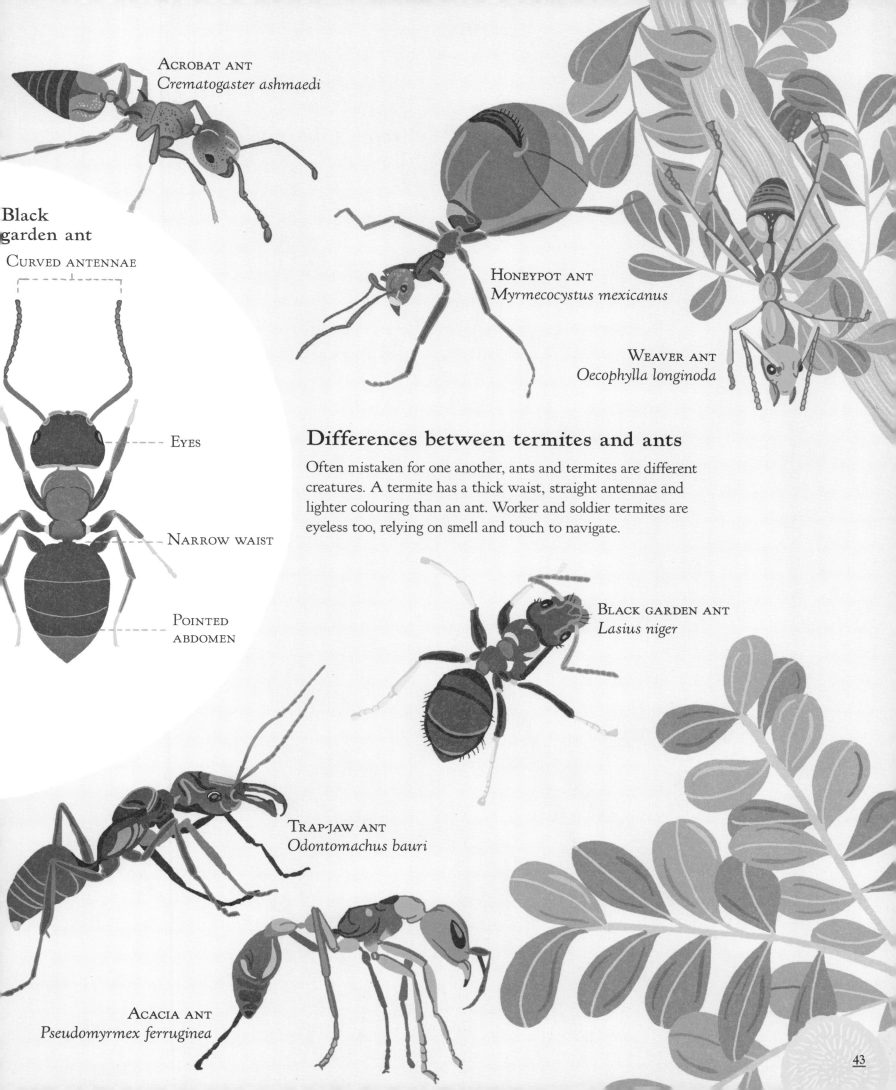

ACROBAT ANT
Crematogaster ashmaedi

Black garden ant

CURVED ANTENNAE

EYES

NARROW WAIST

POINTED ABDOMEN

HONEYPOT ANT
Myrmecocystus mexicanus

WEAVER ANT
Oecophylla longinoda

Differences between termites and ants

Often mistaken for one another, ants and termites are different creatures. A termite has a thick waist, straight antennae and lighter colouring than an ant. Worker and soldier termites are eyeless too, relying on smell and touch to navigate.

BLACK GARDEN ANT
Lasius niger

TRAP-JAW ANT
Odontomachus bauri

ACACIA ANT
Pseudomyrmex ferruginea

Leafcutter ants

A leafcutter ant attacks a plant like a miniature chainsaw. Then it hauls a slice of leaf determinedly onto its back, and joins its ant legion to march home.

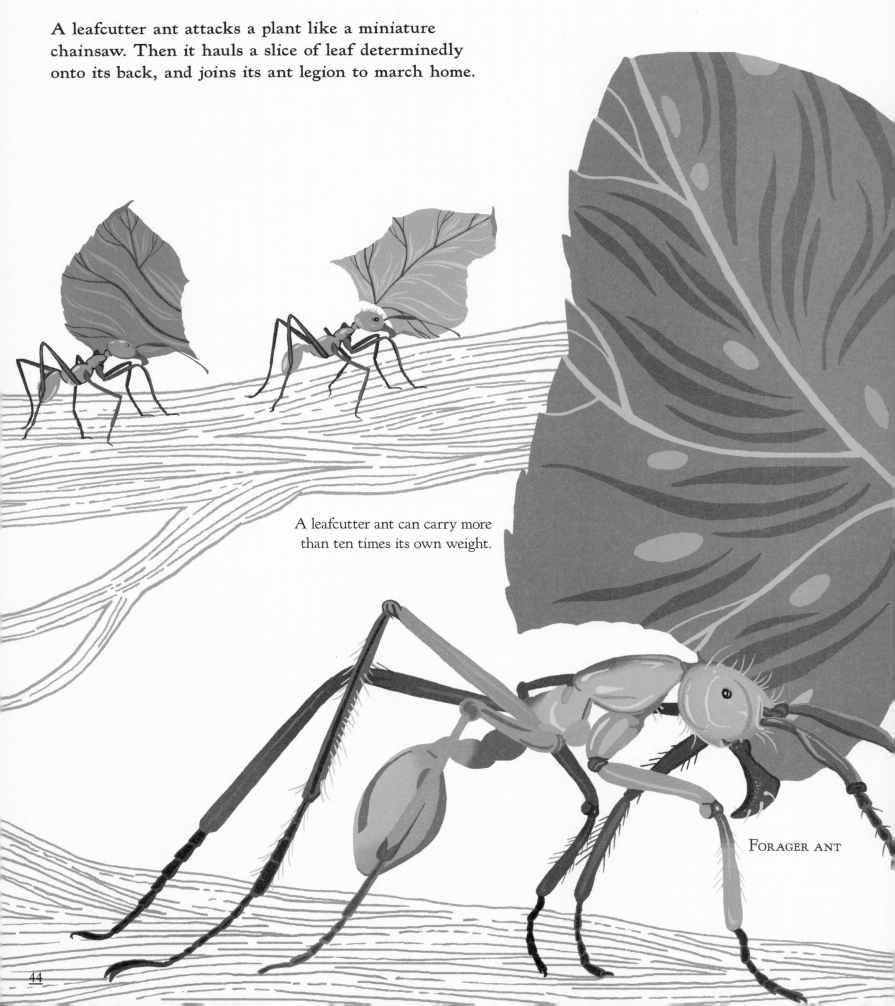

A leafcutter ant can carry more than ten times its own weight.

FORAGER ANT

Leafcutters are farmers – their mission is to feed fungus that the ants themselves will eat. Millions of ants occupy a vast underground nest, pulverising leaves to nourish their fungal gardens, nursing larvae and toiling to keep the place clean. While foragers troop in with leafy loads, soldier ants guard the nest like a fortress.

Giant weta
Deinacrida heteracantha

This hulk of the insect kingdom creeps through forests in the pitch-dark night. The giant weta can outweigh a mouse, and in extreme cases even a sparrow. Females are the heavyweights of this cricket-like species, which is found only on Little Barrier Island, off the coast of New Zealand's North Island.

MALE WETA

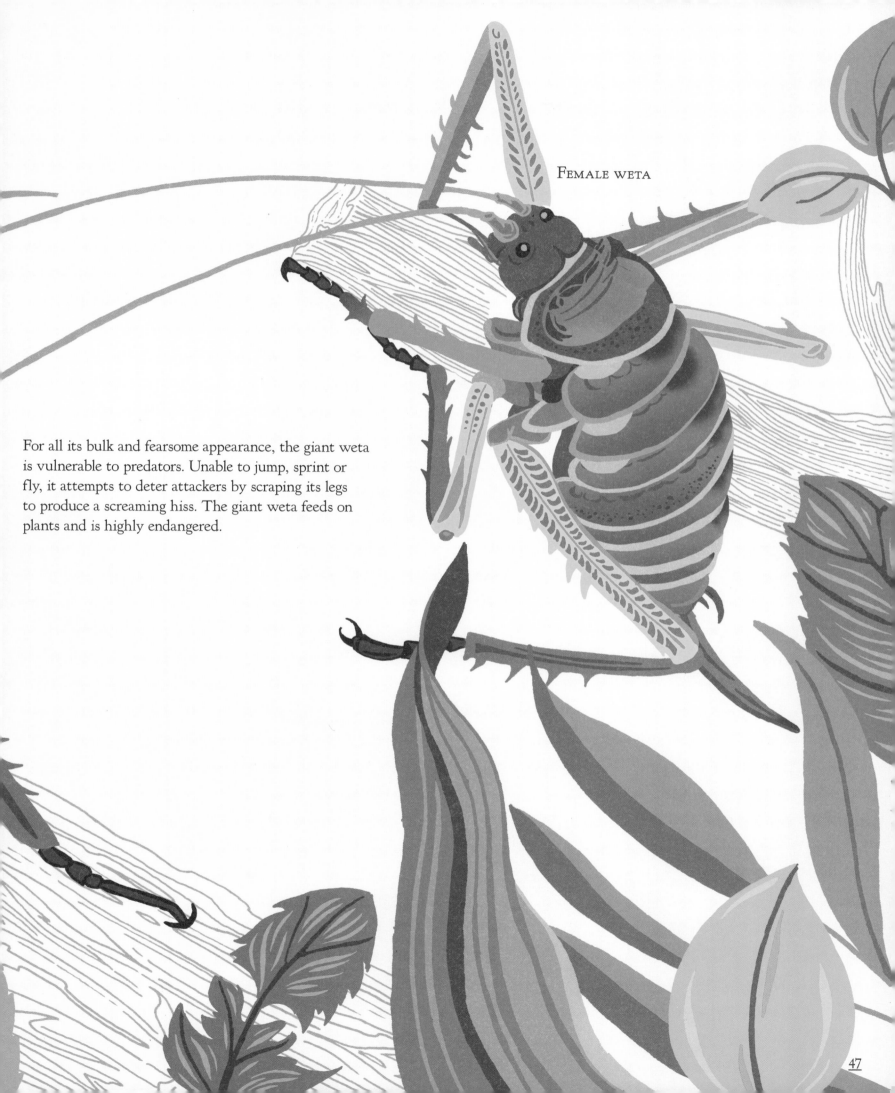

FEMALE WETA

For all its bulk and fearsome appearance, the giant weta is vulnerable to predators. Unable to jump, sprint or fly, it attempts to deter attackers by scraping its legs to produce a screaming hiss. The giant weta feeds on plants and is highly endangered.

47

MALAYSIAN STICK INSECT
Heteropteryx dilatata

GIANT PRICKLY STICK INSECT
Extatosoma tiaratum

Stick insects and leaf insects

The phantoms of the undergrowth, stick insects and leaf insects merge eerily with the foliage around them. Many are armed with a toxic taste or spiny skin – a shock for any predator that's eagle-eyed enough to detect them.

INDIAN STICK INSECT
Carausius morosus

PRICKLY STICK INSECT
Acanthoxyla prasina

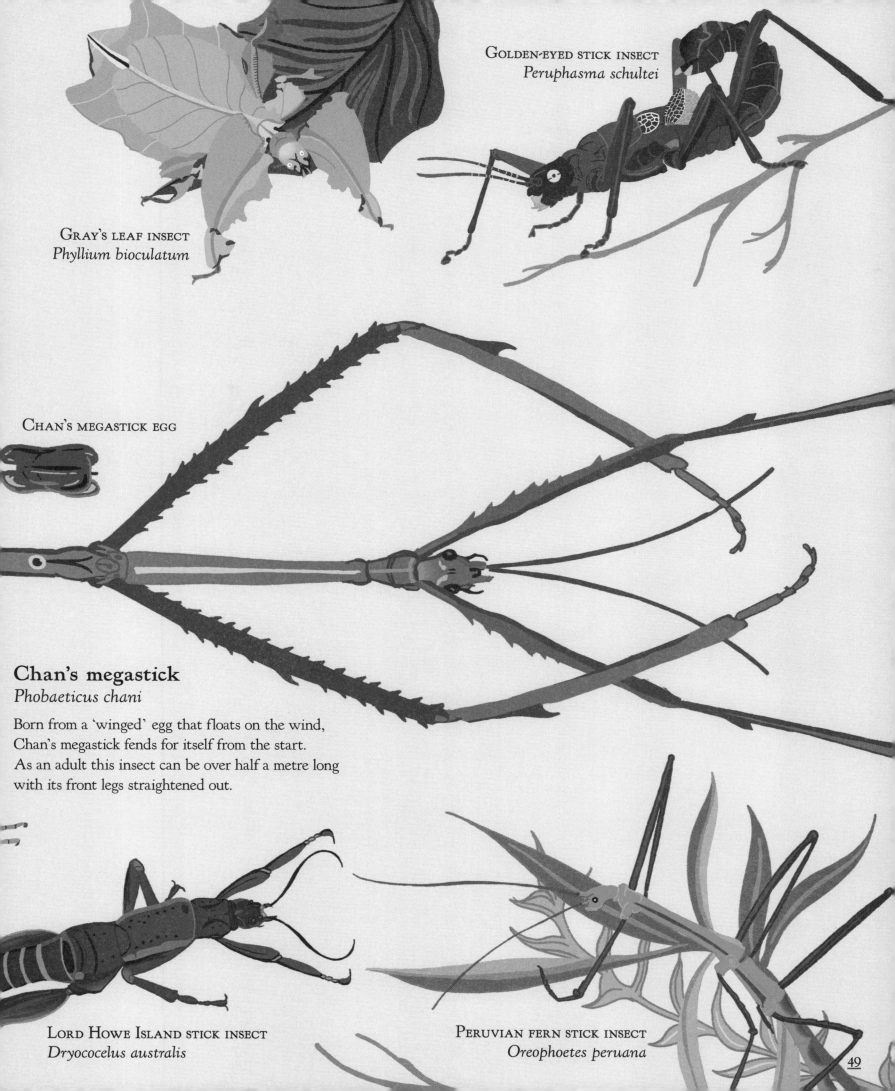

GRAY'S LEAF INSECT
Phyllium bioculatum

GOLDEN-EYED STICK INSECT
Peruphasma schultei

CHAN'S MEGASTICK EGG

Chan's megastick
Phobaeticus chani

Born from a 'winged' egg that floats on the wind,
Chan's megastick fends for itself from the start.
As an adult this insect can be over half a metre long
with its front legs straightened out.

LORD HOWE ISLAND STICK INSECT
Dryococelus australis

PERUVIAN FERN STICK INSECT
Oreophoetes peruana

Grasshoppers

It happens fast. A startled grasshopper springs into the air, powered by its mighty back legs. There is a silvery flash as its wings spread out – then it's gone! The grasshopper drops like a stone as soon as its wings snap shut.

The song of summer is a high-speed strumming, made when grasshoppers scrape their ridged back legs against their forewings. Each type of grasshopper has its own distinctive buzz to help it to attract a mate.

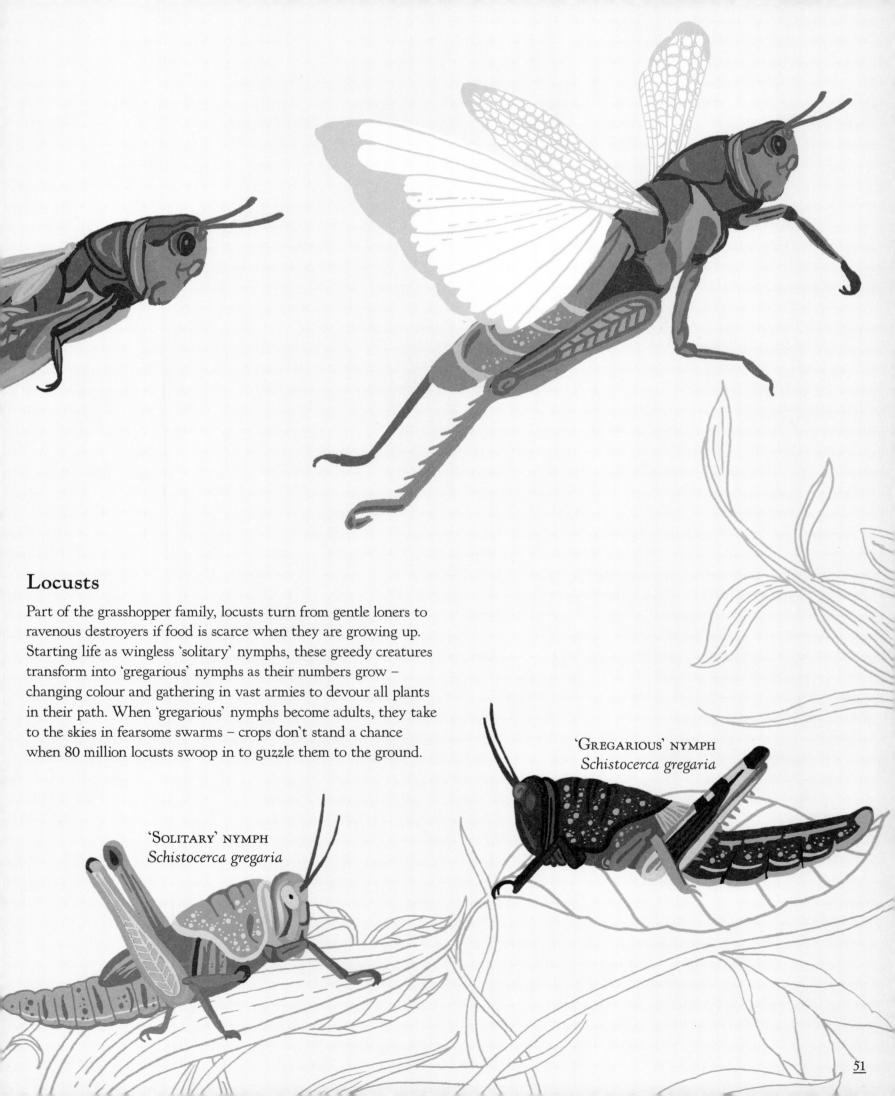

Locusts

Part of the grasshopper family, locusts turn from gentle loners to ravenous destroyers if food is scarce when they are growing up. Starting life as wingless 'solitary' nymphs, these greedy creatures transform into 'gregarious' nymphs as their numbers grow – changing colour and gathering in vast armies to devour all plants in their path. When 'gregarious' nymphs become adults, they take to the skies in fearsome swarms – crops don't stand a chance when 80 million locusts swoop in to guzzle them to the ground.

'GREGARIOUS' NYMPH
Schistocerca gregaria

'SOLITARY' NYMPH
Schistocerca gregaria

51

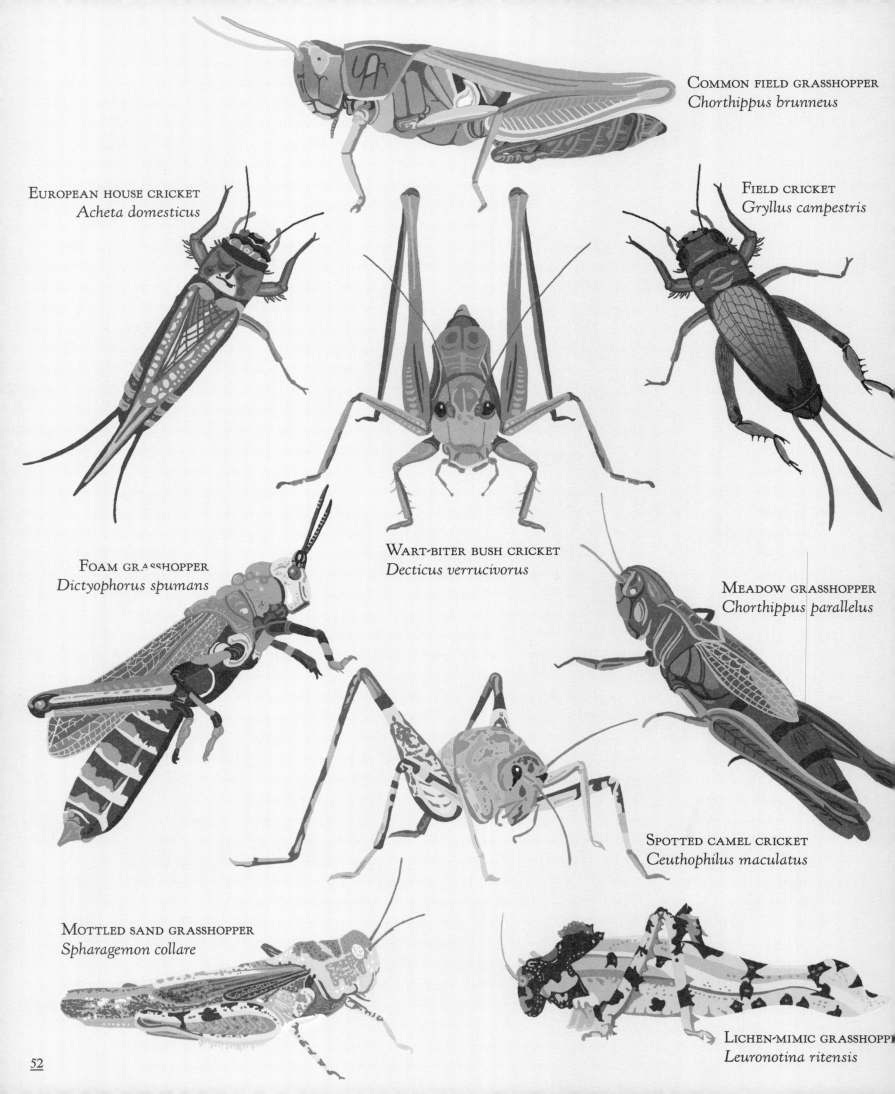

COMMON FIELD GRASSHOPPER
Chorthippus brunneus

EUROPEAN HOUSE CRICKET
Acheta domesticus

FIELD CRICKET
Gryllus campestris

FOAM GRASSHOPPER
Dictyophorus spumans

WART-BITER BUSH CRICKET
Decticus verrucivorus

MEADOW GRASSHOPPER
Chorthippus parallelus

SPOTTED CAMEL CRICKET
Ceuthophilus maculatus

MOTTLED SAND GRASSHOPPER
Spharagemon collare

LICHEN-MIMIC GRASSHOPPER
Leuronotina ritensis

Grasshoppers and crickets

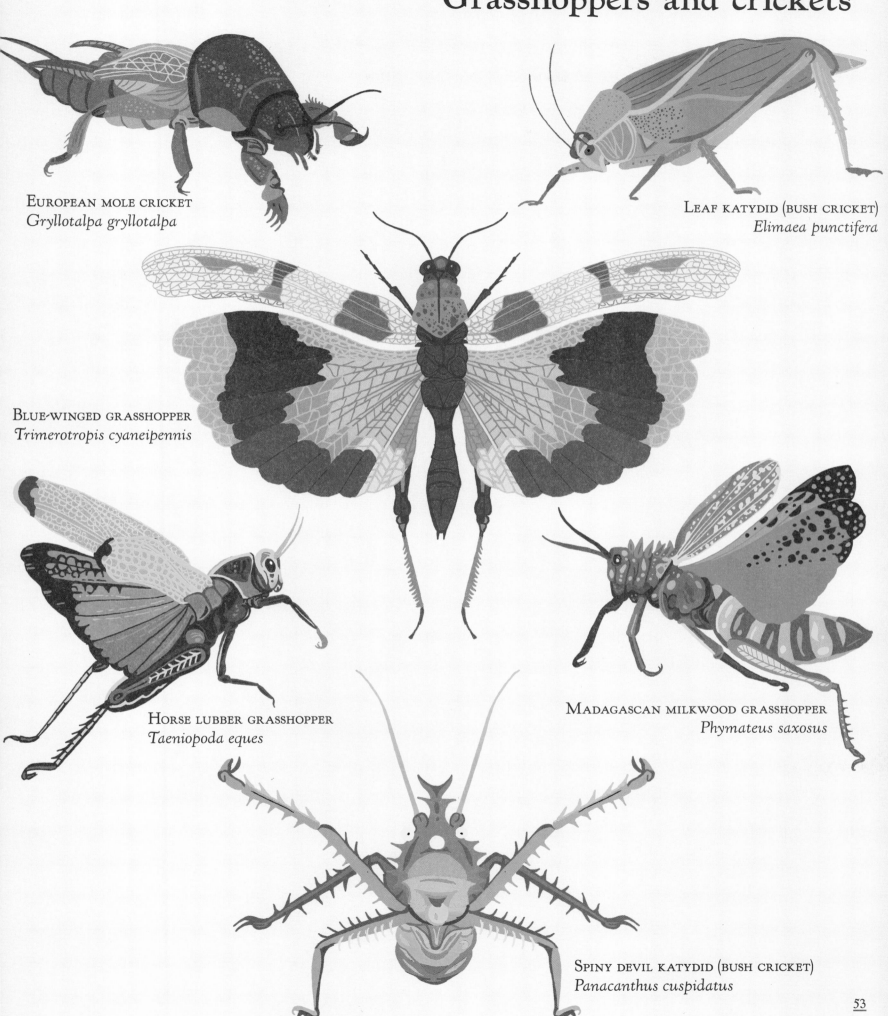

EUROPEAN MOLE CRICKET
Gryllotalpa gryllotalpa

LEAF KATYDID (BUSH CRICKET)
Elimaea punctifera

BLUE-WINGED GRASSHOPPER
Trimerotropis cyaneipennis

HORSE LUBBER GRASSHOPPER
Taeniopoda eques

MADAGASCAN MILKWOOD GRASSHOPPER
Phymateus saxosus

SPINY DEVIL KATYDID (BUSH CRICKET)
Panacanthus cuspidatus

Cockroaches

Fast, nimble and resilient, the cockroach is a ninja of nature. It can vanish in a blink, survive extreme conditions, and even live for weeks without its head.

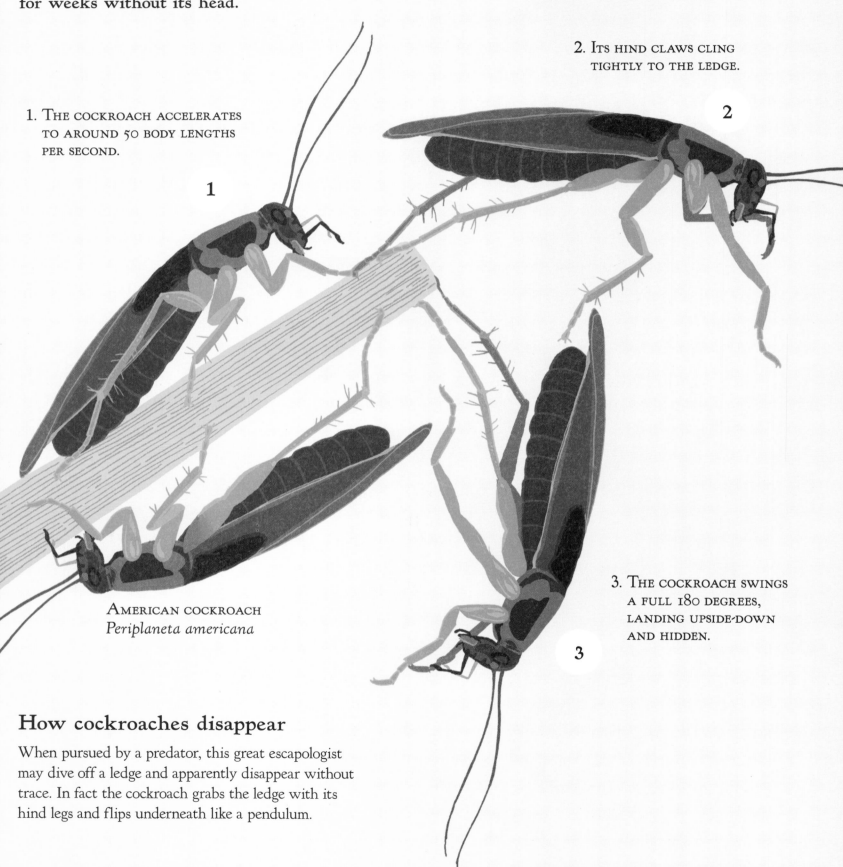

2. ITS HIND CLAWS CLING TIGHTLY TO THE LEDGE.

1. THE COCKROACH ACCELERATES TO AROUND 50 BODY LENGTHS PER SECOND.

AMERICAN COCKROACH
Periplaneta americana

3. THE COCKROACH SWINGS A FULL 180 DEGREES, LANDING UPSIDE-DOWN AND HIDDEN.

How cockroaches disappear

When pursued by a predator, this great escapologist may dive off a ledge and apparently disappear without trace. In fact the cockroach grabs the ledge with its hind legs and flips underneath like a pendulum.

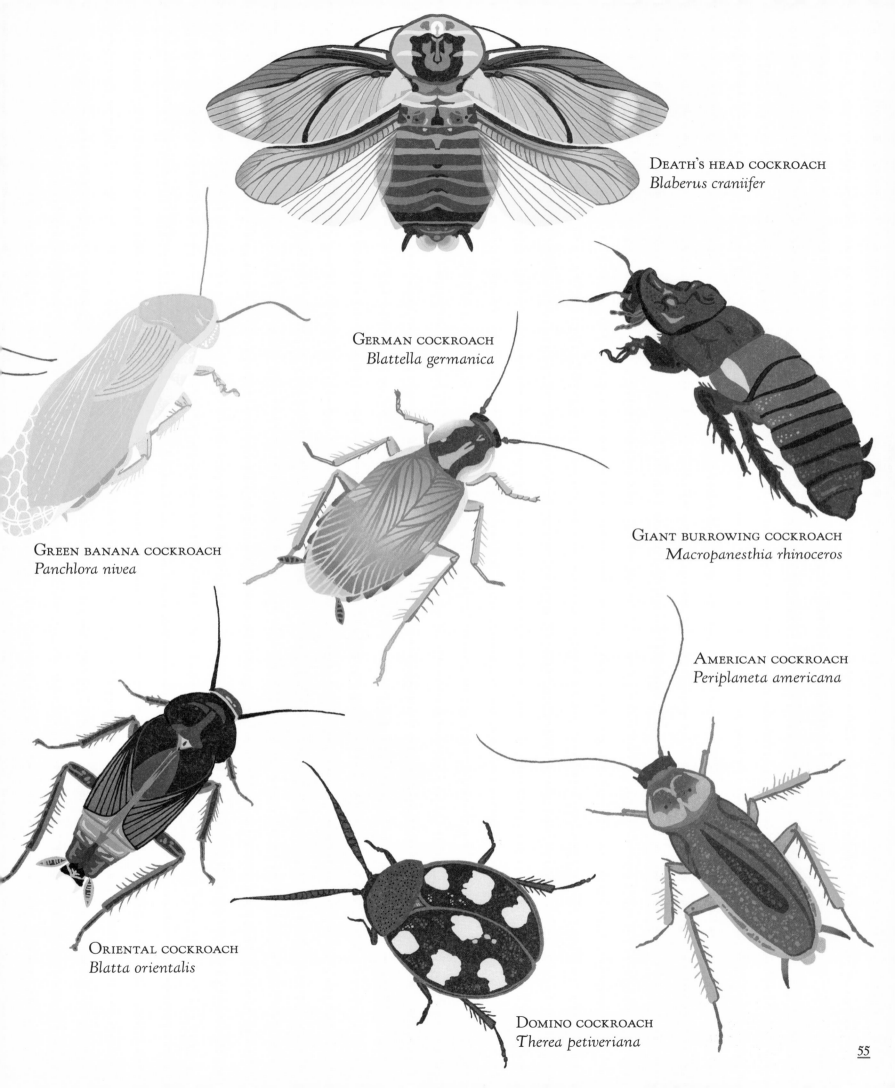

DEATH'S HEAD COCKROACH
Blaberus craniifer

GERMAN COCKROACH
Blattella germanica

GREEN BANANA COCKROACH
Panchlora nivea

GIANT BURROWING COCKROACH
Macropanesthia rhinoceros

AMERICAN COCKROACH
Periplaneta americana

ORIENTAL COCKROACH
Blatta orientalis

DOMINO COCKROACH
Therea petiveriana

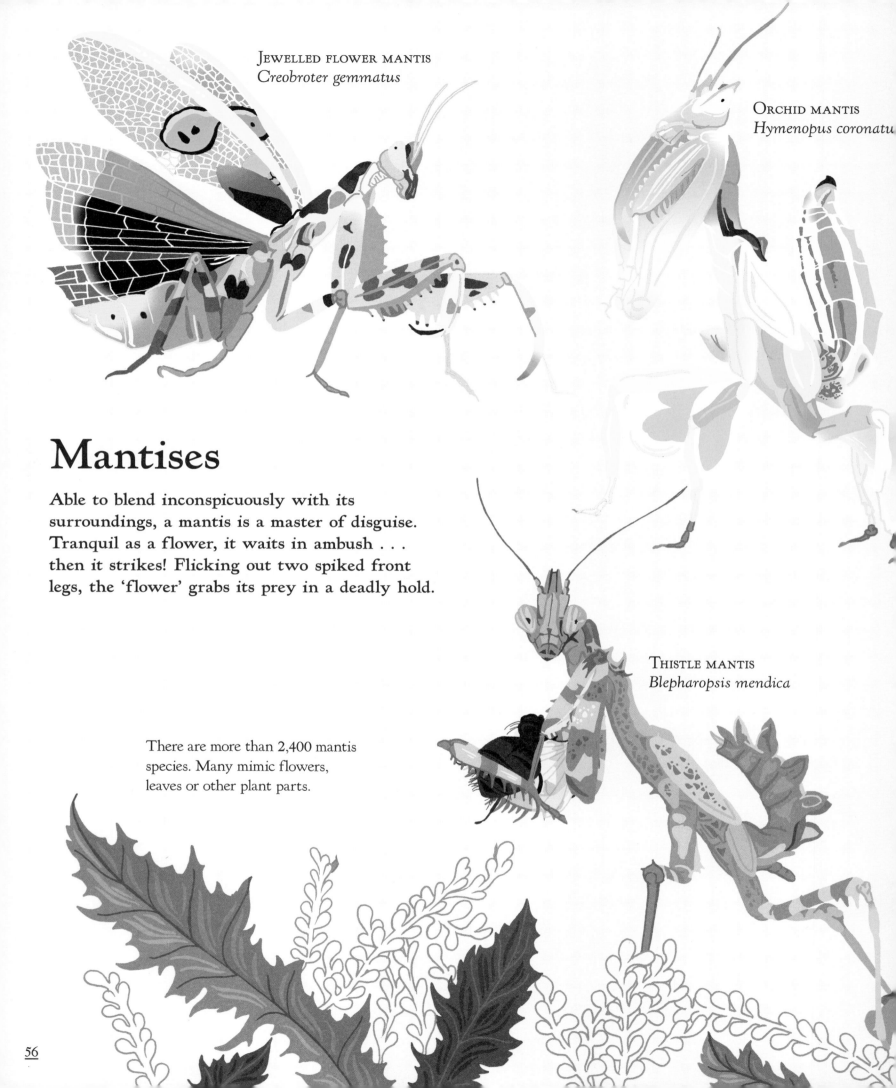

Jewelled flower mantis
Creobroter gemmatus

Orchid mantis
Hymenopus coronatu

Mantises

Able to blend inconspicuously with its
surroundings, a mantis is a master of disguise.
Tranquil as a flower, it waits in ambush . . .
then it strikes! Flicking out two spiked front
legs, the 'flower' grabs its prey in a deadly hold.

Thistle mantis
Blepharopsis mendica

There are more than 2,400 mantis
species. Many mimic flowers,
leaves or other plant parts.

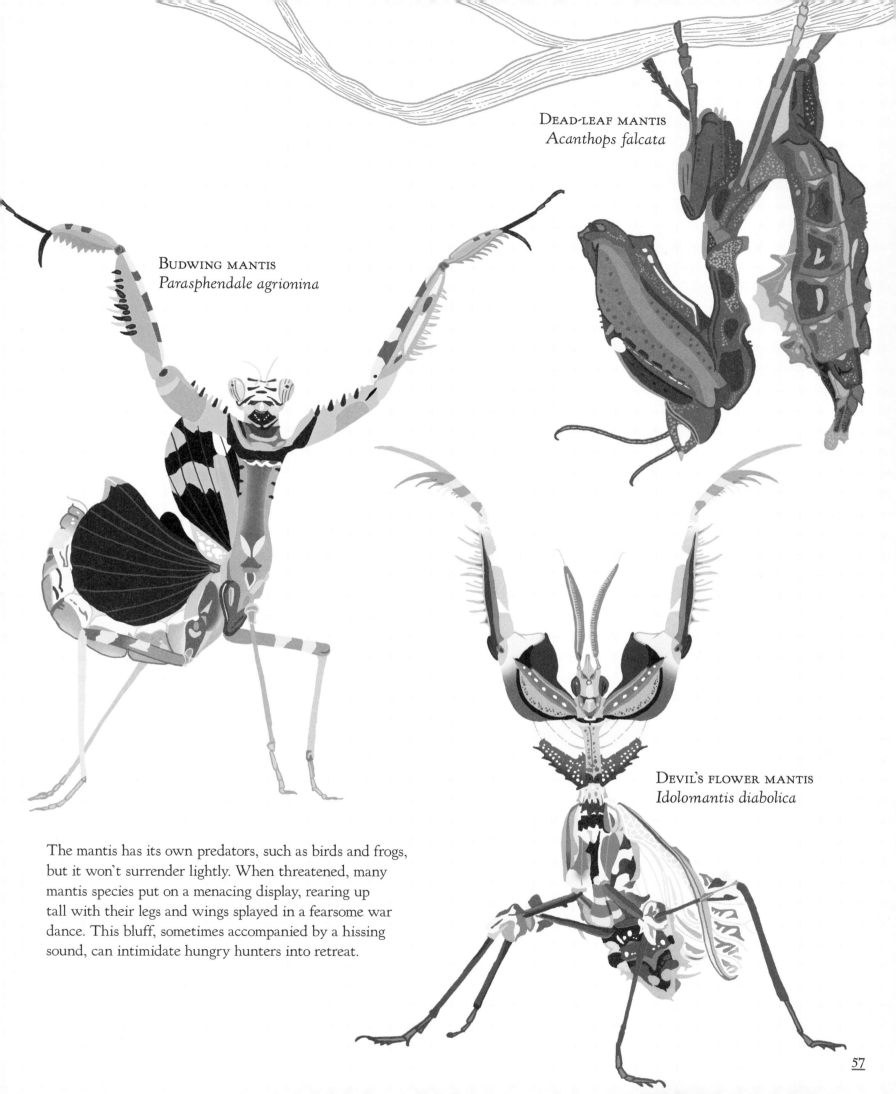

DEAD-LEAF MANTIS
Acanthops falcata

BUDWING MANTIS
Parasphendale agrionina

DEVIL'S FLOWER MANTIS
Idolomantis diabolica

The mantis has its own predators, such as birds and frogs, but it won't surrender lightly. When threatened, many mantis species put on a menacing display, rearing up tall with their legs and wings splayed in a fearsome war dance. This bluff, sometimes accompanied by a hissing sound, can intimidate hungry hunters into retreat.

Amazing insect facts

Wildly diverse and overwhelmingly numerous, insects can astonish us in many ways. Prepare to be startled by some extraordinary facts as you exit the Insect Emporium.

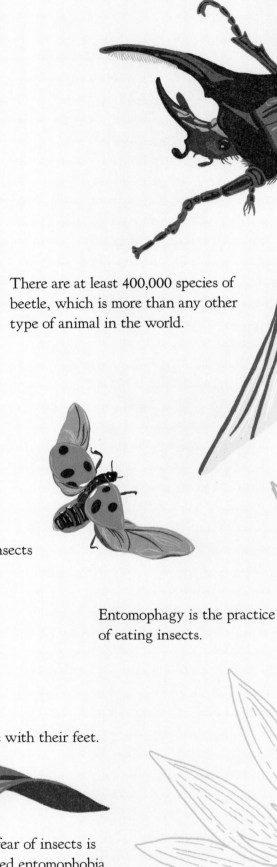

Insect blood, called haemolymph, is usually clear, yellow or green.

There are at least 400,000 species of beetle, which is more than any other type of animal in the world.

Insects appeared on Earth long before the dinosaurs. The oldest insect fossil ever found, *Rhyniognatha hirsti*, dates back 400 million years.

Someone who studies insects is an entomologist.

Entomophagy is the practice of eating insects.

Butterflies taste with their feet.

A fear of insects is called entomophobia.

On a giant set of scales, the world's insects would outweigh the entire human population.

HEAVIEST: Giant weta
(*Deinacrida heteracantha*): 71g

Insect record breakers

SMALLEST: a featherwing beetle (*Scydosella musawasensis*). It is just 0.325mm long.

LOUDEST: Walker's cicada (*Tibicen walkeri*). It can make sounds up to 108.9 decibels, which is louder than a lawnmower!

FASTEST RUNNER: the Australian tiger beetle (*Cicindela hudsoni*). It has clocked 2.5m/s at full sprint. At this speed its vision can't cope, so it has to slow down to see anything.

FASTEST FLIER: a male horsefly of the species *Hybomitra hinei*. One of these horseflies caught a plastic pellet shot from an air rifle at a flight speed of 145km/h.

STRONGEST: the taurus scarab dung beetle (*Onthophagus taurus*). It is is capable of pulling 1,141 times its own weight. A human would have to drag six full double-decker buses to do the same.

HIGHEST LEAPER: the meadow froghopper (*Philaenus spumarius*). It can jump up to about 70cm high, which is more than 100 times its height.

LONGEST: Chan's megastick
(*Phobaeticus chani*): 56.6cm

Glossary

ABDOMEN
The section of the body that contains the digestive and reproductive organs.

ANTENNAE
The two touch sensors on the head of an insect that also detect scents and tastes.

CAMOUFLAGE
The natural colouring or features that allow an animal to blend in with its surroundings.

CARNIVOROUS
Eating only meat.

CHRYSALIS
The protective case inside which an insect, such as a butterfly, transforms itself from larva to adult.

COLONIES
The communities of insects, such as ants or bees, that live and work closely together.

COMPOUND EYES
Eyes made up of numerous visual units, or receptors, that detect information from many directions at once.

CROPS
Plants that are grown by farmers for food or other commercial use.

DIGESTIVE SYSTEM
Body parts that take in food and process it so the body can use it.

ENDANGERED
Threatened, or at risk of extinction.

EXOSKELETON
The rigid, protective covering on the outside of an insect's body.

FUNGUS (plural: fungi)
An organism that produces spores and feeds on decaying plants or other organic material; mushrooms and moulds are types of fungi.

LARVA (plural: larvae)
The immature form of an insect, between egg and pupa.

METAMORPHOSIS
The transformation from one form to another.

MOULT
To shed skin to make way for growth.

MUSCLES
Body parts that enable movement, for example moving wings for flight.

NECTAR
The sugary fluid produced by flowers to attract insects and encourage them to spread pollen; bees collect nectar to make honey.

NYMPH
The immature form of an insect that does not change greatly as it grows, for example a dragonfly.

ORDER
A major group of insects, for example butterflies and moths, or crickets and grasshopppers.

ORGANS
Body parts with a vital function, such as the heart and brain.

POLLEN
The powder produced by plants to allow them to reproduce; insects help this process by spreading pollen from male to female plant parts.

PREDATORS
Animals that hunt and kill other animals for food.

PREY
Animals that are killed and eaten by other animals.

PULP
A soft, wet mass of material.

PUPA (plural: pupae)
The transition stage in an insect's life cycle, between larva and adult.

RECEPTORS
The sense organs that respond to light, heat or other information around them.

SAP
The sugary fluid that circulates inside a plant.

SENSORS
Organs that detect and respond to information such as light, heat or motion.

SPECIES
A type or group of living things with similar characteristics.

THORAX
The middle section of the body, between the head and the abdomen.

TOXIC
Poisonous.

UPPER THORAX
The part of the thorax nearest the head.

Index

GERMAN EAGLES IN SPANISH SKIES

The **Messerschmitt Bf 109** in Service with the Legion Condor during the Spanish Civil War, 1936–39

DAVID JOHNSTON

Schiffer Publishing Ltd

4880 Lower Valley Road • Atglen, PA 19310

Copyright © 2018 by David Johnston

Library of Congress Control Number: 2018937172

Designed by Justin Watkinson
Type set in Bodoni MT/Engravers MT/Minion Pro

ISBN: 978-0-7643-5634-6
Printed in China

Published by Schiffer Publishing, Ltd.
4880 Lower Valley Road
Atglen, PA 19310
Phone: (610) 593-1777; Fax: (610) 593-2002
E-mail: Info@schifferbooks.com
Web: www.schifferbooks.com

For our complete selection of fine books on this and related subjects, please visit our website at www.schifferbooks.com. You may also write for a free catalog.

Schiffer Publishing's titles are available at special discounts for bulk purchases for sales promotions or premiums. Special editions, including personalized covers, corporate imprints, and excerpts, can be created in large quantities for special needs. For more information, contact the publisher.

We are always looking for people to write books on new and related subjects. If you have an idea for a book, please contact us at proposals@schifferbooks.com.

CONTENTS

FOREWORD

Three years before the Second World War, two powers vying for supremacy in Europe clashed for the first time in Spain. The internal Spanish struggle between the extreme Left and the extreme Right turned into open warfare when the Spanish Civil War broke out in the spring of 1936. The Soviet Union on the one side, and the German Reich and Italy on the other, responded positively to requests for aid from the warring parties. The materiel and personnel provided by the two power blocks transformed the civil war in Spain from a minor conflict into one of much-greater dimensions.

When General Francisco Franco approached the German Reich for aid in July 1936, Adolf Hitler immediately said yes. Given his anticommunist stance, this decision was not surprising. It was later claimed that Hitler in part decided to support the Nationalists in order to use the conflict as a testing ground for weapons, but this probably played no part in his initial decision. It was made too spontaneously, and the likely duration of the war and the course of events were too uncertain. At the end of July 1936, the Germans delivered materiel and sent a few troops, who served as advisors at Franco's side. The German volunteers had been discharged from the Wehrmacht before going to Spain. Then, on November 7, 1936, the Legion Condor was brought into being. From then on, the German volunteers played an active role in the fighting at the side of General Franco and the Nationalist forces.

The Legion Condor's fighter unit was J/88, which at first was equipped with He 51s. The aircraft arrived in Spain by sea on November 18, 1936. The German fighter pilots initially flew the He 51 against superior Soviet fighters, but then in December 1936 the first examples of the Bf 109, one of the most modern fighter aircraft of its day, began arriving in Spain.

A number of books have been written about the air war in Spain. They all share a lack of background information, the product of unavailability of original documents. In his book, David Johnston examines the first operational use of what was then the most modern fighter aircraft in the world, in a way that has not been done before. With the aid of previously unseen official documents, he has been able to shed new light on the operational use of the Bf 109 in Spain and the problems that plagued the fighter on its entry into service. His conclusions are thus not supposition but facts, which will have to be considered in future research on the subject. In addition, using diaries, personal recollections, and original documents, he has enabled the men who flew the Bf 109 at the front to speak. The text is supported by many unique photos, most of which have not been published before. I wish the book good success because it closes a gap in aviation history.

Axel Urbanke
Bad Zwischenahn, July 25, 2017

PREFACE

I first became interested in the subject of the Bf 109 during the Spanish Civil War when I came upon Jim Haycraft's *Messerschmitts over Spain*, published in 1970. My interest was spurred further upon reading Karl Ries and Hans Ring's excellent *Legion Condor*, published in 1980. This seminal work by Ries and Ring set the standard for information on the Legion Condor and has, I believe, provided the basis for most books on the subject since it was published. What impressed me most about the book was the authors' use of primary sources, especially accounts of the action written by German pilots. Also invaluable are the appendixes, with their list of victories and casualties. Other sources, such as loss lists and other records, were not listed in the bibliography, but as I discovered when I began researching the subject of the Bf 109 in service with the Legion Condor, these are difficult to come by.

Over the years I amassed a respectable collection of photos of the Bf 109 in Spain, and the study of these began to raise some doubts as to the accuracy of some of the information presented in books on the subject. In particular, photos of the early Bf 109s, usually described either as the B-1 or B-2 variant, raised a number of questions. It was not until a book by Willy Radinger and Walter Schick on the

Bf 109 A to E was published in 1997 that the first concrete information about the existence of the Bf 109 A, and its use in Spain, came to light. Analysis of photos and the Bf 109 B aircraft handbook showed that this subtype differed in a number of respects from the Bf 109 A fighters delivered to the Legion Condor, but further information was lacking. Another claim repeatedly made of the Bf 109s flown by the legion is that a number of examples of the Bf 109 C variant were sent to Spain. This claim appears in just about every book written about the legion; however, never has any proof been provided to substantiate this. Analysis of the Bf 109 C/D aircraft handbook shows that there were significant differences between the C and D, but these differences are confined to the interior of the aircraft, especially beneath the engine cowling and in the cockpit. There seemed to be uncertainty as to the differences between the Jumo-engined Bf 109s, and in the various titles on the Bf 109 in Spain the reader will find the same aircraft identified in various places as a Bf 109 B, C, or D.

I hoped to write something on the Bf 109 in Spain, but without additional sources it seemed that the undertaking was not worthwhile. And then my friend Axel Urbanke of Start-Verlag in Germany provided me with some of the records I had been seeking for so long. These are the daily, weekly, and technical reports compiled by VK/88, the unit that assembled and tested the aircraft sent to the legion, and VJ/88, the experimental fighter unit there. Luckily, these records cover the period from December 5, 1936, to May 14, 1937, and confirm that three prototypes and fourteen Bf 109 A fighters were sent to Spain in late 1936 and early 1937. The daily and weekly reports provide details about all of these early Bf 109s and even the *Werknummer* of a number of Bf 109 As. They also make it possible to follow these machines through their assembly, testing, and modifications until they were sent to the front. Also covered in detail are the struggles with the Bf 109 A's engine cooling, oil system, leading-edge slats, and other systems. Finally, the issue of which prototypes were sent to Spain is also covered in the reports. They show that two of the three prototypes sent to Spain were wrecked in crashes, and even include accident reports for both aircraft that were lost. I believe that this new information will contribute to a better understanding of the Bf 109's career in Spain and, I hope, will spur other researchers to continue the search for those records still unaccounted for.

ACKNOWLEDGMENTS

First and foremost I wish to say thank you to my wife, Betty, for her patience and understanding during the many hours I have spent working on this book. I also wish to thank and acknowledge the help given by a number of friends and colleagues, along with support and photographs. In particular, I am grateful to my friend Axel Urbanke, who led me to the Legion Condor documents that resulted in the writing of this book, and for helping me find photographs and information in Germany. I would also like to thank David Franklin, Christopher Nesbit, Jennifer Graham, Michelle Wilson, and David Brown for their help in obtaining photographs, and for lending their support. I also extend my thanks to Udo Hafner for supplying the handbook illustrations that accompany the text.

INTRODUCTION

The Messerschmitt Bf 109 is undoubtedly one of the most significant fighter aircraft in the history of aviation. As an "ace maker" it had no equal, and more aces flew this type than any other aircraft in any air force. Many of the leading German aces of World War II scored most or all of their victories in the 109. When I asked Luftwaffe pilot Adolf Dickfeld for his thoughts on the aircraft, he replied, "I had absolute confidence in it. I felt that I could do anything in the 109." And it was during the Spanish Civil War that the Bf 109 began its long run of success.

There was some sense of urgency in sending the Bf 109 to Spain, after the He 51 proved inferior to the Soviet I-15 and I-16 fighters in combat. The first Bf 109s sent to Spain were prototypes—the Bf 109 V3, V4, and V6, all arriving there in 1936. The V6 was assembled and then destroyed in a crash during its first takeoff on December 19, 1936. The investigation that followed found the aircraft's pilot to be unfit, and he was sent home. The V3, which differed from the other two prototypes in a number of respects, was flown

for a time, until it too was destroyed in a crash on February 11, 1937. The V4, the sole surviving prototype, was flown by Hannes Trautloft until February 19, 1937. After he left Spain the aircraft was flown by 2.J/88 and then 1.J/88, in whose hands it was written off in a crash landing.

Deliveries of the Bf 109 B to the Legion Condor began in mid-July 1937. Photographs and anecdotal evidence indicate that they were armed with three MG 17 machine guns. Some of the B version survived to enter service with the Spanish air force after the legion received the Bf 109 E.

Despite frequent claims that the Bf 109 C was used in Spain, the author has been unable to find any documentary or photographic evidence to support this. Where these claims originated is uncertain, but it appears that they have simply been repeated without further examination. The Bf 109 C/D aircraft handbook shows that the Jumo 210 G differed from the Jumo 210 D in quite a few respects, and operating a handful of these aircraft would surely have been a maintenance and spare-parts nightmare.

The Bf 109 D began arriving in Spain in March 1938, and together with the surviving Bs and upgraded A versions they equipped J/88 until the arrival of the Bf 109 E (Emil) in December 1938. The Emil outclassed every opposing aircraft in the skies over Spain, but by the time of its arrival, Republican opposition had diminished greatly.

In many respects, fighter operations during the Spanish Civil War were more reminiscent of those of the First World War than the Second World War. Radio was not widely used until the arrival of the Bf 109 E in 1939, and although the *Schwarm* formation may have evolved from experience in Spain, accounts by pilots reveal that the *Kette* was the predominant formation used there, perhaps because of the need to rely on visual signals for communication.

Probably the most enduring legacy of the air war in Spain for Germany was the experience that many of its pilots gained there. Werner Mölders and Adolf Galland, both of whom became *General der Jagdflieger*, served in Spain, Mölders becoming the highest-scoring German pilot there. Many other figures who went on to command units during the Luftwaffe's years of victory had also seen action in Spain (see appendix 2).

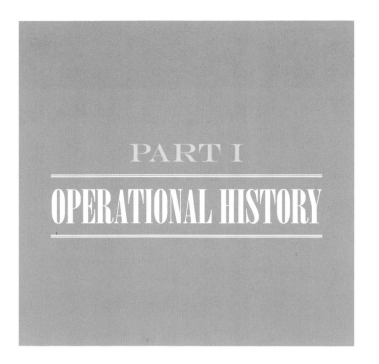

PART I

OPERATIONAL HISTORY

EARLY DAYS

The Bf 109's operational career in Spain began in December 1936,[1] with the arrival of three *Versuchs* (prototype) machines: the V3, V4, and V6. The crates containing the V4 and V6 arrived at Seville-Tablada, where VK/88 was based, on December 5. The V6 survived less than a week; on December 9, it crashed due to pilot error while making its first takeoff.

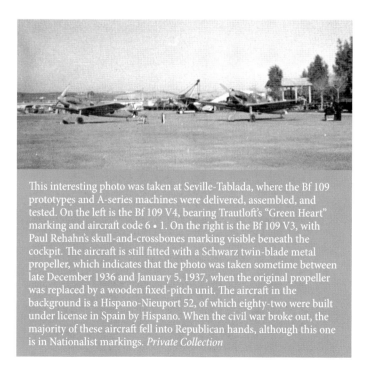

This interesting photo was taken at Seville-Tablada, where the Bf 109 prototypes and A-series machines were delivered, assembled, and tested. On the left is the Bf 109 V4, bearing Trautloft's "Green Heart" marking and aircraft code 6 • 1. On the right is the Bf 109 V3, with Paul Rehahn's skull-and-crossbones marking visible beneath the cockpit. The aircraft is still fitted with a Schwarz twin-blade metal propeller, which indicates that the photo was taken sometime between late December 1936 and January 5, 1937, when the original propeller was replaced by a wooden fixed-pitch unit. The aircraft in the background is a Hispano-Nieuport 52, of which eighty-two were built under license in Spain by Hispano. When the civil war broke out, the majority of these aircraft fell into Republican hands, although this one is in Nationalist markings. *Private Collection*

The damage could not be repaired and the aircraft was subsequently used as a source of spare parts. The aircraft's pilot, Richard Koch, described what happened:[2]

> On December 9, 1936, I took off to test-fly a Me 109 assembled here. Immediately after takeoff, I noticed that the left wing was dropping sharply. Despite full opposite aileron, I was unable to level the wings. As I feared that the left wing was about to touch the ground, I used the elevators to lift it while simultaneously applying full right aileron and reducing power. The aircraft subsequently struck the ground, first the tailwheel, followed by the left wing, and then the right wing.

Engineer Blecher, who was in charge of the flying program, had a somewhat different view of the incident:[3]

> Statement concerning *Gefreiter* Koch's accident report.
> The crash of the Bf 109 was caused by stalling the aircraft during takeoff.
> After a short takeoff run, the aircraft was pulled into a steep climb. In stalled condition, it rolled to the left from a height of 65 to 80 feet.
> With the engine at full power, the aircraft struck the ground, first with the left undercarriage leg and left wing, followed by the right wing.
> The engine was not switched off until the aircraft came to a complete stop. The fuel cock was not closed.
> For damage to the aircraft, see findings report.

The commanding officer was quick to react to the loss of such a valuable machine. He wrote:[4]

> Agree with Blecher's statement. *Gefreiter* Koch is no longer needed and is to be sent home at the earliest opportunity. He has demonstrated that his piloting capabilities are not sufficiently developed to fly modern aircraft.

On December 9, Hannes Trautloft was ordered to Seville to check out on the new Messerschmitt V4. Bad weather delayed his arrival, and it was several days before Trautloft could test-fly the aircraft. He wrote:[5]

> The new Bf 109 looks absolutely fabulous. Alongside it the good old He 51 is like a girl whose beauty has faded, and yet I part with her with a heavy heart.
> Unfortunately, the Bf 109 won't be ready until tomorrow. Its engine is still acting up.
> The Bf 109 won't be ready today after all. The engine is still causing problems. Someone says, "Like a thoroughbred horse, which also bucks at first." As well the right machine gun won't fire, and it lacks warlike markings. Instead of the "Top Hat," I have them paint a green heart: it is a visual representation of Thuringia, Germany's green heart, here in Spain.

Five days later, on December 14, the V4 was ready to fly. Trautloft described his initial impression of the machine:[6]

The Bf 109 is finally ready. The takeoff is somewhat different than I'm used to, but as soon as I'm airborne I immediately feel at home in the new bird. The machine is magnificent. An Italian Fiat is loitering over the airfield. Until now the Fiat has been considered the fastest fighter among the aircraft under General Franco's command, but I come up from behind, overtake him in seconds, and leave him far behind. We should have had a dozen of this type right at the beginning; then things would have been different, and Eberhard and Henrici would probably still be alive.

The Bf 109 V3 was the last of the three prototypes to reach Seville-Tablada, arriving on December 15.[7] Like any new aircraft, the Bf 109 prototypes suffered teething troubles. The V4 had its share of problems, as Trautloft related:[8]

December 14–23

I have been in Seville two weeks already, for the Bf 109 suffers one teething problem after another. It's always something minor. This time there's a problem with the tailwheel, that time the water pump, or the carburetor, or the undercarriage fairings. Repairs always take time and the hours are adding up. Once, while in the circuit, I develop engine trouble and have to make an emergency landing. At least I get down without crashing.

An Italian, flying a Fiat, crashes into the ground while giving a display of aerobatics. Another collides with a Spanish Breguet while landing, and both crash. But in war, where death is all around; one soon becomes hardened to such things. One scarcely speaks about those who have so tragically lost their lives; rather, the main topic is the three new Bf 109s received by our experimental group.

The Bf 109 V3 taxiing at Seville with Paul Rehahn at the controls. Note the pointed spinner and smooth curve of the engine cowling from the spinner to the fuselage. In this photo the V3 still has the metal two-blade propeller with which it was delivered to Spain. This was later replaced by a wooden fixed-pitch unit when the aircraft's Jumo 210 C engine had to be replaced with a Jumo 210 B. Note the cylindrical object beneath the fuselage behind the oil cooler, the purpose of which is not known. Rehahn's skull-and-crossbones marking is visible beneath the cockpit. He had previously shot down two Republican aircraft while flying the He 51. *Private Collection*

Hannes Trautloft and two unidentified companions pose in front of the Bf 109 V4 after his final sortie before returning to Germany. Trautloft's personal emblem, a green heart representing his home state of Thuringia, can be seen beneath the cockpit. The emblem was also present on the port side of the fuselage. The aircraft code, 6 • 1, was positioned aft of the black disc on the fuselage. Note the pitot-venturi forward of the canopy quarter panel. This was later replaced by a pitot under the port wing. *Author's Collection*

While based at Seville, VJ/88, the Legion Condor's experimental fighter unit, had little opportunity to come to grips with the enemy. At the end of December, Trautloft wrote:[9]

> I fly my Bf 109 whenever the weather permits, keeping lookout for the "evil enemy." But he doesn't show himself; he truly is evil. There is little opportunity to add to my list of victories here at Seville. I can take some consolation in the fact that the persistent bad weather grounds my comrades at the front, preventing them from winning more laurels.

Born of a lack of action and continued serviceability problems with the Bf 109 V4, Trautloft's frustration grew:[10]

> I must make another emergency landing in the Bf 109. The continuous heat causes problems with carburetor adjustment and the cooling system. An aircraft destined for Spain need not be as precisely designed as one intended

for Germany. The climatic differences must be taken into consideration and require changes. Today as always, the environment works against technology's tendency to become ever more sophisticated.

> Scarcely a day goes by without a scramble, but I never see a Red in the air. I feel like a hunter who goes to the hunting stand even though he knows he will see nothing. This can't continue in the long run; it wears down even the strongest nerves.

> Cadiz has been bombed twice. Each time I scrambled as soon as the alarm was sounded, but because of the distance I arrived too late. The Reds had already long disappeared over the mountains.

In mid-January the tension was relieved somewhat by a humorous incident:[11]

> On one occasion Fips Radusch accompanies me to Cadiz in his He 112. On the way back I see him low over

the airfield, apparently about to land. Suddenly he begins turning sharply. What is he doing?, I ask myself. The mystery is soon cleared up. Next to our hangar stands a small barracks, home to the weather technicians, and from there a group of men are releasing a red balloon. It soon reaches my height. The "weather frog," as we call the meteorologist, is taking his wind measurements. Often, while sitting at readiness with Fips Radusch, we have watched these wind balloons ascending. Cockily we decide to ram these lovely little things at the first best opportunity. After it! I head toward the "Red" in a turn, raise the nose slightly and it's history. I fly around the weather techs in a wide circle; down below the "weather frog" stands and shakes his fist at me. Obviously he is unwilling to release another balloon until I land. I trick him by making as if about to land. The "weather frog" promptly releases another balloon. I open the throttle, fly toward the balloon, and ram it. The "weather frog" is unlikely to give me any opportunity for additional "victories," so I land. Laughing, the mechanics and Radusch come out to meet me. Like me, he has rammed two balloons. The "weather frog" complains loudly about the fighter pilots, who "are always doing foolish things."

There was plenty of action in the air over the Madrid front, and on January 13, Trautloft was ordered to join a He 51 *Staffel* there. He wrote:[12]

Back from Germany, *Oberstleutnant* von Richthofen meets with General Sperrle in Salamanca. One of their topics is the possible use of our Bf 109 and He 112 on the Madrid front. Impatiently we wait for the outcome. News finally comes, but it affects only me. I am to join another *Staffel* on the Madrid front as soon as my Bf 109 is serviceable—its tailwheel is being repaired. I breathe a sigh of relief; it is as if my spirits are reborn.

Madrid was still the focal point of the war. Franco's previous attempts to take the city had failed. In February and March, he would launch two more offensives aimed at bringing about the fall of the capital. The Battle of Jarama would end in bloody stalemate, while the Italian attack at Guadalajara would end in an embarrassing defeat. In the air, the Republic's new Russian fighters, the Polikarpov I-15 and I-16, had proved superior to the legion's He 51s.

Trautloft and the Bf 109 V4 arrived at the Madrid front on January 14. He described his initial experiences there:[13]

My Bf 109 is ready. The weather is not particularly good; nevertheless I take off for Villa del Prado near Escalona, about 25 miles southwest of Madrid. Flying the Bf 109 is pure joy; more strongly than ever before I feel that, apart from the unavoidable patch of ground below, I am removed from time and space. When I land at Caceres—because the weather has deteriorated sharply—the men with their plodding movements seem to me as foreign as the inhabitants of a distant planet. It takes a while before I am used to being back on earth again.

The Spanish mechanics crowd around my Bf 109; they gaze in wonder at the fast machine.

Every morning when I wake up, I am first to go to the window: How is the weather? This will determine whether

The Bf 109 V3, aircraft code 6–2, at Burgos. By this time the aircraft's original metal propeller had been replaced by a wooden one, indicating that this photo was taken between January 5, 1937 and February 11, when it was destroyed in a crash after taking off from Caceres. Though of poor quality, the photo is of interest because it confirms that the skull and crossbones marking was also present on the starboard side of the fuselage. As well, here engine cowling panels appear to be darker than the rest of the airframe. In the background can be seen the He 112 V4. *Author's Collection*

The He 112 V4 at Seville-Tablada. Like the Bf 109 prototypes, this aircraft was also sent to Spain for evaluation. It was armed with a 20 mm MG C 30 cannon, and *Uffz.* Schulz claimed to have destroyed three Republican tanks with it while flying the aircraft. The He 112 V4 was written off in a crash on July 19, 1937, after developing engine trouble. *Private Collection*

The Bf 109 V3 differed from later prototypes in having wing bulges over the wheel wells as well as a slightly different canopy arrangement. The origins of the skull-and-crossbones emblem under the cockpit are not known, but it was most likely the personal emblem of pilot Paul Rehahn, who was killed when the aircraft was destroyed in a crash at Caceres on February 11, 1937. Though not visible in this photo, the aircraft bore the number 6 • 2. It was originally fitted with a Schwarz twin-blade variable-pitch metal propeller, but after an engine change on January 5, 1937, this was replaced with the fixed-pitch wooden unit seen here. *Private Collection*

The second loss of a Bf 109 in Spain occurred on February 11, 1937, when Paul Rehahn was killed in the crash of the Bf 109 V3. Trautloft wrote:[14]

On my way home I see Fips Radusch's He 112 sitting on the airfield at Almoror. Happy at the prospect of seeing him again, I land at Villa del Prado. I find the old, brave chap at the "fighter pilots' castle." Fips Radusch is unusually serious, and I immediately know that one of our number has bought it. I merely ask, "Who?" His answer is equally brief: "Rehahn." Yes, for reasons unknown, Rehahn, who was supposed to bring the other Bf 109, dove vertically into the ground shortly after taking off from Caceres.

The following account of the crash is from the official accident report:[15]

On February 11, 1937, the He 112 No. 5-1 flown by *Oberleutnant* Radusch and the Bf 109 No. 6-2 flown by *Leutnant* Rehahn took off from Seville at 0930 to fly to Villa del Prado, with a planned stop in Caceres. Prior to takeoff, both aircraft were checked over by the responsible fitters, run up, and reported in order to the technical director, who gave approval for takeoff. The aircraft landed in Caceres at approximately 1040 and refueled there, during which time the pilots remained with their machines. From there the He 112 took off first, at 1126, followed by the Bf 109 one minute later. Both aircraft made a wide 270-degree turn before taking up a roughly northeast heading. By the time the He 112 had almost reached the line of hills that lay in the direction of flight (see map 1), the Bf 109 had just turned on course and was in normal cruising attitude at a height of about 1,200 feet. The undercarriage had been retracted during the climb. At that moment the aircraft pitched forward into a nose-down attitude and, in an almost vertical dive, crashed propeller-first into the ground. The ignition switch was apparently turned off during the dive, since no engine noise was heard during the dive, and the switch was found in position M 1—next to the OFF position and probably moved there only on impact. On initial impact the left wing scraped the ground (see map 2). The aircraft was then turned 90 degrees and bounced approximately 65 feet to the next impact point, where the left wing broke off. The fuselage slid another 65 feet down a slope with a height difference of about 20 feet, tearing off the right wing in the process. Just before the fuselage came to rest, the engine was torn from its mounts.

I go back to sleep or not. Today I am greeted by a wonderful blue sky, something we haven't had for a long time.

I hurry out to the airfield. As of yet the fighter group has no mission orders. The commanding officer gives me permission to fly to the front alone.

At 1000, I am over Madrid at a height of 16,500 feet. Spain's capital city lies beneath me, small and peaceful. I circle over the front for almost an hour without seeing any Reds. My fuel is running low; I must go back. I fly over Torijos to once again demonstrate to the Italians what my Bf 109 can do. There are two Fiats in the air. I roar past them; they look like they're standing still.

In the afternoon, twenty-four Junkers take off to bomb the front between Escorial and Madrid. We and the Italians, a total of forty fighters, fly escort. I stay just above the bombers, the better to spot attacking Reds. But once again those fellows don't put in an appearance. Apparently our numbers, sixty-four aircraft in total, are too imposing for them. And so the bombers are able to drop their "eggs" undisturbed; the effect appears to be devastating.

I land with the tailwheel of my Bf 109 still retracted; this is the second time this has happened to me. The rudder is stove in. Repairs begin immediately, but I am forced to laze about until tomorrow. After much consideration I decide to have the tailwheel locked down. Better to have it not retract at all than to endure repeated repairs.

The pilot was killed instantly.

Trautloft's first encounter with enemy aircraft occurred on February 16, during the Battle of Jarama:[16]

The offensive is about to resume east of Pinto, and early in the morning ten Junkers take off to bomb Red positions. The escort consists of eighteen He 51s plus me.

The Junkers and Heinkels fly at the same height, about 13,000 feet, while I again remain 3,000 feet above them so that I can see everything. I must constantly weave back and forth and reduce power; otherwise my Bf 109 would soon leave the other aircraft far behind. South of Madrid I spot five aircraft about 2,500 feet above me; they are heading north in a long row. They don't appear to have seen me. I move behind them and identify them as Italian Fiats. About 3,000 feet lower I see another gaggle, all heading toward Madrid. Looking back to the Junkers, I find to my surprise that one He 51 *Staffel* is splitting up. The aircraft are flying at irregular intervals and spacings, which suggests that the Reds are preparing to attack our

bombers. I carefully scan in all directions, but I cannot spot any Red machines. To the north there are five black dots high above me, but they would be the five Italians I saw earlier.

Meanwhile the Ju 52s drop their bombs. From this height I cannot determine their effectiveness; all I can see are rising clouds of smoke.

Our bombers and the two fighter *Staffeln* head back, and I remain above them. The only other aircraft are the five Italians, who are flying higher than I. I scan for them. There they are, above me at my five o'clock. I can barely see them through the canopy; also the sun is shining in my face. I begin a gentle turn to the east in order to see better. Suddenly, one of the five peels off toward me. It has no undercarriage, nor does the second, which initiates a half roll and dive. Damn, it's five *Ratas* [the Nationalists' nickname for the Polikarpov I-16 fighter plane; in the plural, Spanish for "rats"]. They all dive on me like hawks. At that moment there is only one thing to do: dive! I make a half roll and put the nose down into a vertical dive. The

The Bf 109 V4 at Seville in the markings of 2.J/88. By the time this photo was taken, the aircraft had been fitted with a metal variable-pitch propeller. Also note the revised style of code, with the number indicating the type in front of the fuselage disc and the individual aircraft number behind it, and the unusual style of the number "1." The V4 returned to Seville-Tablada on April 4, 1937, for partial overhaul and was fitted with the new fuselage-mounted oil tank. *Private Collection*

Ratas are above me; they must start shooting at any second. I instinctively shrink down in my seat; more than anything I would like to make myself into a tiny speck. I am diving at a terrific speed; the earth rushes toward me. I can't see behind, so instead I look to the left and right, my nerves stretched to the utmost. But I see nothing; no tracer, hear no gunfire or bullets striking. Then, at a height of about 3,300 feet, I begin pulling out. God knows, I've never come down from 16,000 feet so fast before. My head is throbbing as if it must explode at any second. Nevertheless, I am able to make several steep turns, during which I recover somewhat. There is no sign of the Reds. Once again I had been lucky, extremely lucky. Nevertheless I am furious that I mistook the Ratas for Italians; I absolutely should have identified them sooner. Only the gods know why those fellows didn't pursue and shoot me down.

Trautloft flew one more mission in the Bf 109 V4 and then was ordered back to Germany. Photographs confirm,

however, that the V4 continued in service with VJ/88 and later 2.J/88 and 1st *Staffel* and was written off while serving with the latter.

ARRIVAL OF THE BF 109 A

March 1937 saw the arrival in Spain of a batch of fourteen Bf 109 A fighters (6 • 3 to 6 • 16).[17] These, together with the surviving prototype (the V4), were allocated to 2.J/88, which was placed under the command of Günther Lützow. The following is from *Bf 109 Technical Experience Report No. 3* for the period February 16 to April 30, 1937:

1. General: fourteen new Bf 109 aircraft arrived during this reporting period. With the three aircraft received the previous November, a total of seventeen have now been delivered; one aircraft (V6) was destroyed in November while being test-flown and was cannibalized here. Another

An unidentified Bf 109 A with what appears to be a ducted spinner. There is no mention of such a spinner in the daily reports submitted by VK/88 and VJ/88; however, it could have been an attempt to resolve the cooling problems that plagued the Jumo 210 engines in the Bf 109 A. The 2.J/88's "Top Hat" emblem is barely visible above the port wing. The aircraft has the original style of engine cowling without cooling cents and has yet to receive the fuselage-mounted oil tank. Also visible in front of the windscreen is the ring of the auxiliary gunsight, part of the Revi 3a/b sight. The auxiliary sight was usually folded down out of the way, but if the gunsight's lamp burned out it could be raised for use as a backup sight. *Private Collection*

An unidentified Bf 109 A during a test flight at Seville. The aircraft appears to be in initial delivery condition with the exception of the vented engine cowling. Judging by the dress of the personnel, the photo was taken during the winter or early spring of 1937. Note the length of the leading-edge slats, extending almost to the outer edge of the mainwheel well. *Private Collection*

(V3) crashed near Caceres on February 11, 1937, while being flown by *Leutnant* Rehahn and was scrapped.

After the new arrivals had been assembled, the fifteen remaining aircraft were used to form a Bf 109 *Staffel*, which was created by merging the former VK/88 test commando and 2nd *Staffel* of *Jagdgruppe* 88 (2nd J/88) under the command of *Oberleutnant* Knüppel and, following his return to Germany, *Oberleutnant* Lützow.

While the aircraft were being assembled, the new pilots had to be familiarized with the flying characteristics of the Bf 109. This proved much simpler than anticipated at home, for all of the pilots assigned to the Bf 109 unit were experienced fighter pilots trained at the fighter school in Schleissheim, for whom converting from the He 51 or Ar 68 onto the Bf 109 presented not the least difficulty. The aircraft mentioned above that was destroyed while being test-flown was flown by a young, inexperienced pilot with no fighter training.

To ensure a smooth *Staffel* operation later on, the formation of a complete military ground organization was carried out. The civilian personnel on hand from before were used to provide instruction and carry out checks.

Following assembly of the aircraft and ferrying to the front, for ongoing maintenance and care of the aircraft, the unit now has one airframe mechanic per aircraft and one armorer for every two aircraft. As well, there is a senior mechanic with a senior armorer, two *Kettenmeister*, and three auxiliary personnel. Also under the senior mechanic are four civilian personnel (two airframe fitters and two engine mechanics), who as specialists are still needed for guidance and checks.

By this time, Franco had come to realize that he lacked the resources to take Madrid. In an attempt to regain the initiative, he now decided to eliminate the Republican enclave in northern Spain. All air forces committed to the campaign were placed under the command of the Legion Condor. To prepare for operations in the north, the legion moved its air park (P/88) from Seville to León, while its headquarters (S/88) transferred from Salamanca to Vitoria. The Messerschmitt fighters were sent north as they became ready.[18] The first three aircraft were delivered to 2.J/88 by *Hptm.* Herwig Knüppel, *Oblt.* Urban Schlaffer, and *Uffz.*

Bf 109 A 6 • 10 photographed at Seville-Tablada. Technicians have jacked up the aircraft's tail in preparation for bore-sighting the guns. Note the long-span leading-edge slats. On the far left of the photo is what appears to be a partially disassembled D.H. 9. Between it and the Messerschmitt is He 51 2 • 42. Finally, on the right is a Breguet XIX, a type used both by the Nationalists and Republicans in the early stages of the conflict. *Private Collection*

Willi Gödecke on March 14.[19] Günther Lützow, the new *Staffelkapitän* who had arrived five days earlier, took one of the new fighters up on a test flight. He recorded his initial impressions in his diary:[20]

Mui rapido! Takeoff normal. Incredible forward stick pressure needed while landing. Turns well, but with constant trim adjustments.

The Nationalist offensive in the north began on March 31, 1937. Republican air strength in the north was weak, and the Nationalists enjoyed air superiority from the outset. The Bf 109s were frequently assigned to escort the Do 17 and He 111 bombers of VB/88, based at Burgos. There was little opportunity for air combat, but on April 6, Lützow scored his first victory, shooting down a *Chato* (a Polikarpov I-15 fighter biplane; Spanish for "snub nose"). It was also the first enemy aircraft shot down by a Messerschmitt 109. Lützow recorded the event in his diary:[21]

First victory. 1715 hours, 7,800 feet, northwest of Ochandiano. Curtiss biplane. . . . Pilot of the downed machine came down by parachute on our side of the lines. Eighteen years old, raw beginner. Stated that he had been on a cross-country flight from Santander to Valencia.

The 2.J/88 achieved its next success on April 22, shooting down two I-15s. One was brought down by *Lt.* Radusch; the other, by *Fw.* Heilmayer. Felipe del Rio, the leading Republican fighter ace in the north with seven victories, was killed in this action.

It was at this time that the first attempts were made to devise a tactical formation better suited to the Messerschmitt's characteristics. While Lützow was in Germany on leave, his deputy *Hptm.* Lothar von Janson commanded the *Staffel.* With insufficient aircraft for the bomber escort role, he adopted two interim measures. First, he led the *Staffel* in a single *Kette*[22] formation; second, he had the remaining fighters operate in pairs (*Rotten*) to the left and right of the

Bf 109 A 6 • 10, probably the most photographed of all the Bf 109s to see action with the Legion Condor. Here it is seen at Calamocha in its initial configuration, with wooden fixed-pitch propeller and closed cowling panels. Beneath the cockpit is the special marking commemorating Günther Lützow's first victory, the first ever by the pilot of a Bf 109. It consists of a number "1" inside a laurel wreath, flanked by the dates 1937 and 1938. Aft of the 2.J/88 emblem is another special marking, a bearded figure drinking from a foaming mug of beer, with the legend *"Pass uff!"* ("Watch out!"). Note that the outer portions of the wooden propeller blades have been painted black. Ironically this was not the aircraft in which Lützow achieved his first victory on April 6, 1937, because 6 • 10 was not flown from Seville to Vitoria until April 29. *Private Collection*

Bf 109 A 6 • 3 back on its feet after coming to grief at Santander-West. Note the damage to the flap, 2.J/88's "Top Hat" emblem, and the aircraft code are entirely aft of the fuselage disc. The engine appears to have been wrenched from its mounts and here is supported by the bed of a truck. Also note the ambulance in the background. *Private Collection*

Bf 109 A 6 • 5 at Vitoria. The aircraft was flown from Seville to 2.J/88 at Vitoria on March 31, 1937. This photo was probably taken soon after its arrival, since it exhibits few signs of wear. The aircraft had not been fitted with the new fuselage oil tank before leaving Seville, because the new tanks did not arrive from Germany until early April. *Private Collection*

command *Kette* and increased the intervals between aircraft. This increased each pilot's ability to maneuver and allowed the *Staffel* to cover a greater amount of airspace.

Following his return to Spain, Lützow continued experimenting. During a morning mission to Bilbao, escorting Ju 52 bombers, he tried von Janson's formation. Afterward he wrote:[23]

> One flight of three, two pairs. Best formation: somewhat tighter *Staffel* wedge with little vertical spacing. Line astern left or right is rubbish!

Lützow soon came to realize that the tactics being taught German fighter pilots were all wrong for the Messerschmitt. Compared to everything that came before, it was a completely different machine. Its strengths were speed, initial climb rate, and diving ability. In a classic dogfight it was vastly inferior both to the Chato biplane and very maneuverable Rata monoplane. The Bf 109 needed plenty of maneuvering room in order to take advantage of its strengths. Lützow later wrote:[24]

> By then we were already operating with significantly greater lateral, longitudinal, and vertical spacing, in order to increase freedom of movement and enable us to search larger areas for enemy aircraft.

The *Kapitän* also devoted much time to practicing fighter versus fighter combat in the Bf 109. He described one such engagement with a Fiat CR.32:[25]

> First aerobatics in the 109. Fabulous roll rate, pull-up into a steep climb poor, fast in the dive. Loops normally. Mock combat with Viotti. Fiat turns better, but not as much so as I expected. Climbs no better than the 109.

When 2.J/88 was not in action, Lützow had every serviceable machine in the air practicing the new formations. Sometimes Lützow led the formation, and sometimes one of the others led while he watched from a distance:[26]

> Morning *Staffel* exercise. Regular nine. *Hptm.* von Janson led; I observed as the tenth machine. Nothing new of significance. During extended turns both *Ketten* remain below the lead *Kette*. Important to commence the turn at the right time during crossovers!

The existing procedures for reversing course in formation were also useless in the Bf 109. As an interim measure, Lützow came up with the idea of having the outer *Ketten* pass over and under the lead *Kette* during changes of direction. He was also coming to realize that the *Kette* formation of three aircraft was just too restrictive for effective combat maneuvers with the Messerschmitt:[27]

The Bf 109 A fighters of 2.J/88 at Vitoria in the summer of 1937. The first aircraft in line is 6 • 16, followed by 6 • 14 and 6 • 7. Aircraft 6 • 16 arrived at Seville on March 23 and made its first flight in Spain on April 8, 1937. It was sent to 2.J/88 at Vitoria on April 16. Aircraft 6 • 16 was one of two Bf 109 As that survived to be handed over to the Spanish Nationalist air force in 1938, the other being 6 • 10. *Private Collection*

Bf 109 A 6 • 16 at 2.J/88's dispersal at Vitoria. The aircraft's *silberweiss* finish appears to be in excellent condition, with no signs of wear. Note the Revi 3 a/b's auxiliary gunsight mechanism forward of the aircraft's windscreen. *Private Collection*

A member of 2.J/88's ground personnel on the wing of 6 • 16 at Vitoria. The hatch over the fuel filler point has been removed and hangs by its chain. The circular hatch over the oil tank filler point is visible just to the left of the man's head. Number 6 • 16 was one of the aircraft that was fitted with the new fuselage-mounted oil tank before leaving Seville to join 2.J/88. *Private Collection*

Air combat practice. Always two against two. Heavy strain on the machines. Turns poorly. Heavy aileron vibration. I against *Hptm.* v. Janson. Outcome indecisive. Fierce battles.

From these simulated combats, Lützow reached the conclusion that the pair, or *Rotte*, should be the basic fighter formation. Two pairs would make a *Schwarm*, and three *Schwärme* would make a *Staffel*. This classic formation would be adopted first by the Luftwaffe and later by most other air forces during World War II.

Bilbao fell on May 17. The outcome in the north was now a foregone conclusion. Encounters with enemy aircraft became rare. That same day, J/88 received a new commanding officer: *Major* Gotthard Handrick, winner of the gold medal in the pentathlon at the 1936 Olympic Games.

The 2.J/88 was kept active escorting the Legion Condor's bombers, but almost a month would pass before another enemy aircraft was shot down. Then, on May 22, while leading a *Kette* with wingmen *Uffz.* Guido Höneß and *Uffz.* Norbert Flegel, Lützow was able to close to within 65 feet of an unsuspecting flight of three I-15s:[28]

I fired, pulled up, turned to the next, and was unable to get in a good shot. I climbed, turned around, and 1,300 feet below saw the first one in flames. Blew apart. No parachute seen. The second and third dove away.

Lineup of 2.J/88 Bf 109s at Vitoria. The second aircraft in line is 6 • 15. It appears to be in its original configuration with wooden propeller and smooth cowling panels with no vents. This aircraft was delivered to 2.J/88 at Almorox on March 31, 1937. It was lost on December 4, 1937, while being flown by *Fw.* Polenz. The aircraft developed engine trouble and Polenz was obliged to make a forced landing in Republican territory. The aircraft was captured by the Republicans and passed to France and eventually the Soviet Union for testing. *Private Collection*

Two more Republican fighters, both Chatos, were shot down by Lützow and *Fw.* Braunschweiger on May 28. These were 2.J/88's last victories before it was called away to the Madrid area. During operations in the north, the *Staffel* had claimed a total of seven Republican aircraft shot down.

Bf 109 A 6 • 12, *Werknummer* 1005, at Vitoria in the summer of 1937. The aircraft is still in initial configuration. Note the external elements of the Revi 3a/b gunsight in front of the windscreen. *Private Collection*

Bf 109 A 6 • 13, *Werknummer* 1006, parked next to the runway at Vitoria in the summer of 1937. The aircraft is still in initial configuration. Note the exhaust staining on the side of the fuselage and the open sliding panel in the canopy. *Private Collection*

Bf 109 A 6 • 14 parked in the grass at Vitoria in the spring of 1937. The aircraft is still in initial configuration with wooden propeller and no vents in the engine cowling. Beyond it is 6 • 10. The photo was obviously taken prior to the application of the special markings commemorating Lützow's first victory. Assembly of 6 • 14 began on March 15, 1937, and was completed on the 24th. It then underwent a comparatively long period of testing and modification, which included an incident in which the aircraft's port undercarriage leg collapsed on landing, and was finally flown to Vitoria on April 16, 1937. *Private Collection*

BRUNETE

On July 6, 1937, Republican forces launched an unexpected attack toward Quijorna and Brunete from the salient west of Madrid. The Nationalist command immediately transferred air units from the northern front to bases near Madrid to counter the offensive. Both sides concentrated their air forces in the area, resulting in the fiercest air battles of the war to date. Altogether the Nationalists assembled about 200 aircraft. Facing them were approximately 400 Republican aircraft, including about 200 Chatos and Ratas. The Nationalist air forces were placed under the command of *Stab*/88.

The 2nd *Staffel* arrived at Avila on July 7. The next day it provided fighter escort for the first mass bombing raid by aircraft of K/88 and A/88. The *Staffel's* first encounter with enemy aircraft took place that same day, with two SB bombers, or *Katiuskas*, shot down by *Lt.* Pingel and *Uffz.* Höneß.

On July 8, *Hptm.* Handrick assumed command of the *Jagdgruppe*, replacing *Hptm.* von Merhart.

More victories followed on July 12. *Lt.* Pingel, *Fw.* Buhl, and *Fw.* Boddem each shot down a Rata, while Pingel also shot down an SB, and *Uffz.* Guido Höneß accounted for two *Pragas*.

One of the *Staffel's* aircraft was written off on July 11, when *Uffz.* Flegel made a forced landing after his aircraft's engine failed. The next day the unit lost another aircraft, when *Uffz.* Guido Höneß was shot down and killed. Two days later, 2.J/88 took part in a fierce air battle resulting in two Republican aircraft shot down. *Feldwebel* Boddem shot down a Chato flown by the American Harold Dahl, who was captured. *Fw.* Braunschweiger also shot down a Rata.

The extreme heat and pace of operations placed a severe strain on the sensitive engines of the Bf 109s. To prevent overheating and water pump failures, pilots were instructed to restrict climb rates to 588 ft./min. (3 m/sec.) until an altitude of 9,842 ft. (3,000 m) was reached. Consequently, it took the *Staffel* about half an hour to reach its operational altitude of 16,400 ft. and make the 30- to 40-mile flight to the combat zone. Lützow wrote:[29]

> I would like to take this opportunity to mention that in the long run the Bf 109's extremely sensitive engine was not capable of handling the stress of so many missions per day. They began running roughly after just three or four days. Sensitivity of the supercharger is the most likely cause. We must not blind ourselves to the fact that the Jumo 210 is extremely delicate and requires much-better and thorough maintenance than does the BMW VI, for example. I am therefore very much against too-frequent aerobatics, mock dogfights, and formation exercises with the Bf 109.

From Bf 109 Experience Report No. 3 (February 16 to April 30, 1937): "To facilitate piston changes and partial overhauls, a BMW VI assembly trestle was set up to accept a Jumo 210. As the illustration [in the report] shows, a running-in bed was fashioned from a wrecked [Bf 109] airframe. The engines are run for four to five hours, including ten minutes at the maximum achievable speed of 2,700 rpm at a boost pressure of 1.27 atm." This photo illustrates the running-in bed referred to in the report. The 2.J/88's "Top Hat" emblem can barely be made out beneath the rear section of the canopy, but the aircraft number is not visible. *Private Collection*

On July 18, *Ofw.* Hillmann shot down a Rata, but another Republican fighter shot down *Uffz.* Harbach. The German pilot parachuted to safely and came down in Nationalist territory.

Feldwebel Boddem was quickly becoming the *Staffel's* most successful pilot, shooting down Ratas on July 21 and 25.

The heavy pace of operations had taken a toll on 2.J/88. On July 21, Lützow described his unit's status:[30]

> 6-16 has to go to Burgos, 6-15's generator is shot, 6-13 is washed up, 6-9 is unserviceable, 6-10 is on patrol. And so I have just three serviceable aircraft for the second mission at 1600 hours.

During the period from July 7 to 25, 2.J/88 claimed a total of sixteen enemy aircraft shot down. Twenty-two new Bf 109 B fighters arrived in Spain in mid-July[31] and were assembled at León, but though badly needed at the front, they could not be delivered to the units until acceptance flights had been carried out.

The Republican offensive was halted, and a Nationalist counterattack launched on July 23 retook Brunete. With the threat near Madrid contained, Franco could again turn his attention to the northern front. Before returning to action, the Legion Condor's aircraft were given a thorough overhaul at León. The recently delivered He 111s and Bf 109s were test-flown, and their crews carried out cross-country flights to gain familiarity with the new machines.

Previous page, top left: Bf 109 A 6 • 4 down in the trees in northern Spain. In the right foreground are the remains of a tree that was snapped off by the aircraft's starboard wingtip. The resulting damage is readily apparent. The aircraft's wings were removed on site and it was transported by oxcart to a nearby road, where further disassembly took place. It was then loaded onto a truck for removal. *Top right*: The Twentieth Century meets the Middle Ages. A team of oxen pulling a cart with wooden wheels carrying 6 • 4's fuselage. *Bottom left*: Another team hauling the aircraft's port wing to a road for recovery. 6 • 4 left for the front before the new oil tanks reached Tablada, and this item was retrofitted in the field. The circular oil filler hatch in the aircraft's port wing can be seen just above the left shoulder of the man whose right hand is resting on the aileron. *Bottom right*: Having reached the road, the aircraft's fuselage is raised onto the bed of a truck. Note the smooth finish on the fuselage. The Bf 109 As were delivered to Seville with fuselage seams puttied and sanded smooth. *Above*: Having reached a road, 6 • 4's fuselage is raised onto the bed of a truck. *Below*: The remains of 6 • 4 and 6 • 5. Note the circular cutout beneath 6 • 4's windscreen for access to the fuselage oil tank's filler hatch and the opening in the fuselage bulkhead. *Private Collection*

Crated Bf 109 B fighters arriving at León. There the aircraft were unpacked, assembled, checked over, and flight tested. *Private Collection*

More Bf 109 Bs in the hangar at León. The aircraft on the right has had its code, 6 • 18, marked on the side of the fuselage in chalk. *Private Collection*

Work on the first batch of Bf 109 B fighters progresses in the hangar at León. Staff have begun applying markings to the aircraft on the left, specifically the black disc on the fuselage. The code of the aircraft on the right has been written in chalk on the fuselage. It appears to be 6 • 30 or 6 • 39. *Private Collection*

The Bf 109 V4 after a crash landing, which resulted in the aircraft being written off. It is wearing the 1st *Staffel* emblem and appears to have been repainted in a color darker than the original *silberweiss*. The aircraft returned to Seville-Tablada on April 15, 1937, for a partial overhaul and perhaps was repainted before returning to the front. The V4 had by far the longest life of any of the Bf 109 prototypes in Spain, the V6 lasting just a few days and the V3 several months before they were written off. *Private Collection*

RETURN TO THE NORTHERN FRONT

With the stabilization of the front in the area of Brunete, Nationalist commanders could again turn their attention to the northern front, which now consisted of the strip of coastline between Bilbao and Gijón.

Before returning to action, the Legion Condor's aircraft were given a thorough overhaul at León. The recently delivered He 111s and Bf 109s were test-flown and their crews carried out cross-country flights to gain familiarity with the new machines.

On July 30, 1938, J/88 moved to Alar del Rey and Callahora. Its strength at that time was nine Bf 109s and eighteen He 51s. Republican strength in the Santander area consisted of two squadrons equipped with Chatos and two with Ratas plus miscellaneous types.

The 2.J/88's equipment situation was still less than rosy. On August 13, Lützow wrote in his diary:[32]

6-8 and 6-9 cannot be repaired. That leaves only ten old MEs (including 6-5). What a mess.

German fighters claimed their first enemy aircraft on the new front on August 13, when *Feldwebel* Boddem shot down a Rata near Santander. The Republican air force was very active, and there were a number of large-scale air battles. In two days of fighting on August 21 and 22, the Nationalists claimed to have shot down thirty Republican aircraft. Three Chatos were claimed by Lützow, Pingel, and Flegel on the twenty-second.

The 1.J/88 began receiving Bf 109s in August, at first operating them alongside its He 51s. Harro Harder scored the *Staffel*'s first kill with the new fighter on August 27. He described the action in his diary:[33]

The Martin bomber is tough, flies wonderfully, and is awfully fast. Sigmund and I peel off to attack while Terry covers the rear. I move in close, dancing in his prop wash, and aim calmly. Just one short burst and the large machine is in flames. I pull up and watch the bomber crash into a field.

A mechanic poses for a photo astride the fuselage of 6 • 3 of 2.J/88 at Vitoria. He wrote on the back of the photo: "As a mechanic with the ME *Staffel* in Vitoria". This aircraft was fitted with an engine-mounted 20 mm MG C30 cannon. It was the only A-series aircraft with a centrally-mounted gun flown by the Legion Condor. The cannon muzzle may be seen in the opening in the spinner tip. The MG C30 was installed on February 21, at Seville during initial assembly. Records also show that the aircraft was delivered with radio equipment, which was subsequently removed. 6 • 3 was one of the first aircraft to join 2.J/88, departing Seville for Almorox on March 14, 1937, along with 6 • 1 and 6 • 4. *Private Collection*

Despite its poor quality, this photo is of interest because it is one of the few to show Bf 109 A 6 • 8 before it was wrecked in a crash. The fuselage-mounted oil tank had not been installed when this photo was taken, as illustrated by the absence of the circular oil filler hatch forward of the cockpit. *Private Collection*

Bf 109 A 6 • 8 down in northern Spain. The aircraft's fuselage has crumpled just aft of the cockpit. Note the 2.J/88 "Top Hat" emblem on the fuselage and the oil tank filler cap on the fuselage side forward of the windscreen. The incident occurred in early August 1937, since on the 13th of that month, Lützow wrote in his diary that the aircraft was beyond repair. *Private Collection*

Bf 109 B 6 • 36 at Llanes airfield in Asturia, with the Sierra del Cuera providing an impressive backdrop. This aircraft was flown by *Hptm.* Harro Harder, *Kapitän* of 1st *Staffel* from April 6 to December 18, 1937. It is finished in the RLM 70/71/65 color scheme. In front of it is Bf 109 A 6 • 15 finished in *silberweiss*. Both aircraft wear the 2nd *Staffel* X marking. Aircraft 6 • 15 was lost on December 7, 1937, and was captured by the Republicans. Visible to the right is aircraft 6 • 20, flown by Fritz Awe. *Private Collection*

Number 6 • 17, the first aircraft from the first batch of Bf 109 Bs delivered to the Legion Condor, in flight over Spain. It is finished in the European scheme of RLM 70/71/65. The 2.J/88's "Top Hat" emblem is barely visible above the port wingtip. This emblem was usually black, but against the dark-green paint of the Bf 109 B, a white version was applied. Since most green-camouflaged Bf 109 Bs went to 1.J/88, there are few examples of the "Top Hat" emblem in white.
Private Collection

On August 24, the Republicans launched an attack in Aragon to divert attention from the northern front. By then, however, the Nationalists were about to enter Santander, so the main point of the attack was lost. On September 1, the objective was shifted from Saragossa to Belchite.[34] The operation turned into another disaster for the Republicans, who lost large quantities of precious armaments, especially tanks, for no gain.

With the threat in Aragon eliminated, the Nationalists were able to concentrate fully on conquering Asturia. In September, 2.J/88 was transferred to Santander. The Republicans continued to resist in the air, and combats were frequent.

Ofw. Seiler shot down the first enemy aircraft over Asturia on September 4. More kills followed, with Boddem shooting down a Rata on September 6, and Harder claiming a French-made twin-engine bomber on the seventh. Harder continued to score, adding a Loire 46 and an I-15 on September 9. *Lt.* Brücker destroyed a Rata on the same day, and Harder shot down another I-15 on September 15. He wrote in his diary:[35]

> With *Fw.* Polenz as wingman, I attacked five Curtisses and three Ratas. The enemy machines were flying in close formation about 6,500 feet higher. They were alerted and came down at us. Polenz was attacked by three enemy fighters and made the mistake of trying to dogfight them. He took hits and flew home. This left me alone. I was repeatedly attacked from above, which I parried by diving straight down followed by a pull-up into a vertical climb. A Bf 109 climbing from below is very difficult to spot, and I was able to surprise a Curtiss in a zoom climb. I closed in, placed the crosshairs on the center of its engine, and fired from point-blank range. The Curtiss abruptly rolled onto its back and spun away. I thought I had shot him down, but then I saw him recover about 1,600 feet below. His armored seat had saved him. We turned like crazy beneath the base of the clouds. Not wanting to lose the altitude I had gained, I pulled back up into the clouds. After a few moments I again gauged the situation. I saw a Curtiss in a steep dive, toward the west and home. I was able to move in behind him unnoticed. I closed slowly, my airspeed indicator showing 340 mph. Once in range, I aimed carefully and fired a short burst. Number 6 crashed burning into the sea. The pilot baled out about 1,000 feet below me, his parachute badly scorched.

A pair of Bf 109 Bs photographed from an He 111 of the K/88. In the lead is aircraft 6 • 28. Both fighters are finished in the RLM 70/71/65 scheme. *Private Collection*

Two photos showing Bf 109 A 6 • 7 after coming to grief at Santander-West while being flown by *Fw*. Norbert Flegel. Written on the reverse of one of the photos is "Emergency landing because of water in the fuel. Santander-West. September 1937."
  Its wings removed, 6 • 7 has been loaded onto a truck for removal. Note the damage to the aircraft's fabric-covered flaps. *Private Collection*

This Bf 109 B, 6 • 36, was flown by *Hptm*. Harro Harder, *Kapitän* of 1st *Staffel* from April 6 to December 18, 1937. In the original photograph four victory bars can be seen on the fin. There was probably another victory bar, as Harder scored his fourth and fifth victories on September 9, 1937, claiming a Loire 46 and a Curtiss. He claimed a total of eleven Republican aircraft shot down, making him the Legion Condor's third most successful fighter pilot after Mölders and Schellmann. *Private Collection*

The 1.J/88's strength at that time was seven Bf 109s and fourteen He 51s. On September 14, Günther Lützow returned to Germany and was replaced as commander of 2.J/88 by *Oblt*. Schlichting. The new commander scored his first kill, a Rata, on September 23. By this time, *Hptm*. Handrick had converted onto the Bf 109. He described his first encounter with enemy fighters:[36]

Our attacks on Gijón were by no means always as smooth and trouble-free. The Rojos offered us considerable resistance in the air, and their Ratas and Curtisses were in no way poor.

Once, during air battle, I engaged a Curtiss. Since this was my first air battle, I was of course convinced that I would shoot the enemy crate down in no time. I was wrong!

Apart from the fact that my guns weren't firing properly for some reason, I must admit that I did not conduct myself all that skillfully.

I attacked the Curtiss from behind—it reversed course. Instead of climbing and then repeating the attack, I immediately continued attacking and managed to get off just ten rounds per pass. The Curtiss, though slower than my machine, was very maneuverable. The enemy pilot flew extremely well and was undoubtedly a damned good shot.

Gradually we moved farther away from the coast, and finally we were a good three miles over the sea, near Gijón. The front was 30 to 35 miles away.

It was therefore high time to put an end to this!

I closed in on the Curtiss, so close that finally there was a great crash—I had collided with it.

My machine had been struck on the wing near the fuselage; also the controls were jammed. I made three or four involuntary rolls in succession before I regained control of my crate. With difficulty I managed to fly straight and level. Should I bale out over the water?

No, thank you. The water is too cold in October.

I headed toward land. If one of them catches me now . . . I dared not continue this thought to its conclusion.

Finally I saw the front; Llanes! I thought to myself: "You're over the airfield. Now you can crash-land the machine without worrying."

Aircraft 6 • 21 photographed after a forced landing. The position of the propeller blades suggests that the aircraft's engine failed in flight. Damage appears to be limited mainly to the engine and radiator. *Private Collection*

Bf 109 B 6 • 24 of 2.J/88 at Llanes airfield in Asturia, with the Sierra del Cuera in the background. The aircraft is finished in the RLM 70/71/65 camouflage scheme. Note the prominent fuel octane triangle beneath the cockpit and the absence of any unit marking. *Private Collection*

Oblt. Rolf Pingel (sitting on the port mainwheel) and another pilot with Bf 109 B 6 • 21, Pingel's aircraft, photographed at Santander-West. Pingel scored a total of six victories while flying with 2.J/88 in Spain. *Author's Collection*

Bf 109 B 6 • 25 after a rough landing at Alar del Rey in July 1937. In the second photo the ground crew has removed the wing root fairing in preparation for removal of the wing. The aircraft is finished in the RLM 70/71/65 scheme. Note the shorter leading-edge slat compared to that of the Bf 109 A. *Private Collection*

Bf 109 B 6 • 28 after coming down in rocky terrain. Its pilot may have been compelled to make a forced landing due to damage sustained in combat, as suggested by the shattered canopy. The identity of this aircraft is something of a mystery as no unit marking is visible. Seven victory bars are painted on the fin. Also note the hinged windscreen quarter panel, seen on early Bf 109 Bs used by the Legion. The aircraft's spinner has a white ring around the base with the rest in a darker color. The aircraft's finish is difficult to identify with certainty, but it may have been one of the machines whose original dark green scheme was overpainted in *silberweiss. Private Collection*

The fuselage of Mosca number "33" has been loaded onto a flatbed truck, while its wings and horizontal tail surfaces have been placed in another truck and covered with tarpaulins. *Private Collection*

This I-16 type 5, aircraft number "33," probably of 3rd *Escuadrilla de Moscas*, was captured by the Germans. Here it is seen sitting in a shed before being partially disassembled and loaded onto trucks for removal. The I-16 type 5 was armed with two 7.62 mm ShKAS machine guns mounted in the wings. *Private Collection*

But then the group commander in me made his presence felt: "Where in the world do you think you'll get a replacement if you crash-land your crate? How are they going to transport it out of here? All the bridges in the rear have been blown; it could be weeks before you get a new aircraft . . ."

These same thoughts spurring me on, I nursed my crippled machine to Santander. Thank God! My height was just 450 feet. I cautiously lowered the undercarriage. As it came down, a piece from the wing of the enemy Curtiss fell out of my machine—a souvenir from my first air battle, which I still have. Now and then I look at it and think: a man has to have luck on his side!

After landing, I got out and looked at my bird. It was pretty banged up: the right wing was a write-off, the fuselage

Bf 109 B 6 • 34, flown by *Oblt*. Erich Woitke of 1.J/88. The man under the wing is attaching a rope from the wing tie-down to a compressed air cylinder. Note the brown oil triangle on the port wing just inside the black walkway line. The Bf 109 B had its oil tank in the wing, whereas the later C, D, and E versions all had fuselage-mounted oil tanks. *Private Collection*

Bf 109 B 6 • 31 of 1.J/88 being serviced at Calamocha. The aircraft's dark-green camouflage certainly stands out against the local terrain. *Private Collection*

Two pilots of 1.J/88 with mascot in front of their Bf 109 Bs at Calamocha. Both aircraft are finished in the RLM 70/71/65 camouflage scheme, and the 1st *Staffel* X marking can be seen on aircraft 6 • 31 in the background. *Private Collection*

was dented, there were a few bullet holes in the rear, and the tail section would have to be replaced. But I was still happy that I'd carried on, since the damage was repaired in two days and my bird was flying again.

Gijón fell on October 21, and the Nationalist forces found four abandoned Ratas and four Chatos. One of the I-16s was dismantled and sent back to Germany. In the air, the Republicans continued to fight bravely despite their hopeless situation.

With the onset of the autumn rainy period, J/88 flew to León, where its aircraft were overhauled by P/88. The 1st *Staffel* was completely equipped with Bf 109s, and a new 4th *Staffel* was formed on He 51s.

During the period July 30 to October 13, the fighters of the Legion Condor shot down thirty-three enemy aircraft.

TERUEL

With the end of the fighting in northern Spain, Franco began planning a winter offensive against Madrid. The chosen start date was December 18, 1937. In preparation for the attack, the Legion Condor established its headquarters in Almazán, while on November 19, the fighter units moved to airfields at Burgo de Osma and Torresavina.

The Messerschmitts were in action soon after their arrival at Burgo de Osma. The 2nd *Staffel* destroyed three Ratas on November 29, and three more the next day.

During the final weeks of 1937, J/88 was moved several times, ending up in the Saragossa area at the end of November. On December 4, *Feldwebel* Otto Polenz made a forced landing in Republican territory. His Bf 109, bearing the code 6 ● 15, was captured by the Republicans. It was

Two Bf 109 Bs of 2.J/88 at Calamocha. Aircraft 6 ● 35 in the background appears to be finished in *silberweiss*, while the machine in the foreground wears the RLM 70/71/65 scheme. By this time the segregation of color schemes by unit may have given way to the need to maintain unit strength levels. *Private Collection*

Two photos of Reinhard Seiler's Bf 109 B 6 • 32 of 2.J/88 during the winter of 1937–38. The aircraft is finished in *silberweiss* applied over the original dark European scheme. Seiler was one of the Legion Condor's most successful fighter pilots, shooting down nine Republican aircraft. He scored his first kill, a Chato, on August 26, 1937. This was followed by a Rata on September 4, 1937; a Rata on November 29, 1937; an SB bomber on January 12, 1938; another Rata on January 22; two SBs on February 7; and finally two I-15s on February 22, 1938. *Private Collection*

subsequently sent via France to the Soviet Union, where it was evaluated. The following account of his last mission and subsequent capture was written by Polenz upon his release at the end of the Spanish Civil War:

> On December 4, 1937, I took off from Saragossa airfield with the 1st *Staffel* on a free-hunt mission into the area around Bujarale. I was flying aircraft 6 ● 15 as wingman to *Lt.* Kühle. We attacked a lone Curtiss, but afterward my engine lagged while climbing. Consequently I fell behind my element leader, who subsequently initiated an attack on a group of Curtisses flying about 3,200 feet lower. I stayed back at a height of 11,500 feet to check my engine, which had begun cutting out now and then. At this time I saw another of our aircraft, 6 ● 50 from the second element, at my altitude. Unfortunately, I was unable to give a signal, and I headed back toward the west, steadily losing altitude.
>
> I was able to keep the engine going by injecting fuel and use of the pressure pump; however, it finally quit for good as I crossed the Ebro River at a height of about 1,000 feet, and I was forced to make a landing at 1155. The right wing of the aircraft suffered minor damage in the process.
>
> As soon as I had landed, three persons appeared about 500 feet away and began running toward me. I was unable to set the aircraft on fire, since I had no matches or other means of starting a fire.

Polenz's account contradicts claims that he had been shot down. Photographs of his machine after capture show no apparent damage, which further supports his version of events.

Another pilot was lost on December 5, when *Ofw.* Leo Sigmund was shot down and captured. On December 10, the Nationalist air forces launched large-scale raids against Republican airfields east of Saragossa. The attacks did not achieve the desired results, however, and large numbers of Republican fighters were waiting. The Messerschmitt pilots found themselves outnumbered by the enemy on almost every occasion, which resulted in growing frustration. Harder wrote:[37]

> December 11 was even worse. We escorted K/88. The Red fighters were already at altitude. Eight Curtisses attacked the bombers; we were able to drive them away. Over the target the bombers made a turn and became bunched up. The *Staffeln* were one above the other when they dropped their bombs. One He 111 was struck by a bomb and blew apart. More and more enemy fighters arrived: here, a unit of eighteen Ratas; there, twenty-eight Curtisses. I climbed, hoping to attack from out of the sun. My altimeter showed 22,000 feet. Eight machines came toward me from the side, even higher than I. Smoke trails began coming from their machine guns while I was still debating what to do. I got out of there as fast as I could. We counted about seventy Red fighters. The Italians claimed to have shot down twenty fighters, and they hadn't flown one meter beyond the front.

The Republicans had learned of the Nationalist plans to strike at their Guadalajara front, however, and they now launched an attack of their own to disrupt Franco's offensive. The chosen target of the attack was the provincial capital of Teruel.[38] The attack began during the night of December 15–16 and caught the Nationalists completely by surprise. To support the attack they had massed six squadrons of Ratas, three of Chatos, four of Katiuskas, and four of *Natachas* (nickname for a Polikarpov R-Z, a Soviet reconnaissance bomber). The harsh winter conditions made operations difficult, and during the cold nights ground crews were forced to warm up the engines of the fighters hourly to make sure they were ready for takeoff come morning. *Oblt.* Schellmann relieved Harro Harder as commander of 1.J/88 on December 19. On the twenty-third, J/88 was transferred to Calamocha. *Hptm.* Handrick described the conditions there:[39]

> The Battle of Teruel was a particularly difficult time for us. It was fought for possession of the town of Teruel, which was at the tip of a Nationalist salient that had projected into enemy territory since the start of the war.
>
> When the battle began I was in Calamocha, a tiny place about 50 miles from Teruel.
>
> The previous summer we had enjoyed more of the famous Spanish sunshine than was good for us, but now, in inhospitable Calamocha, we experienced a brutal Spanish winter. None of us had ever thought it possible that it could ever really be cold in Spain, and the only thing that helped us through the blistering summer heat had been the thought that at least we would enjoy a warm and pleasant winter.
>
> When I took my first drive to the Teruel front on Christmas Eve to look around, the thermometer showed minus 1 degree F.
>
> I will probably think of that Christmas Eve 1937 every time I light the candles on the Christmas tree at home in Germany. I was driving to my headquarters. With me in the car were a few comrades, who like me were looking forward to our warm quarters, where a Christmas tree, greetings from home, and a stiff grog were undoubtedly waiting.
>
> Twenty-five miles from El Burgo, however, the vehicle broke down. The driver looked under the hood and shrugged his shoulders—nothing could be done; the crate wouldn't go.
>
> We scouted the area on foot, but there were no villages to be seen. There was no one around to guide us, and we couldn't rely on our maps, of whose wonderful scale I have already told. We therefore had no choice but to wait. It was the first Christmas Eve of my life that I spent on a country road. Sadly for us, we didn't even have a drink in our baggage with which to console ourselves. All that we could find were three bottles of beer. They made the rounds, but they could do little to warm our bones.

Bf 109 B 6 • 40 of 1.J/88 on an unidentified airfield, possibly Calamocha, still in its European scheme of two greens with pale-blue undersurfaces. *Private Collection*

Bf 109 6 • 41 parked on an unidentified Spanish airfield. It is finished in the 70/71/65 camouflage scheme with white wingtips and rudder. *Private Collection*

Every hour we got out of the vehicle to walk around and warm up a little. And so we spent the night in most unholy conversation. It wasn't until next morning that I arrived at my quarters, where I found everyone still in their warm beds, sleeping off the exertions of Christmas Eve.

Our ground crews had a particularly difficult time in Calamocha. Night after night and hour after hour, a special party had to run up the engines to keep them warm.

J/88's base at Calamocha was also the target of several raids by Republican bombers. Handrick described one such attack:[40]

Morning was just dawning on January 12, when I suddenly heard our antiaircraft guns firing. I rushed onto the balcony, still in my pajamas. I could see shells bursting in the morning sky; then I spotted the Red bombers. I could make out their flight paths clearly. Each bomber was leaving behind a trail of gray smoke. In spite of the bitter cold, I ran half-dressed to the airfield. It was all over by the time I got there. The flak and the alert *Rotte* had done their work very well. Each had brought down two of the Reds.

The two successful fighter pilots were *Ofw.* Seiler and *Uffz.* Staege. Staege's victim was the *Jagdgruppe's* 100th confirmed victory.

Oblt. Schellmann, who would become the Legion Condor's top-scoring fighter pilot for a time, scored his first victory on January 18. He wrote:[41]

My flight of five machines was hanging in the sky at 16,000 feet: a *Kette* on the left, a *Rotte* on the right. I had long since sighted the enemy: a squadron of Curtisses and one of Ratas. They were just what we wanted, but I had to be patient. It wasn't time to go after them yet. First we had to reach a favorable attack position. The enemy aircraft flew to and fro and appeared not to have seen us. We kept pace with them nicely. I climbed to 18,000 feet and worked my way closer. When the enemy reversed course for the fourth time, I waggled my wings. I attacked the machine on the extreme left. My bursts were on target, and flames shot from the Rata. I broke away.

Leutnant Woitke shot down a second Rata from the enemy formation. Two more enemy aircraft were shot down on January 20, a Rata by *Oblt.* Balthasar and a Chato by *Uffz.* Rochel. Balthasar had arrived in Spain as an observer with A/88, the Legion Condor's reconnaissance unit. *Oblt.* Balthasar, who had taken part in numerous bombing and reconnaissance missions with the reconnaissance unit, described his first mission as a fighter pilot:[42]

Move to the front near Madrid. First mission. I still feel somewhat unsure of myself, but I convince myself that nothing will happen on my very first fighter mission, and I will have time to get used to being part of the squadron. Mistake! Before I really know what is happening, I am all alone in the sky, while below the squadron is involved in a wild dogfight with Ratas. Unsure as to what I should do; unable to distinguish friend from foe, I first make a wide turn to get a better look at what is going on and then dive in. But see what happens next! Before I can do anything, one of them turns toward me and opens fire. It can only be the enemy. What now? What was it they told me to do in such a situation? Oh yes, head straight for him and open fire with everything you have. That is what I do. It is now a test of nerve—whose will hold out longer? I am now quite calm, and the uncertainty I felt in the beginning has disappeared. I again feel one with my machine.

Everything happens in fractions of a second; the other grows larger as we close. Then he loses his nerve, rolls over, and dives away. That was a mistake, my boy. After him, and in no time I am on his tail. We are in a vertical dive,

he is in my crosshairs, and my incendiary ammunition reaches out for him. Hurray! A long stream of oil suddenly appears behind him and sprays my windscreen. He's gone! A cloud has swallowed him up. I follow him in, but when I emerge I have to pull up hard, for the ground is damned close. As I streak past I see a fire on the ground. That was probably the Rata. But now it is time to climb back up and rejoin the squadron. They are already all gone, and I fly home alone. My victory has slipped through my fingers, since there is no one to confirm my claim. Very annoying, but there's nothing I can do about it. The same thing has happened to many others. But better one less confirmed victory than one too-many unconfirmed. That is a good German principle. The same thing happens to my second; not until my third is there no doubt.

For the next two weeks the Messerschmitts encountered few enemy aircraft. Then, on February 7, 1938, the *Jagdgruppe* scored its greatest success to date, destroying ten Katiuskas and two Ratas. The successful pilots were Prestele (SB), Seiler (two SB), Quasinowski (SB), Terry (SB), Mayer (I-16, SB), Schlichting (I-16), and Balthasar (four SB).

Hauptmann Handrick described the action:[43]

None of us would have had any good memories of Calamocha if not for February 7, 1938. This day was the date of a very special triumph for my group; on this day we succeeded in shooting down no fewer than twelve enemy machines; namely, ten bombers and two fighters, Martin bombers and Ratas, in the space of five minutes.

Franco's forces had launched an offensive against the Teruel area on February 5 and had pushed in the enemy front in several places. We eagerly took part in the fighting and day after day showered the enemy positions with bombs. On February 7, I was airborne with two squadrons to protect bombers, which were supposed to follow us. I myself was flying with the 1st *Staffel*; the second was far in front of us. No sooner had we crossed the front when we made out a large number of aircraft flying straight toward us from the east. Were they perhaps some of our bombers, returning home after completing their work?

Soon, however, we could see from their blood-red markings that they were enemy bombers. They were Martin aircraft, Soviet-Russian aircraft of American design, not unlike our He 111.

What followed took place much quicker than one can tell about it.

Flying ahead of us, the 2nd *Staffel* immediately attacked the Red bombers. We increased power, getting everything out of the machines that they had. My heart pounded with joy, for I had never seen so many Red bombers before—there were twenty-two of them. It also appeared that the bombers had no fighter escort.

Bf 109 6 • 43, the aircraft of Lt. Walter Adolf of 1.J/88, after it overran the landing field at Llanes. The field, which was a short one situated on a rocky plateau, was a challenge for pilots. These photos provide photographic proof that as used in Spain, the Bf 109 B was armed with three MG 17 machine guns. The three weapons can be seen in both photos, laid out on the port wing. Note 1.J/88's X marking on the fuselage disc. The second photo also shows the seldom-illustrated oil tank filler point, just behind the man sitting on the port wing. The Bf 109 B's oil tank was located in the port wing, but on the subsequent C and D versions this was moved to the fuselage. Also apparent are the shorter-span leading-edge slats compared to those of the Bf 109 A. *Private Collection*

Bf 109 B 6 • 48 after a crash landing. Note the external power socket beneath the cockpit. This was moved farther aft on the fuselage on the C and D and in this position is an identifying feature of the Bf 109 B. The aircraft appears to be one of those whose RLM 70/71/65 scheme was overpainted in *silberweiss. Private Collection*

When the Reds spotted us they turned away, but it was already too late. They were still in the turn when our 2nd *Staffel* caught them, and two machines went down trailing huge banners of smoke. The crews baled out.

The remaining twenty tried to flee, but we were already close enough to open fire. In a single moment, eight Reds began to burn simultaneously and went down like blazing torches.

I had reached a position about 500 feet behind a Martin bomber. The aircraft looked as big as a barn door in my sight. I pressed the trigger, but both guns stopped after fourteen rounds—jammed! I had to leave my victim; I could see the machine gunner plainly as he fired at me like a wild man.

Meanwhile the enemy fighter cover appeared on the stage. Three or four squadrons of Ratas suddenly came down on us like a warm rain. A wild dogfight began, which ended with two enemy fighters sharing the fate of the ten Martin bombers.

Bf 109 B 6 • 49 in flight with Bf 109 A 6 • 6. Both aircraft are presumably finished in *silberweiss* overall, but 6 • 49 appears to be lighter in color compared to 6 • 6. There are four victory bars on 6 • 6's vertical tail. *Private Collection*

It was now time for us to protect our own bombers from the fighters, but the enemy had apparently lost his appetite. He flew off in the direction of Valencia, and our bombers were able to make their bomb runs unhindered.

After we landed, we learned that in addition to the twenty-two Martin bombers, twelve other enemy bombers had attacked without fighter escort. It would have been a feast if we could also have brought our guns to bear on these fat prizes, but in the end we could be satisfied with the day's success.

That 7th of February more than reconciled us with inhospitable Calamocha, especially since several Spanish generals sent wine to congratulate us on our success. It helped us and our Spanish comrades forget the icy cold as we celebrated our victory.

Oblt. Balthasar, formerly of A/88, was undoubtedly the hero of the day. He later wrote:[44]

It was my greatest experience: beginning of February, decisive days in front of Teruel. Four of us are suspended high in the blue sky, while far below the battle rages. We have no time to look down on the fierce struggle. Our attention is glued to the airspace around us, for we must come to grips with the enemy in the air too. We have been aloft for thirty minutes already, circling over enemy territory.

The airfield of Sarrion has just disappeared beneath my wing. Wait, what is that? To our right, a little lower, tiny dots are buzzing about like a swarm of hornets. Now we can clearly see the red markings and typical shape of the Ratas, more than thirty of them. Swinging wide into the sun, we stalk toward the enemy. We have just reached the correct position for a surprise attack. My eyes scan the airspace once more. My three comrades, who were somewhat higher, have begun to attack. There is no time to lose if I am to stay with them. Then suddenly, far off to the left, I see a long column of twin-engine machines. They can only be Martin bombers, heading for the front to sow death among the ranks of our Spanish brothers. A glance at my three comrades shows me that they haven't seen the bombers and are already in combat with the Ratas. I know that it is madness to take on twenty-four well-armed bombers alone, but I must try to keep disaster from befalling the courageous fighters in the front lines. One forgets about one's person in such situations. So I ram the throttle forward and turn. One last look at the guns and instruments to confirm that everything is properly set, and then the dance can begin.

The machines before me quickly grow larger. I can clearly see the broad red stripes. They haven't seen me yet, but soon many machine guns will be shooting at me. Now I am upon them. I dive through the column at a terrific speed and approach the second flight of three from below. Now they've seen me. I become the target of sixty-two guns. Bullets strike my wings. Keep your nerve; don't shoot until you're close! The aircraft on the right of the formation grows large in front of me. I take careful aim at its right engine. My fingers rest on the triggers. I estimate the range to be 60 feet when my three machine guns begin to rattle. There, a flame! I pull up, and the bomber explodes and falls to earth in a mass of flames. I am quite calm. That was number one, I think to myself. The leader of the bomber formation has lost his nerve. He turns and dives away in the direction of home. I am able to cut off his turn, and soon I am behind the aircraft on the left of the formation. Again the shower of return fire surrounds me, but I fly through it and again my machine guns begin their deadly song. Again flames, and I hear the explosion. My machine flies through a cloud of smoke and fire, where seconds ago a proud bomber had flown. That was number two! The surviving machine is now flying alone in front of me. In seconds it is replaced by a fireball, from which pieces tumble toward the earth. That was number three! An entire flight is now missing from the once-proud formation. The rest split up and race for home. As I pursue the leader's flight, I quickly scan the sky. There they come, the Ratas. They are in a very favorable position, and soon they will reach me. But I also see my three loyal comrades. They have grasped the situation, and they heroically try to keep my tail clear against superior numbers. My only thought is that the leader must go down. Before me his flight is still holding good formation. I must pass between the two wingmen. They slide past, close enough to touch. I see the dorsal gunners aiming their machine guns at me; I see blue flashes coming from their muzzles and hear the clatter of bullets striking my machine. But now my guns speak too. The flame I have seen three times again appears, and a comet with a fiery tail falls toward the earth. That was number four and the formation leader!

Suddenly, a strange jolt goes through my machine. The rudder is frozen and thick smoke begins to fill the cockpit. If it turns red, then I will go down like a comet myself. But flyer's luck is stronger. I am able to control the aircraft despite the frozen rudder. My nerves calm themselves, and I find time to look around. Behind me my comrades are locked in battle with the enemy. There's nothing more I can do, for my sick bird is losing power. The oil line must have been hit, since the oil temperature is steadily rising. I turn for home, looking around me. There is a flash behind me and again I hear bullets striking. The Ratas! I stand the crate on its nose and dive. Near the ground I level off. Behind me all is clear, just a black trail of oil mist extending far behind me. The enemy probably thinks he's shot me down. I am determined to keep flying until the engine quits or catches fire. I fly over the countryside at a height of 30 feet. The Teruel church tower serves as a landmark. Will I make it to the front? Then machine gun fire from below. A few more hits. But there, the front! Now I'm home, and I look for somewhere to land. I select a large meadow.

Bf 109 B 6 • 42 in flight over the coast of Spain. According to the information on the back of the photo, the aircraft's pilot was *Major* Werner Mölders, who was attached to 1.J/88 for familiarization on the Bf 109. Taken by Adolf Galland before he left Spain, this was part of a sequence of photos showing a flight of four Bf 109s from 1.J/88, led by Schellmann. The aircraft is finished in the modified 70/71/65 scheme used by 1st *Staffel* for a short time in the summer of 1938. The fuselage has been repainted RLM 63 gray, while areas of the dark greens on the wings and tailplane were overpainted, probably in RLM 63 gray, RLM 62 green, or both. The machine has a yellow spinner, and there is a single victory bar on the tail. *Private Collection*

Schellmann in the cockpit of 6 • 51 in flight over Spain. This is from the sequence of photos taken by Adolf Galland depicting a flight of four Bf 109 Bs of 1.J/88. By this time the repainting process had begun. The fuselage upper surfaces have been painted in RLM 63 gray, while segments of the same color have been applied to the wings and tailplane. There are five victory bars on the fin, indicating that the photo was taken after June 25, 1938, when he shot down a Rata. *Private Collection*

The aircraft rolls to a stop. My nerves abandon me; I'm unable to get out. I look around. The black smoke banners are still in the sky. One—two—five—nine. My comrades have had more luck. It looks like reinforcements are coming. Tired, with trembling hands, I climb out and examine my machine. It's a sieve. The rudder cable is severed, fuel and oil tanks hit, cockpit and wings chopped up. Theoretically I should be in heaven, but for flyer's luck or providence . . . the engagement lasted three minutes. I fired 120 rounds, and sixteen enemy airmen had to give up their lives. It was my 465th and last combat mission in eighteen months, and my fourth to seventh victories. Long live Spain.

On February 14, 1938, Günther Scholz began the journey that would take him to Spain. He wrote:[45]

On February 14, 1938, those of us who had volunteered to serve in Spain were ordered to Bernburg. There had been some changes in Bernburg since my service there. *Jagdgeschwader* 232 had become *Jagdgeschwader* 137, but it still consisted of just a single *Gruppe*.

The so-called 10. *Staffel* was the preparation unit for Spain. It was attached to *Jagdgruppe* Bernburg. The pilots destined for Spain were sent there for about fourteen days. Pilots back from Spain described their experiences in aerial combat. Maps were provided to familiarize us with Spanish geography, and we were taught to identify the different types of enemy aircraft. In addition to the classroom, we also carried out practical exercises. We practiced air combat maneuvers on the Me 109 and low-level attacks on the He 51.

On a rainy morning on March 2, 1938, a group of civilians met at Berlin-Staaken and boarded a Lufthansa Ju 52 as passengers.

These civilians were fighter pilots on their way to Spain. We flew nonstop from Berlin to Rome. We landed at the Italian capital at about 1400 hours. Taxis were waiting to take us to a hotel. An air force office had been set up in the hotel, and each man was issued 300 pesetas. We also received 100 lira for our stay in Rome.

At 1000 hours the next morning we took off for Seville. The flight took us straight across the Mediterranean. These flights were always made by two aircraft, which remained in visual contact. One transport machine had gone missing. The cause remained a mystery, but it was suspected that Red fighters had shot it down over the Spanish coast.

We landed at Seville in magnificent spring weather. In Berlin it was still almost winter. We were driven to the Hotel Christina. The next morning we were supposed to fly on to Burgos in a mail aircraft, departure time 0630.

That night I spent 200 of my 300 pesetas in Seville. With throbbing heads and dead tired, at 0630 we took off for Burgos. The city was the seat of the Franco government. Madrid was still in the hands of the Rojos, the Reds.

In Burgos we were issued Spanish uniforms. In Spain we were upped one step in rank, and I became an *Oberleutnant*. The next day a communications aircraft of the German legion's fighter unit flew us to Saragossa—San Jurga.

The "Legion Condor" was made up of units from all three branches of the Wehrmacht. The air force contributed a fighter group, a bomber group, a dive-bomber group, a reconnaissance group with tactical and strategic reconnaissance machines, and a maritime reconnaissance group. There was also a flak regiment, which operated in the air defense and ground support roles, two signals regiments, and supply units. Personnel, equipment, and aircraft were regularly sent from Germany.

Noncommissioned officers and enlisted men served nine months on average. Officers were relieved after a year. Each soldier continued to be paid in Germany. In Spain we received so-called danger pay, which was based on one's rank and type of duty. Pilots received more than the ground personnel, for example.

This pay was very high, and for a *Leutnant* pilot like me it was 1,200 reichsmark per month. Half of this I received in pesetas, while the other half was deposited into a savings account in Germany. A flying *Leutnant* thus received a total remuneration of 1,500 reichsmark. Money was not a problem for those returning home from Spain.

At that time, 100 pesetas was equal to about 30 reichsmark. Our pay was thus equivalent to 2,000 pesetas. One could live like a king on that sum. Most of those who served in Spain went home with 9,000 to 10,000 reichsmark, and the first thing they did was purchase an automobile.

In later years I asked myself where all this money for the German troops in Spain had come from. It was indirectly paid by Franco. He in turn received it from England, America, and the Vatican. Red Spain, on the other hand, received support from Communist Russia in the form of weapons and personnel and volunteer units from the Communist parties of every nation. There were even Germans fighting on that side.

The Spanish Civil War was practically the first conflict between capitalism and communism, with Hitler and Mussolini occupying a hermaphroditic position. Communism—the common enemy—offset the differences between democracy and dictatorship—but only with respect to Spain and only for the duration of the war. The democracies sent no men or materiel to help Franco, but they remained benevolently neutral and kept track of the communist volunteers sent to Spain from their countries.

At that time, the legion's fighter group was commanded by *Hauptmann* Gotthard Handrick, winner of the gold medal in the modern pentathlon at the 1936 Olympic Games. The *Gruppe* consisted of four *Staffeln* and a headquarters company. The 1st and 2nd *Staffeln* were fighter units flying the Me 109. The 3rd and 4th *Staffeln* were ground attack units equipped with He 51s.

All newcomers were initially assigned to the ground-attack *Staffel* commanded by *Oberleutnant* Adolf Galland. It was designated 3.J/88.

In Spain, Scholz was assigned to the 3rd *Staffel* commanded by Adolf Galland. Flying the He 51, he initially conducted ground attack sorties in support of Nationalist troops,

The *Jagdgruppe*'s next victory did not come until February 19, when *Uffz*. Stange shot down a Chato. Nationalist forces assaulted Teruel on February 17 and after two days of street fighting took the town on the 21st. That day saw heavy fighting in the air, with large numbers of Republican fighters rising to give battle. The 1st *Staffel* shot down three Ratas near La Pueble, and the 2nd *Staffel* destroyed four more near Sarrion and Teruel.

With the fighting at Teruel over, on February 23 J/88 moved to Gallur, northwest of Saragossa on the Ebro River.

THE ARAGON OFFENSIVE

After the defeat of the Republican attack on Teruel, Franco decided to abandon his direct assault on Madrid and instead strike through Aragon, toward the Mediterranean coast.[46] The Republican army had suffered grave losses in men and equipment at Teruel, and the Nationalists were determined to exploit this weakness by striking quickly. The offensive was scheduled to begin on March 9, and preparatory bombing began on the 6th. From the outset the Nationalists enjoyed overwhelming superiority in artillery and air forces.

In the days leading up to the attack, He 111s, Do 17s, and Ju 87s of the Legion Condor struck enemy airfields, headquarters, vehicle concentrations, and bridges, with the Bf 109s providing fighter escort. Contacts with enemy fighters were few, but on March 8, *Oblt*. Schellmann and *Lt*. Awe of the 1st *Staffel* each shot down a Chato. Schellmann wrote:[47]

I spot one little bird that is lagging behind and flying slower than the others. I waggle my wings to signal my wingman—we will go after this fellow. But we are slow to close the distance. I reason that he will have to slow down to land, and then I'll catch him. We fly low over the hilltops and then down into a valley toward the enemy airfield. We close to 600 yards, then 400. A quick burst and the enemy drops a wing and goes down.

We are 25 miles behind the front. Time to climb out and head for home! Suddenly, there is a squadron of Ratas 60 feet above us. Open the throttle and get out of here! My wingman passes me, while I limp along behind him. What's up with my damned engine? I check the instruments. Idiot!

Wolfgang Schellmann's Bf 109 B 6 • 51, photographed at Gallur in its original RLM 70/71/65 scheme. There are two victory bars on the fin, indicating that the photo was taken sometime between March 8, when he shot down a Curtiss for his second victory, and March 24, when he downed another Curtiss for his third. *Private Collection*

The propeller is still set for diving flight! A flick of the lever and the Messerschmitt accelerates to full speed. The enemy is already ticklishly close. I twist and turn and hug the ground, sweeping over hills, olive groves, and a farm. They've been chasing me for four minutes already—an eternity! Finally, there's the front! The enemy suddenly turns back. It's a great relief.

The Chato was Schellmann's second victory.

On the day of the attack, March 9, 1938, the fighters of 1.J/88 escorted the He 111s of K/88 as they attacked enemy positions. Further escort missions followed in support of the Heinkels, Dorniers, and Stukas. Altogether that day, 210 tons of bombs were dropped, a record that would stand for the rest of the war. The heavy bombing demoralized the Republican troops, preventing them from establishing a cohesive defense line.

The next day the bombers of the Legion Condor struck enemy airfields. J/88 attacked Belchite and Jatiel, destroying three I-15s on the ground. In the air, *Fw.* Prestele shot down a Chato, while *Uffz.* Rochel and *Oblt.* Schlichting each destroyed a Rata.

On March 11, 1938, Bf 109s took off to escort a maximum effort by K/88 against Republican targets. None of the bombers

Bf 109 6 • 52 parked on a bleak Spanish airfield. The aircraft is finished in *silberweiss* overall. Note the position of the external power socket beneath the cockpit, identifying the aircraft as a Bf 109 B. *Private Collection*

Bf 109 B 6 • 54 on an unidentified Spanish airfield. The aircraft, which bears the markings of 1st *Staffel*, is receiving fuel from a Mercedes LG 3000 refueling truck. *Private Collection*

Bf 109 B 6 • 54 of 1.J/88 after coming to grief. Though the aft fuselage appears relatively intact, the forward fuselage suffered significant damage. Note the damaged fabric covering of the port flap and aileron. *Private Collection*

were lost, but *Oberleutnant* Graf zu Dohna, who was supposed to replace Schlichting as *Staffelkapitän* of 2.J/88, was shot down by a *Mosca* (the Republicans' nickname for the Polikarpov I-16 fighter plane; Spanish for "fly") and killed.[48]

On March 13, K/88 attacked the city of Caspe and its airfield, with both Bf 109 *Staffeln* providing fighter escort. Republican fighters rose to intercept the raiders, and two Chatos were shot down by *Lt.* Ettling and *Uffz.* Ihlefeld.

Enemy resistance stiffened in front of Caspe, and it was not until March 17 that Nationalist forces were finally able to dislodge the Republican defenders. That evening the entire *Jagdgruppe* assembled at Sanjurjo for a brief respite before resuming operations.

Günther Scholz described another aspect of life in Spain for the German legionnaires:[49]

> The Spanish girls also interested us. The Spaniards were unbelievably devout Catholics. We were not, at least in the opinion of the Spanish. When we were based near the Mediterranean there were dances every Sunday. Sometimes we attended. Whenever we approached a Spanish girl, we were always turned down. They simply didn't want to dance with us.
>
> Bordellos, however, flourished in Spain. When it came to these, the Spanish were suddenly not so serious about their faith. There were so many such installations that they came to be seen as part of everyday life.
>
> Gotthard Handrick, the commander of our *Jagdgruppe*, understood the needs of his men. He approached the owner of one of the bordellos and made an agreement with her. From then on the group had its own bordello. It was set up in a quarter near our airfield. The place had its advantages. For one, conflicts with the Spanish population were avoided, and for another, our men were protected from disease.
>
> For the officers it meant yet another job. From then on, there was the so-called OvB, or bordello duty officer. On one occasion I too had to serve as the OvB. The whole thing took place in the evening, from 1800 until midnight at the latest. As duty officer, one had to keep watch. Anyone wanting to enter had to report to me first. Anyone with alcohol had to surrender it. The use of alcohol was strictly forbidden there. If there were cases of petty jealousy, the officer had to step in and restore order.
>
> This is surely a minor anecdote that is perhaps not all that well known, but that's how it was. Yes, we did more than just fly.

The Nationalist offensive toward the sea resumed on March 22, 1938. The Messerschmitts saw little action until March 24, when improved weather brought a resurgence of activity. The 1.J/88 joined a dogfight between Nationalist CR.32s and a group of Chatos, subsequently claiming three shot down. On March 29, *Lt.* Hans-Karl Mayer claimed his fourth victory, an I-15 brought down near Lerida. This was to be

the *Jagdgruppe*'s last victory for almost six weeks. According to Karl Ries,[50] the month of March saw the arrival in Spain of the first Bf 109 C and D fighters.

t Saragossa, 1st and 2.J/88 received orders to move to a new base at Lanaja on April 4. This seemingly routine transfer flight was marred by tragedy, however, when a midair collision took the life of *Leutnant* Fritz Awe. During a course change, Awe's Messerschmitt was struck by the propeller of the machine flown by his wingman, *Uffz.* Borchers. The blades severed the Bf 109's fuselage, and Awe was killed instantly. Borchers sustained minor injuries when his damaged machine overturned during the ensuing forced landing.

On April 15, General Aranda's Galician Corps and the 4th Navarrese Division took the seaside town of Vinaros, establishing a corridor to the Mediterranean that isolated Catalonia from the rest of Republican Spain.[51] Franco's allies and his Republican foes alike expected that he would follow up his devastating advance through Aragon by seizing Barcelona, Spain's second-largest city and the Catalan capital. But for reasons that are still unclear, the *cuadillo* opted instead to widen his corridor to the sea by advancing south-southwest toward Valencia. At the direction of the German minister of war, General Volkmann urged Franco to advance on Barcelona, but he would not be moved.

The offensive toward Valencia began on April 25. It proved a disaster for the Nationalists. Hastily formed Republican units inflicted heavy casualties on the attackers, and the offensive resulted in defeat for Franco's forces. By the time the offensive ground to a halt in early July, the Nationalists had suffered 20,000 casualties compared to just 5,000 for the Republicans. Franco's decision not to attack toward Barcelona also allowed Republican units falling back from Aragon to regroup and reequip in Catalonia. From there they would attack across the Ebro in the largest Republican offensive of the war.

The Nationalist advance down the coast toward Valencia progressed slowly in the face of stubborn resistance. Operating from their new base at La Sénia, the Bf 109s saw little action until May 11, when *Uffz.* Ihlefeld of 2.J/88 shot down a Rata. On May 18, there was a major air battle, which *Hptm.* Harder described as the largest he had ever experienced. Four Ratas fell to the guns of the Messerschmitts. One was claimed by *Hptm* Handrick, who provided the following description of the action:[52]

> On May 18, 1938, I was supposed to fly back to Germany on leave. Also under my command at that time was a flight of dive bombers, which I was permitted to commit only with a strong fighter escort.
>
> That morning I had the feeling that there was still something brewing for me. I therefore quickly ordered one more sortie before my takeoff for Germany.
>
> My adjutant and I calmly flew along the coast. Suddenly I couldn't believe my eyes: a dense swarm of enemy aircraft

were approaching from the direction of Valencia. I climbed to 18,000 feet and counted: there were twelve Martin bombers and fifteen to twenty Ratas. Unfortunately, I was unable to prevent the fellows from dropping their bombs on our territory. I therefore allowed them to pass beneath us and thought to myself: "Go ahead, drop your bombs—when you're finished, I'm going to take one of you."

Soon it was time. Covered by my adjutant, I selected one of the enemy. I closed to 65 feet and fired. Seventy rounds may have left my guns when the enemy went down vertically in flames.

The aircraft fell on enemy territory. Soon afterward, however, the area was taken, and my people were able to determine that the pilot of the downed aircraft was an American. The back of the pilot's seat was armored, but it had been pierced by the bullets from my machine guns.

The hectic pace of operations since the winter of 1937–38 had seriously affected the *Jagdgruppe*'s available strength, which by the end of May had fallen to just sixteen Bf 109s. Replacement aircraft were badly needed, but the flow of

Bf 109 B 6 • 20 at Santander-West. The 1st *Staffel*'s unit marking, the X in the black disc on the fuselage, is clearly visible. The aircraft has been positioned, tail raised, in preparation for bore-sighting its three MG 17 machine guns. The arrangement in this photo is almost identical to the illustration in the aircraft manual. Bf 109 6 • 20 was flown by *Leutnant* Fritz Awe until it was destroyed in a midair collision on April 4, 1938. *Author's Collection*

Though of indifferent quality, this photo is of great interest. It shows *Lt.* Fritz Awe's Bf 109 B 6 • 20 with other aircraft of 1.J/88 prior to taking off from Saragossa for Lanaja on April 4, 1938. During the flight, Awe's aircraft collided with that of his wingman and he was killed. Three victory bars can be seen on the aircraft's rudder. Awe had scored his third and final victory a little over a week earlier, when he shot down an I-15. Note the framing on the folding portion of the canopy, which is a lighter color than the rest of the aircraft. It may have been a replacement from a *silberweiss* aircraft. *Private Collection*

This series of photos shows the recovery of Bf 109 B 6 • 44 after a forced landing in a marshy area. Ground personnel have begun the recovery effort. Note the rearview mirror on the left side of the windscreen. The aircraft's spinner is finished in three colors (yellow with a red base plate and white ring around front). In the following photos, 6 • 44 can be seen at the waterside, with mechanics readying a tripod with block and tackle for removal of the engine, and the engine being loaded into a small boat. The aircraft's original RLM 70/71/65 camouflage scheme has been greatly modified, with the fuselage upper surfaces painted RLM 63 gray, and the two greens on the upper wing surfaces augmented with lighter colors (also see photo at the bottom of page 151). *Private Collection*

materiel to the Legion Condor had diminished as the Wehrmacht prepared for its move into Austria.

On June 2, Republican aircraft attacked La Sénia. Bf 109s intercepted the raiders and shot down four Katiuskas. A fifth was downed by the airfield's antiaircraft guns. At this time the fighters began using satellite airfields to avoid the threat of enemy bombing raids on La Sénia.

The pace of operations increased, and the *Jagdgruppe* was kept busy escorting bombers and conducting fighter sweeps. J/88 also had to maintain a so-called "alert" *Schwarm*, a flight of four fighters ready to take off at a moment's notice to intercept incoming raids. On June 10, the "alert" *Schwarm* was scrambled to intercept a formation of bombers with fighter escort. Two Ratas and a Katiuska were shot down.

While escorting He 111s of K/88 on the evening of June 13, the Bf 109s of 1st and 2.J/88 scored a major success, shooting down six I-15s and two I-16s. The next day brought a turn in the *Jagdgruppe*'s fortunes, however. While escorting Stukas, *Lt.* Priebe's aircraft was shot up by a Chato. Wounded in the shoulder, he just managed to nurse his damaged aircraft back to base. *Lt.* Henz's Bf 109 was shot up by Ratas south of Castellon, and he was obliged to make a forced landing in Republican territory. Henz was taken prisoner, but other Messerschmitts strafed his largely intact machine and set it alight before it could be removed by the Republicans.

After these losses, J/88's equipment strength fell to disastrous levels, with just eleven Bf 109s between the two *Staffeln*. On the ground the advance had ground to a halt. Meanwhile, the air units of the Legion Condor were grounded from June 17 to 22. Operations resumed on June 25, when *Oblt.* Schellmann and *Fw.* Ihlefeld flew escort for aircraft of K/88 and A/88 attacking enemy positions near Sagunto. Enemy fighters rose to intercept, and in the ensuing combat each German pilot destroyed a Rata.

At this time J/88 finally began receiving new aircraft.[53] This enabled the *Jagdgruppe* to equip the 3rd *Staffel*, now under the command of *Oblt.* Mölders, with Bf 109s. Mölders's biographer wrote:[54]

> At the beginning of July, *Staffel* commander Mölders received news that his unit was to convert to the Messerschmitt Bf 109, in order to bolster Nationalist air superiority. The news excited the entire *Staffel*, especially the pilots. Now they would be able to test themselves against the Curtisses, Ratas, and Martins like their comrades in the 1st and 2nd *Staffel*. The new aircraft soon arrived from Germany, and reassembly began in León. The *Staffel* sent a party of mechanics and technicians to help prepare the new aircraft for operations. While they waited, Mölders and his men studied everything they could get their hands on about the new fighter.
>
> The first four Messerschmitts arrived at La Sénia, where they were test-flown and their guns harmonized. Mölders was impatient to put the machines to use, but as

inexperienced "olive pickers" they at first had to fly with the "old hands" of the 1st and 2nd *Staffel*.

In early July 1938, 3rd *Staffel*, now under the command of Werner Mölders, was equipped with Bf 109s. Günther Scholz wrote:[55]

> Now the 3rd *Staffel* also received the modern Me 109. Low-level attacks were abandoned because of heavy losses.
>
> From then on, we flew escort for the bombers or conducted fighter sweeps. We regularly became involved in air battles, something that had almost never happened in the previous months when we were a low-level attack *Staffel*.
>
> Werner Mölders was a Catholic and a very religious man. Nowadays they call him a criminal, and not only him, but all those who fought in Spain. Mölders was no different than the rest of us. We were pilots, fighter pilots, who performed the tasks that went along with being such.

By July 15, Mölders's unit had six Bf 109s on strength. On that day he led the *Staffel* on its first solo mission, providing fighter escort for He 111s of K/88. He wrote:[56]

> For a second I hold my breath. In the distance near Valencia I see numerous tiny dots . . . enemy aircraft! The moment I have been waiting for is at hand. I climb 1,600 feet higher and repeatedly give the signal to attack. The dots come closer. I recognize them as Curtisses, about forty to forty-five. There are six of us, all inexperienced, but they haven't seen us. After them! I make a beautiful approach, but out of excitement I open fire too soon. The fellow reverses and heads straight for me. I see muzzle flashes from his four machine guns.
>
> My God, what a shock: shooting down an enemy isn't as simple as I thought. There, a parachute, a burning Curtiss—my *Staffel*'s first victory. Who could it have been? Around my machine, smoke trails. Two Curtisses come toward me; I'm sweating like a pig. There, a Messerschmitt going down vertically; hopefully it will pull out. Please don't let me lose anyone in my first combat. Forty-five to six, I curse myself for attacking. Keep going, just fight! Then, suddenly, I am perfectly calm. I survey the airspace around me. I see two Curtisses climbing. I dive then come up from below. The rear one sees me and dives away, but I have the other one in my sight; 165 feet. I open fire with all machine guns. He rears up then rolls over and dives with me behind him. I fire again and he begins to smoke and then burn. My first air victory. I am overjoyed—where are my Messerschmitts?
>
> The Curtisses all have fled. I assemble four of my aircraft and head for home. When we reach the airfield, I roar low over the landing strip waggling my wings (the signal for a victory). Behind me another aircraft does the same. It is *Leutnant* Lippert, who scored the *Staffel*'s first

OPERATIONAL HISTORY

Another recovery effort, this time involving Bf 109 B 6 • 50, which crashed and burned on a Spanish beach. This aircraft also wears one of 1.J/88's modified RLM 70/71/65 schemes, with the upper fuselage surfaces painted RLM 63 gray, and the two greens on the wing upper surfaces broken up by patches of lighter colors. There are five victory bars on the aircraft's tail. In the last two photographs the aircraft's engine has been placed on one of the wings and is being hauled away by a team of horses. *Private Collection*

An unidentified Bf 109 A sits in the bright sunlight at La Sénia. With its vented engine cowling and metal propeller, this aircraft could easily be mistaken for a Bf 109 B, but the position of the oil cooler beneath the port wing clearly identifies it as an A. It is still finished in *silberweiss* overall. *Private Collection*

victory. Below I see my mechanics jumping for joy. My faithful crew chief Meier is able to paint the first white victory bar on the tail of my machine. *Leutnant* Oesau also shot down his first, and I am able to proudly report to my commanding officer that we have recorded three victories in our first engagement.

Altogether the escorting fighters claimed nine Chatos destroyed. Two were shot down by *Fw.* Ihlefeld of 2nd *Staffel*, raising his victory total to nine. This successful pilot's regular aircraft was 6 ● 6, an upgraded Bf 109 A, which was one of the oldest fighters still flying with the Legion Condor. In recognition of his success as a fighter pilot, on July 16 Ihlefeld was promoted from the ranks to *Leutnant*.

On July 17, the *Jagdgruppe*'s fighters accounted for six more of the enemy, three of them falling to pilots of the 3rd *Staffel*. Mölders wrote:[57]

The next day there was no activity over the front, but on July 17, while on the way home, I again sighted two squadrons of Curtisses approaching from the direction of Valencia. I immediately led my *Staffel* after them. Flying beside me, *Unteroffizier* Bauer shot down a Curtiss on the initial pass. It was his first victory. The enemy pilot took to his parachute after the first burst. Seconds later it was my turn. I opened fire on a Curtiss, and it quickly began to burn. Its right wing fell off, and the rest of the machine

crashed in flames. My opponent must have been killed by my first burst. *Leutnant* Oesau also brought down an enemy machine in this combat.

Three more Ratas were shot down on July 18, and the next day the 3rd *Staffel* encountered a large force of Republican bombers with fighter escort near Sagunto. Mölders described what followed:[58]

The next day was again quiet; then on the afternoon of the 19th the *Staffel* was ordered to escort a squadron of bombers. I was just about to turn for home when I saw bombs bursting on the Italian corner of the front. Seconds later I spotted about eighteen Martin bombers with an escort of three Rata squadrons heading away from us. This was our first encounter with the Rata, and we soon discovered that these bumblebees were damned fast and difficult to shoot down. Lippert, Bauer, and Goy were forced to take violent evasive action when they suddenly found several diving onto their tails. *Leutnant* Ebbighausen shot down a Rata on the first pass, his first victory, while *Leutnant* Tietzen and I each downed one on the second pass. I had to pour a lot of bullets into the fuselage of mine before it began to smoke. Tietzen's victim blew up. I was especially happy for Jakob Tietzen, since it was his birthday.

Obergefreiter Hien also shot down his first in this engagement, which was also his first contact with the

The starboard side of Werner Mölders' Bf 109 D 6 • 79. Two of the D series' identifying features can be seen: the access panel over the wing-mounted MG 17 machine gun is in the open position, and the oxygen filler point and external power socket are farther aft compared to their positions on the earlier Bf 109 B. The name *Luchs* (Lynx) appears on the engine cowling in front of the cockpit. The significance of this name is not known. Mölders appears to be in conversation with another pilot with a bandaged hand. *Private Collection*

The aft fuselage and tail of *Hptm.* Werner Mölders' Bf 109 D 6 • 79. There are twelve victory bars on the aircraft's fin. This is something of a mystery, since Mölders scored his twelfth and thirteenth victories on the same day, October 31, 1938. Perhaps one of the victory bars represents a claim that was not confirmed. Note 3.J/88's "Mickey Mouse" with revolver emblem on the fuselage. In the background is a lineup of He 111s of K/88. *Private Collection*

enemy. Afterward he was tremendously excited: "I don't know if it was a Curtiss or a Rata; I didn't see any wheels, but there were big red discs on top—well, then I just fired!"

I got a terrible fright when my engine began sputtering while I was still over enemy territory. I calculated that I would not be able to glide back to base, but fortunately my faithful kite recovered.

As the Nationalist forces slowly advanced, disturbing reports began coming in about a Republican buildup in the north at the bend in the Ebro. Meanwhile, operations in support of the offensive continued, and on July 23 there was another large air battle involving all three Bf 109 *Staffeln*. Mölders wrote in his diary:[59]

Today is a wonderful day. Bomber escort again, and toward the end of our flying time I see the 2nd Squadron north of Viver in combat with Curtisses and Ratas, about forty enemy aircraft. I quickly lead my squadron into the fray, but the Curtisses have learned a lot; they skillfully descend to about 3,300 feet and circle there. With them are the Ratas, which repeatedly zoom upward. By now the 1st *Staffel* has also arrived. A fresh squadron of Curtisses appears, and I want to use this opportunity to give my wingman Jänisch a chance to engage. But he comes too late, and as well the 1st *Staffel* pounces on them and throws off our entire attack.

All of the MEs are now more or less above this circus, diving into the swarm of bees and shooting from impossible distances, but without success. In fact I don't see a single one go down. Again and again we spray them with machine gun fire from above, but when one dives down on one of them, one soon has three or four others on his tail blazing away. There are devilish situations. One often ended up sitting in the middle of a bunch of these fellows and had to take violent evasive action to avoid their fire.

Finally, I got a Curtiss in a favorable position in front of me. I crept up on him in a wide arc; 650 feet—325 feet—160 feet. He doesn't see me. The machine is sitting perfectly in my sight; what an opportunity. I watch the unsuspecting pilot looking to his ten o'clock. There's no way I can miss now. I press the trigger. What's this? Not a shot comes out. The enemy continues to fly straight and level in front of me. I recharge the guns—not a shot comes out. I work like crazy on my guns, the other still in my sights. The red light isn't on; there's a short circuit in my electrical cocking mechanism. I fly past the enemy, unable to shoot. Shocked, he cringes then dives away. You certainly have a guardian angel, my boy! What to do? Fly home? That's out of the question since the air battle is still raging. As leader of the *Staffel* I can't just fly away, but it's a damned uncomfortable situation to be flying around among enemy aircraft with no weapons to defend oneself, having to depend solely on one's own maneuverability.

Six of our pilots are successful in this battle. From my *Staffel* there's *Leutnant* Lippert and *Unteroffizier* Boer, but neither has a witness. Unfortunate; because of this there will be difficulties obtaining confirmation. Boer, the poor chap, took a bullet that went through the wing and then the undercarriage. At first he waggled his wings cheerfully to signal his victory, but then he was unable to get his gear down and had to make a belly landing. He put our good ME down on the airfield.

Tietzen had taken hits too, in the wing spar, and the wing had to be replaced. Lippert had a bullet hole in one slat. The chaps must learn to be more careful.

Despite growing indications of an imminent Republican offensive across the Ebro, the Legion Condor continued operations in support of Nationalist forces attacking toward Valencia. The *Jagdgruppe*'s fighters continued to see action, claiming three Ratas and a Curtiss on July 23.

BATTLE OF THE EBRO

During the early hours of July 25, 1938, Republican commandos crossed the Ebro River and eliminated the Nationalist sentries on the other side. Soon afterward, six Republican divisions began crossing the Ebro between Fayón and Cherta. The objective of the offensive was to recapture the Nationalist corridor to the sea and rejoin the two parts of Republican Spain. The Republicans had formed an army of the Ebro for the offensive; however, after the losses in Aragon its equipment was lacking in several key areas, especially artillery. All available air forces were concentrated in the area of the offensive, resulting in the largest air battles of the entire war. This final great exertion by the Republicans would end in failure, however, and bring about their ultimate defeat.[60]

For the fighters of the Legion Condor, the period of the Ebro offensive and the ensuing Nationalist counterattack (July 25 to November 16) was their most fruitful of the entire war. During that 113-day period, the pilots of the *Jagdgruppe* would claim ninety-nine enemy aircraft shot down. This was in part a reflection of its increased strength—three *Staffeln*—but also of the intensity of the fighting. In the beginning the bridges across the Ebro were the primary target for the legion's bombers and Stukas. Operating from La Sénia, J/88 was ordered to support the bombers of K/88 and "attack ground targets if the situation permits." Mölders wrote in his diary:[61]

The situation has changed. The enemy has attacked at the Ebro, crossed it in several places, and gained some ground, especially in the direction of Gandesa. Our entire air force is being committed. The *Stubos* (dive bombers) are particularly active, dropping their deadly eggs up to four times per day. We fly escort, without seeing a single enemy machine. At present we don't know where the enemy air force is hiding. Actually an air raid on our airfield tomorrow morning wouldn't be completely out of the question. Well, wait and see.

The Republican air force was seldom seen in the early days of the offensive. Mölders wrote:[61]

There have been no enemy bombing raids. We have been flying over the Ebro for days. Since there are no enemy aircraft about, we have limited ourselves to ground orientation and observing the fall of the bombs. Our bomber squadrons and Stukas, along with the Italians and Spaniards, continuously bomb the Red-Spanish area of penetration, while five divisions gradually prepare to counterattack. The Maroquis Corps is there. The crossings are bombed all day long. The effect on morale must be colossal, and this mass action must be causing some material damage somewhere. Only we fighters are able to take it easy on our machines. . . .

We have now seen the film of the Olympiad. The appearance of *Hauptmann* Herrmann [Handrick] received enthusiastic applause. The offensive begins tomorrow, and the entire Spanish Nationalist air force has been placed under our commanding officer. Hopefully we'll soon be advancing on Valencia.

Bf 109 A 6 • 6 has its guns bore sighted. This improvised set-up was necessary at the spartan forward airfields used by the legion. The mainwheels were rolled into a trench dug in the ground, then jacks were used to level the fuselage. Note the plumb line beneath the fuselage under the aircraft number "6." The rear fuselage appears to be supported by a trestle atop a large stone, which in turn is resting on a compressed air cart. The name *Holzauge* (Wooden Eye) can be seen on the radiator housing. By this time the aircraft has vented engine cowling panels and a metal variable-pitch propeller. Aircraft 6 • 6 had a long life with the Legion Condor but was finally written off in a crash landing at Tortosa on July 28, 1938. *Private Collection*

A member of the ground crew poses for a photo on the wing of Bf 109 A 6 • 6, which has been serviced and is ready for its next sortie. When this photo was taken the aircraft was serving with 2.J/88 and appears to be finished in its original *silberweiss* finish. Note the covers over the mainwheels and the pilot's parachute on the horizontal stabilizer. The name *Holzauge* is again present on the radiator housing. This machine was flown by a number of pilots during its long career with J/88. *Private Collection*

On July 28, 1938, one of J/88's three remaining Bf 109 A fighters was written off. On July 30, Mölders wrote:[62]

> The day before yesterday Jänisch wrote off our 6-6. Supercharger trouble on the other side; he managed to cross the front to the airfield at Tortola but crashed. He was under antiaircraft fire when the problem first appeared, and he may well have over-revved something.

The first engagements with enemy aircraft took place on August 1, when three I-15s were shot down by Jaenisch, Bauer, and Ebbighausen. Mölders wrote of this action:[63]

> We're still escorting bomber squadrons, reconnaissance squadrons, and dive bombers attacking the Ebro crossings. The Stukas have proved very effective at destroying bridges. In any case the enemy's supply system has been crippled.
>
> We now know that most of the enemy's air force is up here now, but only once has our squadron had contact with the enemy, two squadrons of Curtisses. I initiated the attack and when in favorable firing range peeled off, because I suddenly remembered promising my *Katschmarek* [wingman] a chance. Unfortunately, my actions irritated Scholz, who was upset at missing such an opportunity. Ebbighausen and Bauer each shot one down. The one Ebbighausen shot down burned. The pilot baled out, his parachute slightly scorched by the flames. Jaenisch's victim also baled out. Bauer, the wild man, continued dogfighting at a height of 3,300 feet. Fiats also took part in the operation; since then, however, we haven't seen any sign of the enemy. *Oberleutnant* Kroeck is the only one to have claimed a

victory, his first Rata shot down over the Ebro. [on Aug. 2; *Author*]

The next major combat occurred on August 12, when the 1st *Staffel* destroyed three SB bombers and two I-16s. Otto Bertram, who scored his first kill in this action, wrote:[64]

> I'm flying in the *Staffel* commander's *Kette*, behind and to his left. Schellmann waggles his wings: a squadron of Martin bombers! Attack! The two aircraft flying on the right go down. Damn, Schellmann can shoot! I go after the third one. A short burst—there, one of them bales out; a cloud of fuel swirls about the starboard engine. Break away. Five Ratas move in slowly. A stupid attack—they are trapped by the next *Kette*. Where is my wingman? He has just attacked a bomber. The crew bales out, tiny figures swinging beneath their parachutes. Ratas poke their noses in. An odd feeling to be chased by those fat radial engines. Break away! Dogfight! I have but a single thought—I must get one of them! There's a lonely hare. Man, why don't you keep a better lookout? I get behind him and fire off a burst. The Rata continues to climb. I become incensed. He must go down! My bullets saw through the Rata's left wing until it breaks away. Suddenly, bullets whiz past my cockpit. Now I'm in for it! Then, suddenly, divine stillness. "My first kill!" I shout to myself.

Bertram was credited with only one enemy aircraft shot down, the Rata; apparently the SB was only damaged. *Hptm.* Schellmann destroyed two SB bombers in this action.

Further heavy fighting took place on August 14, and the Messerschmitts tangled with twenty I-16s. Six victories were claimed, and *Uffz.* Szuggar gave the following account of the action:[65]

> Schellmann's *Staffel* has been given the job of escorting reconnaissance aircraft over the area of the enemy penetration. They roar in the direction of Tarragona at 15,000 feet. The *Staffel* is flying in two flights of four aircraft and one of two machines.... There, below us, Red fighters! They haven't seen us yet. Schellmann is first off the mark. He pushes the stick forward and goes into a dive. Schellmann's Me dives on the Rata like a winged bullet. With his first burst, bright flames spurt from the Red fighter. The Rata spins away. I cover Schellmann's tail against the other Ratas. One attacks the *Staffelkapitän*. A sharp turn to the left places him in the reticle of my gunsight. The Rata dives away vertically and escapes my burst. I dive after him. There are still Ratas behind me. Engines howling, we dive vertically toward the earth. I take aim. Three times I have the Rata in my crosshairs. Bursts hammer from my machine guns. After the third burst the Rata begins to smoke. Flames leap out. I have hit his fuel tank. The left wing breaks off and the Rata spins away on fire.

Schellmann's Bf 109 B 6 • 51 at La Sénia. There are four victory bars on the fin, indicating that this photo was taken sometime between June 13, 1938, when Schellmann destroyed a Rata for his fourth victory, and the 25th of the same month, when he claimed his fifth victory, another Rata. The machine's wings and tailplane are still finished in the modified 70/71 scheme. *Private Collection*

Wolfgang Schellmann's Bf 109 B 6 • 51 at La Sénia. The aircraft's wings have been removed, as have the engine cowling and spinner. There are six victory bars on the tailplane, indicating that this photo was taken sometime after July 18, 1938, when Schellmann destroyed a Rata for his sixth victory. Note the light-colored band on the upper part of the undercarriage leg. Schellmann ultimately became the second-highest-scoring fighter pilot of the Legion Condor, shooting down a total of twelve Republican machines. The positions of the external power socket and oxygen filler hatch beneath the cockpit clearly identify the aircraft as a Bf 109 B. The aircraft in the background, 6 • 65, is a Bf 109 D, as indicated by the position of its external power socket farther aft on the fuselage. *Private Collection*

The Messerschmitts used a number of forward bases during this period, including Zaidin and Poma. These well-camouflaged airfields enabled the German fighters to take off unseen. After becoming airborne, they flew into one of the valleys and then stayed low until just short of the mountains, where they climbed into the sun and headed for the front. Using this tactic, on August 15 the 1st *Staffel* was able to surprise three squadrons of SB bombers flying at 12,000 feet and three of I-16s at 3,300 feet. The Messerschmitts immediately attacked and came home with three victories, for which pilots Oesau, Bertram, and Küll each received a case of beer.[66]

On August 19, 1938, seven Nationalist divisions launched a counterattack toward Fatarelle in an effort to clear the area of the Republican penetration, but the attack resulted in only minor gains. That same day, west of Flix on the Ebro, Günther Scholz scored his first victory. He wrote:[67]

The majority of the pilots who served in Spain failed to achieve a single victory, and most of those who did got one or at most two.

My victory was more a stroke of luck. Our principal opponents were the Russian Ratas. These machines were extremely maneuverable but were not as fast as the Messerschmitt. By then we had become an efficient, tight-knit *Staffel*. When we were attacked, and the Ratas usually outnumbered us, we formed a so-called defensive circle. Flying in a circle, we were able to provide mutual cover. Anyone who tried to enter the circle immediately found one of us on his tail. It was thus extremely difficult for the enemy fighters to achieve a victory.

On that day we were again attacked by a numerically superior force of Ratas. Mölders ordered us to form a defensive circle. I had the impression that our opponents were quite inexperienced. Again and again, they blithely flew into our circle and tried to shoot one of us down. In this they failed, succeeding only in placing themselves in danger.

Suddenly I saw a Rata drop down right in front of me. It flew into the defensive circle with the intention of shooting down the man ahead of me. He was right in front of my nose, perhaps 100 feet away. I pressed the firing button and watched my explosive bullets strike home. Fatally damaged, the Rata spun down and crashed. It was no great feat. There had been no dogfight. He simply came down from above and placed himself right in front of my guns.

Werner Mölders described Scholz's victory on August 19th and the actions that took place on that and the following day:[68]

The enemy air force has again received new equipment here at the Ebro, and recently there have been frequent combats. One time the 1st *Staffel* intercepted Martin bombers, and *Hauptmann* Schellmann destroyed two and *Unteroffizier* Brucks one. Bertram brought down a Rata.

Luck was with my 3rd *Staffel* again on August 19. I saw three squadrons of Ratas approaching from the direction of Tarragona and was able to lead my *Staffel* into position for a surprise attack. The engagement began west of Flix on the Ebro. Scholz shot down his first, and I shot a Rata down in flames for my fourth victory. The poor chap who was flying it burned with his aircraft.

On the afternoon of the 20th, there took place the finest dogfight I have experienced to date. Far away to the northeast, coming from the direction of Reus, I saw two enemy formations against the clouds. As we got closer I lost sight of them, until suddenly I saw a Rata squadron below me, but it was already engaged with twelve machines of our 1st *Staffel*. We attacked, but then suddenly two squadrons of Curtisses and one of Ratas joined the fight—from where only God knows. All of my Messerschmitts bravely remained above, and now and then one of us caught a Rata as it climbed.

I got behind a Rata, placed my sights on him, and fired. I still don't know why he didn't go down. Seconds later I was on the tail of a Curtiss. Their pilots flew well, repeatedly climbing and attacking us from below. I closed in, firing, until I finally passed over it to avoid a collision. As I did so I saw that the Curtiss had taken many hits. But then it disappeared beneath my wing and I didn't see it again.

Then another Curtiss came from the side. Once again I was able to get in an accurate burst, and I clearly saw hits in its tail section. But it was as if I was jinxed that day: they simply wouldn't go down. If the enemy aircraft didn't burn, one was rarely able to claim a kill. Despite this, I enjoyed this engagement immensely; it was like something out of a book. Unfortunately, Ebbighausen was badly shot up by the Curtisses and took eight hits. He managed to get home and made a safe landing, but the aircraft's fuselage was stove in as a result and put out of action for some time. Despite being in combat for a good twenty minutes, not a single enemy aircraft was seen to be shot down.

As the month of August 1938 came to a close, on the ground the Nationalist forces made slow progress against the Republicans, who resisted fiercely. On the 23rd, Mölders shot down an SB bomber but narrowly escaped being shot down himself. He wrote:[69]

The 23rd of August was a day when everything went wrong—yet I was incredibly lucky.

A fighter sweep by the 1st and 3rd *Staffeln* was planned for the morning, to catch the Martin bombers. And they came promptly, but we were still on the ground since our operations staff had delayed our fighter sweep by an hour. It would have been an opportunity, but now flying held little prospect, since the enemy never came two times in a row. That day our 1st and 2nd *Staffeln* went to a forward airfield, and I requested a *freie Jagd* mission for the period 1315 to 1400.

Everything went according to plan, we waited in the air like falcons, and the Martin bombers came. I saw them far away at a moment that was very unfavorable given the position of my *Staffel*. We were in a turn, reversing course, at a point farthest away from the front. As a result, some of my pilots did not even see my signal to attack, and for the first time my formation became scattered.

As we approached the Martins the flak placed such a curtain of fire in front of our noses that we had to fly around it. Finally, I picked my way alone through the small black clouds to close with the bombers. My *Kette* was late in following me, and therefore Scholz was the only one who saw me pursuing the Martins. He also saw a Rata squadron giving chase behind me.

I was closing with the fat bombers when I saw a Rata squadron above and to my right. I had to decide—would I rather me be behind the bombers or the Ratas behind me. I decided in my favor, and ultimately I moved toward the Martins, rapidly closing the distance. Deep in enemy territory I saw the bombers split up into two flights of three aircraft. This enabled me to get in close very quickly, and from a range of about 200 yards I opened fire at the inside man in the right formation. Tracer from the bomber's rear gunner was soon flying past my cockpit. I answered and the firing immediately stopped. After a second burst the bomber spurted oil and my windscreen was covered. I roared over the bomber and was able to see a huge flame under its port engine. Then I took aim at the formation leader.

At that instant I saw a Rata coming toward me from the right. I turned toward it and saw two more Ratas diving toward me from the other side. I evaded them and, as I did so, noticed two more Ratas pursuing me. Like a hunted animal I turned and spun down between the enemy aircraft. But they stayed on my tail like a swarm of bees. Ultimately, however, I must have lost them low among the valleys.

Flying 30 feet above the ground, I raced back in the direction of the front. My only thought was of my engine; I hoped it would not fail me. When I was convinced that there was no one behind me, I reduced power and then covered the 30 miles of enemy territory flying fast and low. On the way, I flew over a main road on which a column of troop trucks was driving. I descended to just above the ground and skimmed over them. They all waved to me. They seemed mightily impressed. I climbed back up to 30 feet and flew over empty terrain. And then I had to fly over the positions at the Ebro.

I saw the river glimmering near Fraga and once again pushed my machine quite close to the ground. I roared over the enemy trenches, surprising the people inside. Then I swept across the Ebro and was out. I breathed a sigh of relief and soon afterward landed at La Sénia. Jaenisch, who had seen the Ratas behind me, probably never thought he'd see me again. My victory, the only evidence of which was the oil on my windscreen, probably won't be confirmed.

Incidentally, the gunner in the enemy bomber scored a hit on my propeller spinner during this operation.

On August 24, a Republican pilot crash-landed his I-16 at Saragossa. Mölders described the incident and the subsequent interrogation of the enemy pilot:[70]

> On August 24, an enemy pilot who had become lost after combat with Fiats came down at Saragossa and made a passable crash landing. Unfortunately, as a result the Rata did not fall into our hands intact. We commanders interrogated the fellow yesterday; he was very green, twenty-one years of age, and we didn't get much new information out of him. He had little flying experience, since he was only on his fourth operational sortie. We found it interesting that he had been flying at 18,000 feet without oxygen, and that the other side—if this young airman's account was to be believed—is again receiving new aircraft. It was also interesting to learn that he had received five months' training abroad, as was his claim that the squadrons had been moved in from south to north. He said that they had flown over the sea, about 6 miles off the coast, at a height of 13,000 feet. Almost all of the enemy squadrons were based individually and were assembled [in the air] only to carry out their various combat assignments. They had different ground personnel at each airfield.

September began as August had ended. On September 5, fifty Republican fighters, Moscas and Chatos, attacked German fighters and bombers. A gunner in an He 111 destroyed an I-16, while *Lt.* Ensslen accounted for a Chato. Two days later "Otsch" Bertram shot down a pair of I-16 fighters. He described the action as follows:[71]

> I am on patrol with two pairs of fighters, dead tired and fed up. I'm at 20,000 feet, oxygen tube in my mouth, my mouth dry, no saliva. I see an enemy squadron, and then a wave of aircraft comes rolling in: five squadrons! Handrick and Oesau attack, and a wild dogfight develops. I force myself to be calm because to attack too soon is rubbish. I'm just about to tackle the squadron of Curtisses flying at 12,500 feet when a lonely trio of Ratas comes along at 16,000 feet. Change of target! Soon I am on the tail of the one on the right. It goes down with no sign of fire; no one bales out. Time to go home—or is it? Where is my wingman? Not there. Should I try it again? I am alone, but it's taking me straight to the front. And it works: another goes down, this time in flames!

September 9, 1938, was another eventful day. While Mölders recorded his sixth victory, *Uffz.* Kiening was obliged to make a forced landing north of Gandesa after his aircraft was damaged by fire from a Chato, and *Lt.* Lutz was shot down. Mölders wrote in his diary:[72]

Bf 109 D 6 • 62 after a rough forced landing. The aircraft appears to be finished in the late-war 63/65 camouflage scheme. Note the 1st *Staffel* marking on the fuselage disc and the four victory bars on the fin. Two of the aircraft's four MG 17 machine guns have been removed and placed in the cockpit. *Private Collection*

enemy aircraft. Finally I spotted Curtisses circling 1,600 feet below us. These fellows were shooting at us from below by pulling up into a vertical climb. Now and then they landed a chance hit, as had just happened to Kiening. He crash-landed near Batea, and I later picked him up at Alcanis. His machine had taken five hits: three in the wings, one in the coolant tank, and one in the oil line. That was enough!

The enemy is quite active, but we failed to catch them again today. The 2nd *Staffel* missed some Curtisses, and we arrived ten minutes later after Martin bombers had dropped their bombs.

Among those who took part in the operation on September 9 was a recent arrival in Spain, *Leutnant* "Joschko" Fözö. His account of the action reveals the anxiety he felt while striving to achieve his first victory:[73]

A gray September day has broken; heavy cloud fills the sky. But we aren't cold. The same oppressive heat bakes the plateau on which our airfield is situated. The mission order for September 9, 1938: fighter sweep over the bend in the Ebro.

Long since, I have not needed to look at the map. I know every twist and curve of the earth. I am as familiar with the route to the combat area as the alley where I played as a child. It is strange to observe the land from a height of 18,000 feet. It actually resembles a painted map. I have completely lost any impression of the "terrain." When I fly over it, I see nothing more than a faithful enlargement of my flight map, and only the final objective, the front, alters its position every few days, hardly noticeable to airmen used to thinking in hundreds of miles.

The clock shows 1215. As we climb, there is a flat cloud layer, like a stretched bed sheet, at 21,000 feet. Fighter sweep? It is a hunt with no prey. Too bad that the other side hasn't the same desire to go hunting as we.

I have gradually gotten rid of the calm. I have become a veteran Spanish flier, and I no longer see enemy aircraft where there are none. I have grown used to not looking back every few seconds to see if someone is sneaking up behind me. No, I calmly keep station behind the *Staffelkapitän*, the perpetual wingman.

Today we ran into the enemy again. The 2nd *Staffel* returned at about 1230 hours, and my *Staffel* and I took off on the next fighter sweep. We flew over the sea into the area, and at 1300 hours I saw a squadron of Ratas coming from Tarragona.

As of late the enemy has been flying broad arcs and turn continually over the front. No longer do they fly in a straight line as before. I therefore followed the same arc. Though it took rather longer, I closed on the trailing one undetected and shot down a Rata over Flix. I probably hit the pilot, since the aircraft's movements as it went down were uncontrolled.

Soon afterward I saw *Unteroffizier* Kiening beside me suddenly turn for home, trailing white smoke. My first instinct was to cover his tail, since I suspected that Ratas were behind him. At first, however, I couldn't see any

Bf 109 A 6 • 16 photographed later in the war. By this time it has been fitted with a metal variable-pitch propeller. There are seven victory bars on the tail of the aircraft. Among those who scored victories in 6 • 16 were *Lt.* Fözö and *Fw.* Fleischmann, the latter scoring all three of his victories in Spain flying this machine. The aircraft is still wearing its original *silberweiss* finish, which is quite worn in some places, with evidence of overpainting. *Private Collection*

There is just one thing I don't know: combat and victory. Mölders, too, has had no luck. It is as if we are jinxed.

We have reached the curve of the Ebro; once again nothing to be seen. Try as I might, as we circle I can't conjure up the enemy.

"There—what is that?"

For the first time I see Mölders's machine briefly waggle its wings—one, two, three times in succession. Alarm? Enemy fighters in sight?

Where?

I strain to see the enemy. Mölders must be mistaken, for as hard as I try I cannot make out a black dot in the sky. I look back, to the left, to the right, below, above—no Ratas, no Curtisses, nothing at all.

"What's going on?" I ask myself. "Am I blind? Don't I have a pair of what are acknowledged to be keen eyes in my head?"

At that moment, Mölders's machine suddenly pulls ahead. It goes through me like an electric shock: Horridoh!

A combat must be in the offing, even if I, the innocent bunny, still can't make out the enemy. I stick to my *Staffelkapitän*'s bird, engine at full power. Just don't get there too late! Don't miss it!

Where is the enemy?

My heart is pounding as if it must burst. The pressure on my chest is such that I can scarcely breathe. My breath comes in short gasps . . .

Where is the enemy?

Now Mölders is climbing. Just then I spot the enemy, heading straight for his machine. Mölders is already above him, makes a tight turn, and dives below the enemy aircraft. I recognize it as a Rata. Then two, three, six, eight appear one after another. With a quick glance from wide-open eyes I make them out.

Mölders is already within shooting distance. Thirty yards at most separate him from the enemy machine. I see the ammunition come from his barrels in a few brief bursts. A brief jet of reddish-yellow flame spurts from the engine of the enemy aircraft; it staggers, smokes, rights itself once more, and then falls away in a steep dive.

"He's finished!" I celebrate, as if it were my own victory.

The next Rata has closed to within firing range. We are at the same altitude, and I have him in my Revi obliquely from the side. I aim carefully, feeling as if I must suffocate from excitement.

Go! Press the button! Just don't let the guns jam! No, all of my guns are firing. I have a hit! A tiny point of light close to the engine builds into a circle of flame. It's burning! I remove my hand from the firing button: I've done it! Done it!

But what is this? The Rata calmly flies past me. I turn to follow . . . Nothing? No smoke cloud? No flames?

What in my overheated excitement I took to be a spurt of flame was nothing more than a spark caused by one of my bullets striking the outer skin.

I ram the throttle forward and set off after the despicable fellow who fooled me so miserably. He—me? I made a fool of myself. Damn! Damn! It's all too late. He is diving away at a terrific speed. He is gone.

Ashamed and disgruntled, I make my way back to rejoin my people. There's Mölders in front of me. For some time he has been circling calmly and safely. He positions himself in front of his *Staffel*, which, without scoring additional victories, has driven the enemy away.

We roar home. On the way I blame myself harshly. "Didn't you see, Josef," my better self says to me, "how your

A group of Spanish civilians and military personnel pose in front of Handrick's Bf 109 B 6 • 56 at La Sénia. The marking on the aircraft's spinner commemorates the gold medal that Handrick won in the men's modern pentathlon at the 1936 Olympic Games in Berlin. His was one of thirty-three gold medals won by the German team, nine more than its closest rival, the United States. *Private Collection*

Bf 109 B 6 • 56 after it passed to *Hptm.* Walter Grabmann. Handrick's "H" was replaced by a "G" on the fuselage disc. There are three victory bars on the fin, indicating that the photo was taken between September 23, 1938, when Grabmann destroyed a Curtiss (I-15) and a Rata for his second and third victories, and October 10, when he scored his fourth victory. Grabmann commanded J/88 from September 10, 1938, until the end of the war and scored a total of seven victories over Republican aircraft. *Private Collection*

The 1.J/88's new *Staffel* emblem, the so-called *Holzauge* or Wooden Eye emblem, was introduced when Siebelt Reents took over as commander of the unit in September 1938. *Private Collection*

Staffelkapitän did it? Close, close, fire and finished. It is the simplest thing in the world, you idiot! Don't take him from the side, like you did, and don't open fire too soon! Mölders said, 'Not until it's time!' And you? You just move in sloppily and press the button when you are still 250 or 300 feet away? Why, you moron? They're going to laugh at you when you get home. Let them!" . . .

We near the airfield that we took off from. Mölders roars low over the strip and waggles his wings. I come down close behind him and see the tremendous uproar on the field. Caps are tossed into the air; arms wave. I almost convince myself that I can hear the din down there.

I taxi to a stop and climb out. On seeing the empty spaces in my ammunition belts, my armorer says, "Too bad, *Herr Leutnant*."

"Oh well," I say and try to grin. "Another time."

"I'm certain of it," declares my armorer trustingly. "I'm not the least bit worried about it."

The noise has eased now, and I walk over to Mölders. He is stretched out in a deck chair, his sleeves rolled up. I congratulate him. He extends his hand, and after a brief and beaming "Thanks!" he looks at me long and hard. Then, in a display of good-natured banter, he says, "An opportunity is no opportunity. The next time we will practice it again, and then you'll do it better than me, right?"

I have to laugh. But the words "next time" remain behind like a small barb. When will the next time be? Tomorrow? Or in three weeks? Or never?

On September 10, 1938, *Hptm.* Handrick was relieved as commander of *Jagdgruppe* 88. His replacement was *Hptm.* Grabmann. At this time about half of the Legion Condor's veteran fighter pilots were relieved and sent home, where they were urgently needed because of the growing crisis over Czechoslovakia. Schellmann was among those who returned to Germany, and Reents replaced him as leader of 1st *Staffel*.

On September 13, Mölders shot down a Rata. He wrote in his diary:[74]

A wonderful day. The Nationalists tried a new attack. The entire air force was over the enemy positions until 1030. Then there was also artillery fire, and the attack was supposed to begin at 1100. My 3rd *Staffel* took off on a

Bf 109 D 6 • 64 of 2.J/88 at La Sénia. The name "Peter" can be seen beneath the cockpit sill. The brown oil triangle is just visible next to the man sitting in front of the cockpit. *Private Collection*

79

Two photos of Bf 109 D 6 • 60 in the familiar gun harmonization position, with tail raised and mainwheels in a trench. This is the aircraft of *Uffz.* Herbert Schob, who scored a total of six victories in Spain. This photo was taken sometime between November 3, 1938, when Schob scored his third victory, and November 16, when he recorded his fourth. Several features are visible that identify the machine as a Bf 109 D: the external power socket and oxygen filler point hatches on the fuselage aft of the cockpit, the gun ports for the wing-mounted MG 17 machine guns, and the oil triangle next to the filler point for the fuselage-mounted oil tank. The presence of the steam separators atop the coolant tank confirm that the aircraft is a D and not a C, which had a larger horseshoe-shaped coolant tank. *Private Collection*

fighter sweep at that time. I again made my approach from over the sea and at 1120 I saw a Rata squadron exactly where they had been circling over the front on September 9. We got behind them nicely. I opened fire at the bird flying on the outside of the trailing flight of three. It absorbed bullets from all my machine guns and spurted oil. Then it fell. I immediately turned my attention to the formation leader. I hit him too, but I do not know if he went down, since afterward Ebbighausen saw only one parachute, and it must have been from the first one.

Another Rata landed at a Nationalist airfield near Lerida. Desertions by Republican pilots were becoming more common. During this period the front remained largely static. Nationalist forces made minor gains, but these were eliminated by Republican counterattacks. For two weeks there were daily air battles, during which the Republican fighters were very aggressive.

On September 23, Mölders had another close shave. He described the action and also wrote about the new *Gruppenkommandeur*'s first contact with the enemy:[75]

On September 23, an *Unteroffizier* of my *Staffel* saved my bacon. I had just shot down my eighth enemy aircraft and was in a climbing right turn, when I suddenly saw muzzle flashes from the four machine guns of a Rata. I turned, but the fellow remained behind me. His aim was poor; I saw everything passing behind me, but at any moment he must have me, I thought. At that moment a Messerschmitt opened fire on the Rata from above—I saw the smoke trails from its bullets. The Rata reared up and fell off into a spin, leaving behind a growing trail of smoke. I had been saved at the last second. Well done! It was *Unteroffizier* Mart, and the Rata was his first victory. Afterward I gratefully shook his hand. We often helped each other out of trouble, and surviving such air battles together produced a deep comradeship.

Uffz. Werner Schob sitting on the cockpit sill of his aircraft 6 • 60 of 2.J/88. Between his legs can be seen part of his personal marking, the letters NNWW, which stood for *Nur Nicht Weich Werden* (literally translated: "Just don't go soft"). Schob, who was known to his comrades as "the Fat One," is in black face for reasons not known. Note the oil triangle beside the oil filler hatch and the raised access panel over the wing-mounted MG 17, two features of the Bf 109 D series. *Private Collection*

Bf 109 D 6 • 66 of 1.J/88 on an unidentified Spanish airfield. The oil triangle beside the filler hatch for the fuselage-mounted oil tank and long ejector stubs clearly identify the aircraft as a Bf 109 D. *Private Collection*

Not long afterward I was able to keep two *Ratas* from shooting down our commanding officer. He had recently arrived from Germany and was flying with me for familiarization.

One evening the two of us were cruising above the bend in the Ebro at 16,000 feet; below us were circling three squadrons of Italian Fiats. Once again there was something in the air, and I soon spotted three squadrons of Ratas at our altitude coming from the direction of Tarragona. I gave the alert signal, climbed another 1,500 feet, and positioned myself behind the Ratas. They flew past without noticing us, but just as I was about to attack the trailing squadron the Ratas spotted the Fiats and fell upon the Italians like a waterfall. The result was a fierce air battle in which the enemy was always in the most favorable position.

I gave the attack signal and dived into the fray. I moved into position behind two Ratas, but just as I was about to fire, my commanding officer roared past, chasing a Rata. It was his first aerial combat. I looked on somewhat anxiously and then saw two Ratas diving after my commanding officer. I turned away from mine and moved between the two Ratas. The rear one dove away; the one in front was about 100 feet behind the commanding officer. Rushing in, I put a burst between the commanding officer and the Rata and roared just over the enemy machine. He rolled

over and dove away. When I climbed back up there were no enemy aircraft to be seen. The sudden appearance of two German Messerschmitts had been enough to cause thirty Ratas to flee the combat area. Those fellows were terribly afraid of us in those days, something confirmed by prisoner statements.

Bf 109 D 6 • 67 of 2.J/88 parked at La Sénia. This was the aircraft flown by *Oberleutnant* Otto Bertram. Note the three victory bars on the aircraft's fin and the 2nd *Staffel* marking on the fuselage disc. Bertram scored his third victory on August 15, 1938, shooting down a Rata. Next to Bertram's aircraft is 6 • 51, the Bf 109 B flown by Wolfgang Schellmann. *Private Collection*

Aircraft 6 • 67 parked under trees at La Sénia. Note the position of the external power socket and oxygen filler point on the fuselage and the long exhaust stubs, identifying features of the Bf 109 D. *Oblt.* Bertram was shot down in this aircraft on October 4, 1938, becoming a prisoner of war. *Private Collection*

The new commanding officer was terribly eager, but one had to keep a close eye on him.

On October 4, *Jagdgruppe* 88 suffered a painful loss when *Leutnant* Bertram, a rising star with seven victories to his credit, was shot down. He later described what happened:[76]

Scramble! It's five o'clock. Out of the bunk. It begins—a squadron of Curtisses. I select a machine that will be my eighth victory, and prepare to attack. Select propeller pitch. Radiator flap up. Supercharger on. I look left and right—my wingmen are there, in we go! Ten seconds later I feel stinging impacts on my face, a rattling and crashing, and flames spurt from the engine. Instinctively I raise my arm in front of my face, which burns like fire. With my left hand I jettison the hood, while my right releases the safety belt. Subconsciously I recognize that the ground is above me, the earth is going to land on my head. I pull the parachute release. There is a jerk and I am swaying as if on a giant swing; the huge canopy is above me. I reproach myself as I descend: "You ass, allowing yourself to be shot down!" Down below is the Ebro—and there I see my faithful 6-67 spinning away. There will be no eighth victory bar painted on you today. Farewell!

The enemy fighters circle around me. This is probably my final hour! I am a living target. I rummage in my pockets because I have plenty of time. I was at 12,000 feet, which means a descent of a quarter of an hour. The Reds don't shoot at me; instead they wave and disappear. I destroy my legion identity card, letters—do I have any insignia anywhere? My helmet is who knows where, and my leather vest won't tell them anything. It is the *Staffel*'s traditional vest and has lived through twenty victories already. Below an automobile follows my progress; the welcoming committee. Watch out! I draw up my legs and then crash against a wall in the middle of an olive grove. My knee hurts terribly Two soldiers free me from my parachute. I stagger to my feet and, helped by the two men, hobble to the car. Captured!

An I-16 flown by *Teniente* Sabino Cortizo had climbed onto Bertram's tail and shot him down from below. That same day, SB bombers attacked the airfield at La Sénia, destroying one Bf 109 and damaging several others. The bombers and their escort of twenty Ratas appeared over the airfield at about 0745. "Joschko" Fözö described the day's events:[77]

There was a black day. Not every day can bring boredom or victories. Three of us were sitting in the car, leisurely making our way through the valley toward the airfield. There was low cloud. Several girls stood in front of the houses and smiled at us. We saluted; that was it.

Then: "Stop!" I shout to our Spanish driver. He brakes. "Switch off!" I call. I had heard a noise just then. It was a noise that quite clearly drowned out the rattling of our own engine. I scan the sky and listen: it was the sound of a bomber, unmistakable!

There! Isn't that a formation of aircraft in the air? Perhaps a squadron of bombers without our escort, passing over our airfield on its way home?

They descend. No, I'm not familiar with this type, and the sound is not that of our machines. It sounds foreign, lacking the deep, reassuring drone of our engines.

"Enemy bombers! Go, drive like the devil, boy! Avanti!" We were supposed to be at the airfield in five seconds . . . Yes, if it hadn't been so far away.

"Signal, signal! Clear the road! We have to get there before disaster strikes!"

Too late. We didn't hear the whistle; we saw only the massive mushroom cloud rising into the air, and we heard and felt the force of a powerful explosion. Then another, a third, a fourth!

We are almost on the airfield. Something is burning somewhere. Pillars of fire rise into the sky. Fragments fly about, light, as if they were straw . . .

Then, finally, our flak goes into action, the heavy guns making a loud boom, boom; the light ones, a bang, bang, bang. Clouds fill the sky. Ten, twenty, a hundred.

The bombers leave the airfield, climbing, turning, beating a retreat. Are there no machines ready to take off and give chase, to follow their scent? A powerless rage grips us all as we roar onto the airfield.

One of our precious machines is burning. Hidden beneath the olive trees, only its nose was visible to the enemy. Had they seen it, or was it just a lucky hit? It doesn't matter: the aircraft is ablaze; its wingtips rise as if they want to touch. The fuselage bursts. The air is filled with loud banging, clattering, and crackling.

And the other bombs?

With the nearby antiaircraft guns banging away, we can't understand a word. Then they fall silent, one after another. The enemy is out of range.

We search the airfield. It had been hit by four bombs. The mushroom clouds are still smoldering in the air. Moved to and fro by a gentle wind, they look like giants doing a native dance in slow motion.

We roar over to the scene: a bomb crater barely a meter deep? It can be filled in again by noon.

All right, no damage done.

The next smoke cloud is hanging over the olive grove at the south end of the airfield.

No damage.

The fourth came down on a narrow dirt road some distance from the airfield.

No damage here either.

We breathe a sigh of relief and head back . . . There they are carrying a man's body from the grove, toward the first-aid barrack. A tall blonde youth, one of our black

The remains of an unidentified Bf 109 D, still burning after a Republican bombing raid on La Sénia. *Private Collection*

Two photos of Bf 109 D 6 • 70 of 1.J/88 on an unidentified Spanish airfield. These photos reveal three of the major changes introduced by the D series. The first was replacement of the B series' wing-mounted oil tank with a fuselage-mounted tank, with a filler point on the side of the fuselage forward of the cockpit accompanied by a brown servicing triangle. The second was the addition of two wing-mounted MG 17 machine guns, and the third was the presence of projecting curved exhaust stubs. The aircraft is finished in the late-war scheme of RLM 63/65. Note the two victory bars on the fin and the "X" marking used by 1.J/88. *Private Collection*

men; he was attached to the 1st *Staffel*'s ground personnel. His arms are hanging lifelessly. A fragment struck him in the chest. The only sign is a thin trickle of blood, but he has been mortally wounded. Poor lad! Now we will lay the remains of what was once an excellent comrade and aircraft mechanic in the lead coffin; a ship will take him home.

Mölders is there. With the commanding officer, he had just inspected the airfield, ranted, cursed, and shaken his head. Now he stands before the dead man and removes his cap.

The dead man is given a fitting farewell. A hundred silent men surround the coffin in a salute of gratitude . . .

That same morning the 1st *Staffel*, which lost the aircraft and mechanic, takes to the air to take revenge.

When they return, *Leutnant* B. [Otto Bertram] is missing. We ask the *Staffelkapitän*. He just nods gloomily.

Bf 109 D 6 • 68 after a forced landing in a field. The brown oil triangle can be seen beneath the windscreen, as can the muzzle opening of the MG 17 in the port wing. There are two victory bars on the aircraft's fin. Note the *Holzauge* (Wooden Eye) emblem on the fuselage, which was adopted by 1.J/88 after *Hptm.* Siebelt Reents took command of the unit in September 1938. *Private Collection*

Shot down, the wonderful B.? Is his burned body lying somewhere on the ground? Charred amid the wreckage of his aircraft?

Three days later we hear the happiest news on Radio Madrid, to which we always listen: "After crashing in no man's land, a German fighter pilot trying to escape to Franco was captured and is now a captive."

On October 10, Mölders and his *Staffel* encountered Republican SB bombers. Mölders wrote about the action that followed in his diary:[78]

Finally, Martin bombers again. My *Staffel* was flying escort for our own bombers, which constantly bombed the enemy positions at the fiercely contested road fork at Venta de Camposines. After the bombers flew away we loitered in the area for a time.

I was ready to head for home when, in the distance, I saw five dots in the direction of Tarragona. That could only be the enemy! I led my *Staffel* up to 20,000 feet and flew in an arc into enemy territory in order to allow the Martin bombers—which is what they had turned out to be—to reach the front. As we got nearer I sighted two squadrons of Ratas right and left of the bombers at 18,000 feet. I was just about to begin the attack by my *Staffel* when another squadron of Ratas appeared at 20,000 feet. There

were about thirty-five enemy fighters, all to protect five bombers. I had just ten Messerschmitts.

My *Schwarm* first had to attack the enemy fighters to draw them away from the bombers, and then my other pilots would have to try to get to the bombers. We were flying in the sun; apparently the enemy hadn't spotted us yet. I had just given the signal to attack the highest Rata squadron when a lone aircraft rolled over and dove away. The fellow had spotted us and was going to warn the bombers. Wait, my dear chap! I was able to head him off, took him from the side, and fired from a distance of about 200 feet. I saw how this unsettled the rest of the Ratas, and they dove on me, but my Messerschmitts were already behind them. My opponent must have been hit immediately, for he rolled onto his back and dove away. I was so close that I could have rammed him. I got my sights on him again and in a vertical dive I fired all four machine guns. He began to burn and went down like a blazing torch.

When I looked around I saw Ratas everywhere behind me. My speed was very high, and I used it to gain altitude. Around me, Messerschmitts were locked in a fierce battle with the enemy fighters. Some distance away the five bombers flew on alone—no, there were two small dots behind them. One bomber began to burn and then a second went down trailing smoke. My wooden-eye pair (two pilots I always had fly above my *Staffel* over the Ebro) had broken through to the bombers, then flying alone, and each shot down a Martin bomber. Now only three enemy bombers returned, and unfortunately I never encountered them again.

October 15 brought more large-scale air battles. German fighters claimed four enemy machines shot down, two of them by Mölders. The *Staffelkapitän* was held in very high esteem by his pilots. Günther Scholz later wrote of him:[79]

Werner Mölders remained in Spain until the beginning of November 1938. He left the theater as the most successful fighter pilot of the German "Legion Condor," with fourteen confirmed victories.

Whenever one of us shot down an enemy aircraft, on returning to base he flew a so-called honor circuit of the airfield while waggling his wings. Mölders always added to this, roaring low over the airfield before suddenly pulling his machine into a vertical climb and performing a roll. He was a virtuoso pilot.

I personally tried a number of times to perform a roll, especially later in my career, but I was never able to really complete the maneuver 100 percent. The required hand movements literally had to merge with flesh and blood. In those fractions of a second there was simply no time to think about how to operate the elevator and rudder. This maneuver, which Mölders began from a low pass, left not the slightest margin for error and from that height could have cost him his life. I simply admired him.

Poor weather hampered flying operations, and it would be more than two weeks before German fighters made their next victory claims. On October 31, a large force of Ratas and Chatos took to the air to intercept German raiders. They shot down one He 111 but suffered heavy losses.

Bf 109 A 6 • 16 at La Sénia. The aircraft wears a very worn *silberweiss* finish and has seven victory bars on its fin. Josef Fözö flew this aircraft when he first joined 3.J/88 and also scored his first victory with it. In his book he described the aircraft's color as "silver gray." *Private Collection*

German fighters claimed nine Ratas and a single Chato shot down. On this day, *Leutnant* "Joschko" Fözö finally scored his first victory.[82] He later wrote:[83]

One period of bad weather has followed the other, but finally, the last day of October brings a bright blue sky, the harbinger of future deeds, promising victory, heralding luck. Spirits, marked by melancholia, are suddenly transformed. All eyes look as if freshly polished. Faded hopes bloom: action!

After weeks of inactivity, the entire *Gruppe* takes to the air. Our orders are to provide escort for a formation of bombers: the Bolshevik positions near Pinell, which have been stubbornly resisting Franco's forces, are to be pounded until the enemy can neither hear nor see.

We rendezvous with the bomber group, take up our positions, and sail into the blue day. My thirst for fame has long since given way to carrying out my duty as a matter of course. Modesty? It may be better. But does not unopposed, raging success make a man harder and cause him to become straighter and more soldierly? I know for sure: if I return home again without a victory, I will be a little sad. But the anger, the chagrin, the desperate obsession; I no longer feel it as before.

The singing of our machines mingles with the droning of the twin-engine bombers into a harmony filled with pride and power. Seen from below, the sight must be unforgettable. In perfect order, the fighters and bombers sail onward in secure formation. A flight of Fiats passes us in the distance.

"Good hunting, comrades!"

They are following the same course as we, but they are to the east, flying along the sea. We took off at 0820. The instrument panel clock shows 0845. We are nearing the target. Have we taken them by surprise?

No, in the hazy background the dots we have longed for are slowly and steadily rising to our altitude: enemy fighters! They are still too far away to count.

The wings of our *Staffelkapitän*'s machine waggle incessantly: "Attention, get ready for a big fight!"

Grasping the stick tighter, sitting a little lower in the seat, this is the same to us as "tighten helmet straps" to the infantryman.

The enemy in front of us has reached our altitude. Meanwhile our bombers are over their targets and drop their bombs. Fountains of dust and smoke whirl into the air—the steel seed is terrible; the iron harvest, enormous. The first enemy positions in front of Pinell are no more.

Now Franco's troops down below can breathe freely; now they can attack and dash forward to secure the ripe harvest.

Why am I wasting time thinking about this? The *Staffelkapitän* is preparing to attack. Almost a mile still separates us from the enemy, but already Mölders has begun a steep climb. We follow. I make a rough calculation of the enemy's strength: three squadrons. There must be between thirty-five and forty aircraft.

But what kind of machine is that? I don't recognize it; it is neither a Curtiss nor a Rata. It is a new, compact, and sleek design; fast, much faster than the Ratas. Will we be faster?

We are. And we are stronger. It is not speed that decides; rather, it is the quality of man and machine. But we are Germans in German fighter aircraft.

A cloud of aircraft climbs and splits up to attack. I stick with Mölders to cover his tail. Then he dives on the first, which is trying to take him from the side. From all his machine guns he sends a stream of bullets at the enemy aircraft, which also raises its nose to fire. The pilot must be hit: I see the enemy machine pull up sharply then sluggishly and helplessly fall away into a spin. This makes it clear enough that the aircraft is no longer being controlled.

My brain works with a feverish clarity. I recognize a thousand details, seeing them as if it is no more than a film strip running before me at tremendous speed. I climb after the next enemy and try to stay with him, but he turns into me and veers to the side. Should I follow?

As I am about to haul the stick around and apply full throttle, a second enemy machine rises directly in front of me—a gift from heaven. Less than a few hundred feet separate us. I can dive away beneath it, I can fly past it, or I can also take it on. Is it time? Fractions of a second decide.

I press myself down behind the gunsight; every fiber of my being is possessed by a single imperative: to fight. Time races.

Now, the enemy sits fat in my sight. Eyes, don't fail me; brain, remain clear. Hand, press the buttons! If only my guns don't jam! Just this one time. Victory is certain.

I press the firing buttons. A stream of bullets hisses from the barrels. I follow the tracer. There, it's on target, close to the nose in the center of the engine. Where I have aimed is where the bullets strike. Unless a miracle saves him he is done for.

The first tiny darting flames demonstrate the effect of my fire. Gray smoke creeping from beneath the cowling forms a tiny puff and then grows into a banner. The aircraft falls away and goes down, down!

I look back. Left and right my comrades are whizzing through the air. Gosh, this is a proper fight! Each is behind an enemy aircraft. Just don't collide. Aircraft turn and fire, and the sky is filled with smoke and flame.

I follow the doomed enemy machine for a few hundred yards. The fire has eaten its way to the wings. My first victim becomes one ball of flames.

Friend, comrade! You who should witness my first victory, did you—like me—see him? Look here, how the machine goes down in a steep dive and smashes into the ground in a cloud of dust and flame.

"Victory," I celebrate to myself.

But this is no time to celebrate shooting down an enemy aircraft. I must climb back up and again engage the enemy, who still outnumbers us.

I breathe heavily. Soaked with sweat, my clothing sticks to my body. I rub away the sweat that has run down my forehead into my eyes. I have to see clearly.

The dogfight breaks up into small and smaller groups. Two of our fighters are mixing it up with seven enemy machines. There. One of them has caught fire, which spews from the cockpit. His oil line must be burning. Black smoke pours out, licked by bright flames that spread into a huge fire. He's had it. The aircraft rolls to the right and its nose drops. The pilot tries once again to get away, but his bird somersaults and he's gone. I don't see it crash, but its end is certain.

Can I score a second? Why couldn't this be the day I come home with two victories? I position myself behind an aircraft from my flight that is pursuing three of the enemy. I ram the throttle forward; don't arrive too late! I close to within 300 feet of my comrade, and we are close to the enemy, but the others hurriedly descend several hundred feet and pull into an extremely tight turn. It almost looks as if the last two will collide. Then, one behind the other, they reach safety behind the rugged mountain range.

We climb to rejoin. My machine gives a triumphant cry as I apply power to climb. I climb skyward, nothing but blue sky above me. I could keep on climbing like this, toward the sun. I feel like master of the world, and I am.

I rejoin my comrades. We have caught up with the bomber formation and head for home, quiet and calm, a little battle weary and grateful for this, our busiest day. There is the airfield.

But now! Now! Should I give you a thrill, my black boys? I know, like me you have been waiting for this moment for months. Like me, when you saw the pot of black paint you averted your gaze, because you had no reason to use it.

Once again you stand waiting in front of your workshop huts and watch for me: Will I come home in one piece? And how will I return?

Watch this! This is how someone who has scored his first victory approaches the airfield. He dives and roars over the airfield. Only the machine of a successful fighter pilot waggles its wings.

I land and unfasten my seat belts. I laugh. I step onto the airfield; I am clownish. What should I do? I clap my people on the shoulder—my fuel technician, the mechanics, the armorers. From up close, I look into their eyes. I have to see my happiness reflected there. . . .

Mölders is there: "Finally, Joschko!" he shouts to me, and I hear the deep and pure joy with which he greets me. "Tell!" I stutter, repeat myself, but finally manage to make my report. Then I say, "Thank you, *Herr Hauptmann*."

"For what?" asks Mölders.

Members of the ground crew work on Bf 109 D 6 • 73 at La Sénia. Note the single victory bar on the aircraft's fin and the 2nd *Staffel* "Top Hat" emblem. *Private Collection*

Bf 109 D 6 • 79, photographed at León after delivery to Spain. The aircraft was apparently repainted and its unit emblem, in this case 3.J/88's "Mickey Mouse," was applied there. The aircraft in the background, 6 • 7 ?, is wearing 2.J/88's "Top Hat" emblem. After delivery to 3.J/88, 6 • 79 was assigned to *Staffelkapitän* Werner Mölders. *Private Collection*

A *Schwarm* of Bf 109s flying low over the airfield at La Sénia. The lead aircraft, 6 • 79, is that of Werner Mölders, *Staffelkapitän* of *3.J/88*. *Private Collection*

"For everything I've learned."

"Oh!" says Mölders, and with a heedless movement of his hand deflects my gratitude, almost embarrassed.

"What? *Feldwebel* Fleischmann and *Unteroffizier* König have also brought down their first? Come lads, give me your hand." And a firm handshake unites the three first timers.

"And the chief?"

Mölders has shot down his twelfth. Now I am almost embarrassed for not asking about it when I had the opportunity. I catch up with him and offer my congratulations. He laughs his boyish laugh. "Well," he says, "there were plenty to choose from. By the way, we have five in total. What do you have to say about that? Bolz also earned his first victory bar today. And what did you think of the new kites they were flying today? We must have a good look at them the next chance we get."

Mölders and *Fw*. Fleischmann each claimed two enemy fighters shot down that day. Fleischmann, who was flying Bf 109 A 6 • 16, described his two victories as follows:[84]

The 3rd *Staffel* took off at 0820 on October 31, 1938, to escort K/88 into the area of the Red penetration. I was in the highest *Rotte* with *Lt*. Fözö flying at 20,000 feet. Forty minutes after takeoff, the formation flying below us made contact with three squadrons of Ratas. We maintained our altitude to provide cover against an attack from above. My element leader made several undercutting turns in quick succession, and I was left about 300 yards behind. Suddenly, I saw five or six individual Ratas. They were below us and trying to get on my leader's tail. I attacked a lone Rata from behind and above. When he saw me he tried to shake me by making several half rolls and dives. I dove after him. When we reached an altitude of about 13,000 feet, the Rata pilot thought he was alone and began climbing in a turn to the left. Because of my Me's greatly superior speed I closed to within 150 feet of the Rata. From above and behind I fired four or five short bursts, aiming in front of his engine. The Rata went straight up, reached a vertical position, and then slowly fell backward. I believe I hit the pilot, because this maneuver appeared to be unaided and did not look controlled. The aircraft went straight down for about 3,300 feet and then began to spin. Since there were no other Ratas in the area, I was able to closely follow the spin until the aircraft hit the ground. It crashed northeast of Perello.

The 3rd *Staffel* took off at 1415 on October 31, 1938, to escort K/88 into the area of the Red penetration. I was flying in the lowest formation in a pair with *Lt*. Fözö. By making an overlapping turn I stayed about 300 yards behind him. We were flying in the direction of Tarragona at an altitude of 20,000 feet. At 1500, several aircraft approached us from a distance of 1,500–2,000 yards. At first glance I took them to be Me 109s. Because we were

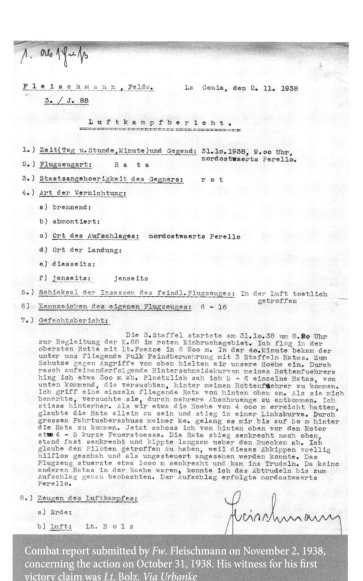

Combat report submitted by *Fw.* Fleischmann on November 2, 1938, concerning the action on October 31, 1938. His witness for his first victory claim was *Lt.* Bolz. *Via Urbanke*

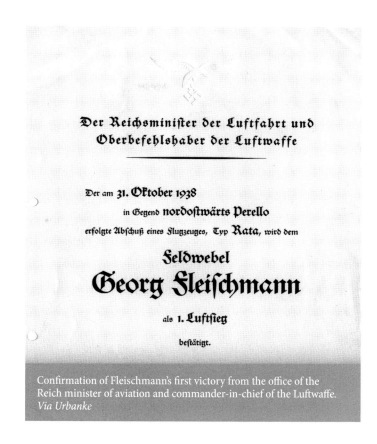

Confirmation of Fleischmann's first victory from the office of the Reich minister of aviation and commander-in-chief of the Luftwaffe. *Via Urbanke*

flying right toward each other, they closed very quickly and turned out to be Ratas. Two Ratas attacked my element. One Rata passed over my element leader by 150 feet and climbed. The second Rata came toward me at my altitude and fired from medium range. I fired right at his radial engine. When we were about 150 feet apart, the Rata put its nose down, passed under my machine, and dove away. I made a split-S and chased after him, and from a distance of 100 yards I opened fire, aiming ahead of the engine. The aircraft went straight down for about 3,300 feet and then went into a spin. I watched it go down for about five seconds, and at the end I saw a white line behind the spinning aircraft. At that moment I was attacked by a Rata, which came down in a vertical dive, and I was unable to see the aircraft crash.

At this time, German pilots reported meeting a new "Curtiss" fighter that was almost as fast as the Bf 109 and possessed an excellent rate of climb. Mölders described his encounter with the "new" type:[85, 86]

In the next few days, new enemy aircraft suddenly appeared that were almost as fast as us and had an excellent rate of climb. They came down at us from over 25,000 feet and used the same flight tactics as we; however, they didn't carry out their attacks as aggressively as we German pilots do when we have an enemy aircraft in front of us. Because of this, several pilots who were attacked by surprise were able to return home in spite of being hit.

It was extremely unpleasant because none of us could properly identify the enemy.

Finally, on October 31, my tactic worked. I had led my squadron far out over the sea and flew into enemy territory from behind at an altitude of 21,000 feet. The (mythical) enemy squadron was still climbing toward the front, and I got it in front of me at 16,000 feet as it approached the Ebro. But these fellows were so fast that we closed only slowly. I could have positioned my entire squadron for a surprise attack on the enemy, had two new Rata squadrons not appeared on our flank at that moment. On spotting us they immediately turned and fled, apparently having no desire to get to know us better. As a result, I made the first attack with just my own flight (*Schwarm*).

My twelfth went down and then there was a terrific dogfight with these new enemy aircraft. The better German pilots came out on top. Five enemy machines went down.

This Chato (Polikarpov I-15), CA-108, was delivered to La Sénia by its pilot *Sargento* Marcelino Arranza. Here a throng of German personnel get their first close-up look at one of the Legion Condor's principal opponents in the air war. Werner Mölders test-flew the aircraft soon after its arrival. *Author's Collection*

CA-108 again, this time after its Republican markings had been overpainted. *Author's Collection*

Leutnant Fözö, *Feldwebel* Fleischmann, and *Unteroffizier* Kiening scored their first kills. I added number thirteen to go with my twelfth. On fire, the enemy aircraft flew straight and level for a while, allowing me to move in close and get a good look at the type from the side. Then it stalled and went down like a torch. The spell of this new enemy had thus been broken.

On November 1, *Sargento* Marcelino Arranza deserted to the Nationalists, landing his Chato at La Sénia airfield. Werner Mölders immediately took the opportunity to test-fly a machine he had met in the air so many times. "Joschko" Fözö wrote:[87]

The next day brought us a very unusual surprise, which, in the manner in which it was presented to us, was surely unique and most astonishing.

We were lying in deck chairs, wrapped in blankets since the day had brought cool air. Then something drew our attention: a noise in the air. It grew louder and approached quickly. Then a black dot was spotted against the blue sky. Mölders had his binoculars in his hands.

"I'll be damned, a Curtiss! Up men!"

Mölders raced to the car and steered it toward the airfield. I jumped in beside him. A pair of fighters would be sufficient to bring this fellow down. But look, he's coming lower. What's the fellow up to? Mechanical trouble? It doesn't sound like it. What's wrong with him?

Then, what is that? The pilot is waving a white cloth. He means to land, to surrender? Good, let him land. We can wait.

The fighter—which can now clearly be seen to be an enemy aircraft—flies straight toward our airfield, makes his approach, and taxis to a stop. Well, his landing was no act of heroism.

Four men race to the machine. The pilot makes no effort to escape. He calmly hands over his pistol and allows himself to be led to the command post.

The interpreter enters the barrack with the *Staffelkapitän*. Moments later, Mölders emerges and laughs.

"Gentlemen, that man didn't walk across the lines to desert, he flew! Upon my soul! The fellow is all of twenty-one years old and already so war weary. He'd had enough and simply delivered his machine to us; he was probably too lazy to walk. They're going to question him a little more inside and try to learn what he has to say about his comrades in the front. Anyway, in the meantime there's something I want to do . . ."

He goes over to his crew chief and exchanges a few words with him. Then the Curtiss is refueled; the mechanics check every nut, bolt, and screw and examine the entire crate. Finally Mölders climbs in and we witness the most extraordinary display of flying as our *Staffelkapitän* throws the enemy bird around the sky.

Before taking off, he shouted to Julio Bolz and me: "Don't be daft and shoot me down!" He makes one turn after another. He cautiously pulls the nose up and climbs, then he rolls over, spins, waggles the wings, and comes in for a landing.

When he lands he is bathed in sweat. He joins us on the deck chairs and wraps himself in a blanket. He shivers from the cold. We admire the daring he showed in climbing into the completely unfamiliar enemy crate.

"I learned something new, gentlemen!" he said cheerfully. "We already know plenty about them from observing them closely in combat. But the thing still holds plenty of secrets, which they over there haven't shown me yet. By the way, the kite can turn like crazy! But just to remove all doubt, boys, I much prefer our crates!"

Boyishly enthused by what he has just learned, he works out new tactics for us.

"There, you see," he says after a thorough inspection of the red-painted bird, "here is a weak point in its design. If one can score a hit here, he is gone in seconds. We should be grateful to that cowardly dog in there for the new information he has provided us. So, gentlemen, I will shoot down my next Curtiss with wisdom, understanding, and precise knowledge about its design. So that I don't get any complaints!"

He laughed his irrepressible and infectious laugh.

On November 3, after their first major breakthrough on the Ebro front, Nationalist forces took the town of Pinell. *Jagdgruppe* 88 had another successful day, claiming six enemy aircraft destroyed, five of them Ratas. Mölders recorded his fourteenth victory; Oesau, his ninth. Two days later, *Gefr.* Nirminger was slightly wounded and had to make a crash landing. On the night of November 6–7, the Republicans attacked across the Segre River in an attempt

Bf 109 D 6 • 75 at La Sénia. The ground crewman has opened the hatch cover over the oxygen filler point and is preparing to top off the aircraft's oxygen tank. The position of this access point and the external power socket to its left identifies the machine as a Bf 109 D. *Private Collection*

Bf 109 D 6 • 76 at La Sénia. Note the position of the external power socket in front of the aircraft number, "76." The mountains in the background were an obstacle that the pilots had to negotiate every time they flew to the Ebro front. *Private Collection*

to relieve the pressure on the Ebro front. By the 16th of November the Nationalists had regained all the territory they had lost.

The three and a half months of fighting on the Ebro had cost the Republicans more than 300 aircraft, about a third of which fell to *Jagdgruppe* 88. Mölders's 3rd *Staffel* alone had claimed forty-two victories.

On November 10, during a mission over Republican territory, Werner Mölders' aircraft developed engine trouble and he was forced to land at an abandoned Republican airfield at Villa Lames. He returned to his relieved unit later that night. "Joschko" Fözö described the incident:[88]

It is not always enemy fire that brings a machine to grief. The smallest defect—if it affects an important part of the engine—can bring disaster.

We have a *Staffelkapitän*, perhaps the best shot the earth has ever seen, the most complete flier the air has ever borne.

One day we are flying escort to the north. All of the aircraft have been inspected; nothing has been missed.

And yet a break has been developing for a long time. At first it was only an insignificant crack, invisible to the naked eye. During flight, with every part of the machine under the greatest stress, the crack becomes larger and larger. Then a piece of steel breaks into two useless parts, which grind and rub against each other. The damage eats further; the end is near.

Mölders is flying ahead of us. Nothing suggests that the destructive situation will show itself in a matter of seconds . . .

The enemy's antiaircraft guns send up their shells; we fly past and through them. Shells burst to our left and right, but they can't stop us.

Then—we have just cleared the flak belt—Mölders peels away and begins to descend. The aircraft still looks all right, but then a small white stream of vapor appears from the left side.

Flak hit? At that moment who can say? All can I see is the small stream turning into a long coolant trail. Failure or hit, no matter, the *Staffelkapitän* is in danger.

Should we peel away with him? Can we?

The same is true for every mission: "Carry on, carry out the mission no matter what happens!" With heavy hearts we fly on. Below us the aircraft of our *Hauptmann* continues to descend. Now it is trailing a huge banner.

Will he make it? Will he be able to land before his engine flies to pieces? I can't see him any longer. I clench my teeth and carry on.

Later, back at the airfield, a search for the *Kapitän* is organized. A flight of four aircraft takes off to circle the area where Mölders left formation.

Mölders's version of what happened was slightly less dramatic:[89]

Today, on November 10, we took part in a combined operation with a bomber squadron on the southern front in front of Nules. The bombers draw heavy antiaircraft fire, and every day some return home with flak damage. Shortly after overflying the front on the way home, I developed engine trouble but was able to land safely at Villa Lames. Water in the cylinder. If it had happened fifteen minutes earlier over Valencia!

Feldwebel Fleischmann scored his third victory on November 12. Once again his aircraft was 6 • 16, one of two Bf 109 A fighters still in service with the *Jagdgruppe*. Fleischmann described the action in his combat report:

The 3rd *Staffel* took off at 1500 on November 12, 1938, to escort K/88 into the area of the Red penetration. Twenty minutes after takeoff, we spotted a squadron of Curtisses circling south of Asco at about 11,500 feet and attacked it from behind. However, the Curtiss squadron realized that we were about to attack, broke up, and dove away. I gave chase to a lone Curtiss and fired at it from above. The Curtiss turned so tightly that I was forced to break off my attack. At that moment I was fired on by several Curtisses climbing almost vertically from beneath me. I regained altitude and tried to reestablish contact with my *Staffel*, which was about 3,300 feet away and heading north. When I had reached an altitude of 10,000 feet, 1,500 feet below my nose I saw a lone Curtiss in a climb. I only had to put the nose down and he was in my sights. After several longish bursts the Curtiss rolled onto its back, somersaulted several times, and went straight down. I was able to follow its descent until it crashed. The machine burned neither in the air nor on the ground. It crashed in a valley south of the mountain El Mont Sant.

November 16 is generally regarded as the date on which the Battle of the Ebro ended. On November 17, the units

Mölders' Bf 109 D 6 • 79 undergoes repairs on the abandoned Republican airfield at Villa Lames. During a mission over the Ebro front on November 10, 1938, Mölders' aircraft developed a problem with its cooling system, and an overheating engine forced him to land there. The aircraft's spinner appears to be yellow with the base plate painted white. *Private Collection*

Bf 109 D 6 • 80 after a wheels-up landing at La Sénia. Mölders' aircraft, 6 • 79, can be seen in the distance. Note the open access panel over the starboard MG 17 wing machine gun. *Private Collection*

This photo of 6 • 80 was taken somewhat later. The rudder and horizontal tail surfaces have been removed, as have the folding canopy and fixed aft section. The wing root fairing has also been taken off, probably in preparation for removal of the wing. The aircraft's rudder is lying on the ground at the bottom left of the photo. Strangely, there is no unit badge of any kind on the aircraft. *Private Collection*

Another of 2.J/88's Bf 109 Ds, coded 6 • 81. Its smiling pilot is wearing a woman's dress, for reasons unknown, with a seat parachute. The man on the left appears to be working on the wing-mounted machine gun. *Private Collection*

of the Legion Condor were ordered to rest until December 1, and the time was to be used to bring them back up to full operational readiness. The only units that remained at combat readiness during this period were one *Staffel* from each of K/88 and J/88, plus two reconnaissance aircraft of A/88. J/88 claimed no victories between November 16 and December 20. On December 5, 1938, Werner Mölders was relieved as *Staffelkapitän* of 3.J/88 by *Oblt.* von Bonin. "Joschko" Fözö described the day of Mölders's departure:[90]

There comes a day that, for weeks, we have been anticipating without joy: it brings the *Staffelkapitän's* departure. After having been in Spain for a long time, Mölders and our doctor Appel have been called home. What Mölders accomplished down here, he will now have to build upon at home through tireless training. None of his flights were in vain: at home, hundreds and thousands of young men wait for this most experienced of fighter pilots, who will tell them what was learned here and the lessons derived from it.

We know well that he might probably be more important at home than he is here. But it pains us to see our comrade leave our ranks. He has been more than our *Staffelkapitän*. In the hot months of the fighting in Spain, he has become the master of fighter pilots. He leaves the battlefield with fourteen victories, and he lightheartedly and readily left many certain victories to comrades who needed them more badly than he.

To us he was the builder of the new school of flying, its champion and chief instructor in one. He had completed what Galland began before him.

We planned a farewell party for the night before his departure, but it became an assembly of mourners. We sang the old songs and passed around the old jokes, but the joy was forced and not from the heart. We exchanged tales of our experiences to cheer us up, but it was as if they had grown stale overnight. Nothing could make us happy.

The next morning we stood before the passenger aircraft. He laughed and waved his unauthorized bouquet of flowers that his people had brought to him at the airfield. He shouted "Horridoh!" and climbed into the aircraft. We knew that Mölders felt no better than we.

Four fighters flew escort until his aircraft was far out over the sea. The rest of us watched from the ground as the machine made a sweeping turn after departure and then disappeared into the distance.

By mid-December, the *Jagdgruppe's* strength was down to thirty-seven Bf 109 A, B, and D fighters, but word had arrived that the first of the new Bf 109 E series would soon be arriving. Republican fighter strength stood at about 140 aircraft, Ratas and Chatos. Deliveries of I-16s from Russia had virtually stopped, and a factory in Alicante delivered just twelve of a planned series of 100 aircraft by war's end. Chatos were more readily available, since the factory in Reus was producing one aircraft per day.

After the failure of the Ebro offensive, the Republican side's prospects were indeed bleak. Anthony Beevor described the situation as follows:[91]

The onset of winter in Republican Spain was bleak. Food supplies had diminished even further; industrial

Four Bf 109s parked on a Spanish airfield, possibly León. The two aircraft on the left, 6 • 86 and 6 • 69, are Bf 109 Ds of 1st *Staffel*, while the other two, 6 • 87 and 6 • 89, are Bf 109 Es with no visible unit markings. *Private Collection*

production was down to about one-tenth of 1936 levels as a result of raw material shortages and the lack of electricity in Barcelona. There was little fuel for heating. Cigarettes and soap had been generally unobtainable for many months. Defeatism was rife, and even those who, in desperation, convinced themselves that the struggle would eventually end in victory could not now avoid the truth. They realized that the next battle would be the last, and faced the prospect with bitter resignation.

Republican bombers struck La Sénia again on December 16, destroying two Bf 109s. "Joschko" Fözö wrote:[92]

> Cold rain fell from the sky, day after day. We suffered terribly from the cold. All day long we played stupid, senseless games. We wrote letters, ate, drank, and slept, and yet every day there remained time enough to complain about our inactivity. It was almost a relief when an attack by enemy bombers ripped us from our forlornness:
>
> "Martins, Martins! A whole formation!"
>
> They approached beneath a solid cloud deck. But after the first attack on our airfield the people on the ground were wide awake. The enemy formation was approaching at an altitude of more than 23,000 feet, but our flak filled their path with a hail of exploding steel that made them forget about bombing.
>
> Hearts pounding, we watched the spectacle through our binoculars. Should we take off? No point. They would disappear into the heavy cloud before we could reach them. We had to rely on the barrage being thrown up by the antiaircraft guns, whose shells were drawing nearer to the Martins.
>
> Then one of the bombers staggered. It looked like it was flapping its wings, trying to stay in the air. It wobbled like this for a few seconds. Its gyrations became more violent and it went down, down, down. Seeing this, the other bombers turned away. A dot appeared in the sky. It fell earthward, then after a while canopy opened and slowed its descent. The pilot had baled out. His parachute opened just as the machine struck the ground not far from the airfield. We saw the jet of flame, which rose more than 300 feet. Then dust and smoke filled the air.
>
> Two of our cars were standing by. We climbed in to go and get the enemy pilot, wherever he had come down. The wind was blowing him roughly toward the spot where a pillar of smoke was still rising.
>
> The smoke cloud showed us the way. We drove into the valley, up and downhill, racing over the rough dirt road. The car bounced and shook as it rolled over the cart tracks. Finally we were there.
>
> The pilot was attempting to get hold of his parachute when we spotted him in a cornfield. He was fighting desperately against the entanglement of the hundred belts and lines. His whole body was shaking, sweat was running down from under his cap, and his hands were racing. His

boots and trousers were singed. No more than a tiny lad of nineteen, he stood there, looking around with cheerless eyes, and allowed us to help him. We soon had him free from his entanglement. He asked for a cigarette and we gave him one. He eagerly inhaled the smoke. Then he followed us to the car.

> The remains of his aircraft were still burning on the other side of a small grove that bordered the field. We took the "little Soviet bomber" with us to the crash site. Acrid smoke filled the air and made us cough. Thick swaths of smoke wafted over the site.
>
> Scarcely fifteen minutes ago, a valuable combat instrument had flown over this spot. Now it was no more than a pitiful, twisted pile of wreckage. Charred frames, struts, and spars rose up like octopus tentacles. Fire licked them. Pieces of the propeller and engine had broken off from the nose and were lying on the ground 150 feet from the wreck. Tubes, wires, and stiffeners were scattered everywhere. Part of the wing had broken off and was stuck to the bottom branch of a cork oak; a shocking sight. Of the bomb aimer, who was in the aircraft when it crashed, nothing can be seen.
>
> We look at the young man, who stands before us as pale as a corpse. His upper body is bent over as he stares into the hissing, sizzling sea of flames, searching for his comrade. Then he looks at us, covers his face with his hands, and drops to his knees.
>
> We help him up, but as we are taking him to the camp an uncontrollable shaking seizes his body.
>
> With an uncomprehending and almost animallike look, he says in Spanish: "It was my first combat mission." Over and over he says: "My first combat mission."

The Nationalist offensive into Catalonia was delayed until December 23. Its ultimate objective was to drive the Republicans back toward Barcelona.

With less opposition in the air, the fighters of the Legion Condor increased their attacks against enemy airfields. *Oberfeldwebel* Fleischmann of 3.J/88 described one such attack:

> The evening before, the *Staffel* commander held a briefing. A brief explanation of our mission: the White air force is going to destroy the Red air force on the ground at its bases. Our *Jagdstaffel* was to attack the Red airfield of Muñoz, 25 miles north of Tarragona, at low level. Reconnaissance aircraft have found that there are many aircraft—fighters, reconnaissance machines, and some bombers—on the airfield. We know where the enemy aircraft are located from photos taken by the reconnaissance aircraft.
>
> We are shown a map with our route of flight, and the commander goes over our flight profile, attack time, and plan of attack, as well as our response in the event of contact with enemy aircraft. We are under strict orders to avoid aerial combat.

The next morning we take off punctually at the appointed time, in almost total darkness. I am flying in the number two position behind the *Staffel* leader in the specified echelon right formation. I can barely make out the position lamp of the first aircraft. We must pay close attention because we must fly just a few yards above the ground.

After a few minutes we are over the open sea, make a left turn, and then head north about 3 miles off the coast. A magnificent flight! To our left is the white coast. Beyond the tall mountains is the bend of the Ebro River. It begins to get light. Tarragona appears. We pass the first fishing boats with their billowing white sails. They are not far away—but we don't shoot. The water changes color every minute—the waves are becoming higher. I listen attentively to the engine. Will it keep going? Our target is almost 60 miles behind the Red front. The slightest engine trouble means capture and the destruction of the aircraft. Left turn—I look around—everyone is still there. Now we are heading toward the coast. We fly over white houses—who might be living there? Some people look up at us curiously, then they take cover when they see our Nationalist insignia. Vendrell, a lovely coastal town; then we fly over a small valley. We must soon reach the airfield. It is not fully light yet; good navigation by the *Staffel* commander. He pulls up in front of me. I can't make out the airfield yet, since I am still too far away, and I wait for the aircraft in front of me to peel off before pulling up. Damn—now I've lost sight of him. While diving toward the airfield I see tracer from his guns, but then he must pull up. I can still see the tracer, but it can't be his. My first thought is that it must be from antiaircraft machine guns on the airfield. I still don't see any aircraft, so

I fire into the middle of the tracer—my machine guns function perfectly. I pull up into a left turn and almost collide with a biplane. Retracted undercarriage—I've never seen one before—it must be a Red Delphin. Its pilot is just as shocked as I am, and he peels off into a dive. Where is the *Staffel* leader? Far in front I see a low-wing monoplane. I look for the other aircraft. Above me another monoplane is circling beneath a layer of cloud. A Messerschmitt; no, fat fuselage, a Rata, hateful bird. Another appears. Where are they coming from? They seem to have an excellent warning system. I remember the order not to attack, so I decide to get out of there. I dive away and see behind me the last Red fighters taking off. A few feet above the ground, I set a rough course for the sea. I join up with one, then two of our fighters and after a few miles find the *Staffel* commander. Soon we are over our airfield and land. Everyone breathes a sigh of relief when the last one is on the ground. It could easily have gone wrong.

There is great puzzlement during the debriefing. How is it possible that the Red fighters got airborne so early? The mystery is soon cleared up. Another fighter *Staffel* lost its way and passed over the airfield a short time before our attack, spooking the Red fighters.

FINAL MONTHS OF THE WAR

The 3.J/88 was now led by *Oblt.* von Bonin, and it had received the new Bf 109 E, the first version of the Messerschmitt fighter to fly in Spain with radio equipment. *Lt.* Fözö wrote:[93]

Bf 109 E 6 • 99 photographed on the airfield at Barcience-Toledo. It is finished in the RLM 63/65 scheme with black-painted exhaust and wing root. Note 3.J/88's "Mickey Mouse" emblem forward of the fuselage code, and the pilot's parachute on the tailplane. *Private Collection*

Hauptmann von Bonin is our new commanding officer. He has flown with us to familiarize himself with his new position and now leads the *Staffel* quietly, surely, and correctly.

On the day after the holidays, we take off once again for Zaidin. While it is not far from our old base of operations, the landscape is very different: more rugged and difficult, more subdued in shape, and less furrowed. The colors are also less vivid than in Aragon. Or does it only seem so because we arrived in the new area of the Lerida front in winter, whereas it was summer when we first arrived in La Sénia?

A mission sends us up: we are told that we will be meeting up with Italian aircraft. When we climb through a solid layer of cloud at many thousands of feet, we in fact find a flight of fighters in the air. Our orders are to assemble with our Italian comrades so as to fly to the front together.

Our new *Staffelkapitän* approaches the flight of fighters in a wide turn. But suddenly we see that there are four times as many as we were told to expect. Instead of nine aircraft there are thirty-five or forty fighters, heading toward us. Are they Fiats? No, no, no! The gaggle of aircraft splits up, peeling off to the left and right, creeping up on us.

We hear the voice of the *Staffelkapitän*: "Curtisses!"

We have been ambushed. Then we see the Fiats approaching from the other side. Will they help us?

We are caught in the midst of confusion and are seriously threatened. A devilish dogfight breaks out. It is almost impossible to tell friend from foe. It is nothing more than a swarm of angry hornets. A fierce battle rages in the sea of clouds.

The fight moves higher. Our oxygen has been working for some time, so thin has the air around us become. I turn toward the group of enemy biplanes on my right. Time after time I position myself behind the enemy machines, but the enemy pilots are as alert as foxes, running away and coming back again. It is a cat-and-mouse game, previously known only in legend.

Again and again, I seek a fresh victim. Each time the fellow escapes me just as I am about to pepper his tail. Furious because my attacks show no results, I want to dive into the midst of the swarm. As I am about to do so, I hear Mölders's voice say to me clearly and calmly: "Don't go into the middle, Joschko! Stay to the outside!"

At the last second I veer away and again try to get on the tail of a lone enemy fighter. One rises just in front of me. I have him! I have him! Nothing's missing!

Then—an ear-shattering crash in my crate, a frightful blow against my chest. Almost out loud, I say, "Shot down! It's all over, just a matter of seconds. Can I at least take one of these fellows with me?" I would feel better if I could. No Joschko, it wasn't Mölders who spoke to you before. It was his good sense, which you rightly remembered. Mölders is at home! . . . Bonin, Bonin, are you all OK? Thunder, what is with me? I have to get down. Perhaps it is the last strength I have. Can I still land? Do I have time?

All of this went through my feverishly working brain in a fraction of a second. Here and there I still see the Curtisses and Fiats dogfighting, and see our brave boys locked in combat with the Ratas. I peel away from the swarm and push the nose down. Through my flight suit I touch the spot on my chest where I can still feel the pain from the terrible blow. I hold up my hand to see if there is blood on it.

There is none. I am not wounded. I continue diving. Who can say if there is one behind me? I am below 10,000 feet, and that is my salvation. Had I remained above, after a few seconds more, fatal unconsciousness would have taken me in its arms, since the blow I felt came from the cover of the oxygen equipment, which hangs before me. One of the enemy must have shot the device to pieces.

I am extremely glad. My heart, which had been pounding, has returned to a normal beat. But I can't return to the battle still raging above me. I have to turn, reverse course, fly home.

I slowly head for home, endeavoring to retain my machine's goodwill at least until I can land. It works. My *Staffel* has long since broken off the air battle, without claiming any of the enemy, but without loss. High in the sky they formed up for the flight home, and no one saw Joschko carefully nursing his machine homeward at low altitude.

Surely they have given me up for lost and in their minds are working on my eulogy. No, I won't give you that pleasure. Here! The one making the miserable landing, that is Joschko Fözö, *Leutnant* and flight leader in the *Legion Condor*, only slightly damaged and—all in all—still good to use.

Poor weather hampered operations, but on New Year's Day 1939, 3.J/88 fought an inconclusive battle with a group of Republican fighters. "Joschko" Fözö later described the action:[94]

I survived New Year's Day. It was a tough one for me. Once again I just managed to escape death.

We flew three tough missions. The weather that day turned out to be magnificent. The sky was clear and the bright sun was hard on the eyes.

In the afternoon we took off in the cold; the harsh rays of the sun blinded our eyes. This demanded extreme vigilance. At any minute they come at us from out of the light, and we would be at a disadvantage if we saw them too late.

And that is exactly what happened! Enemy fighters, already formed up for the attack, came racing toward us.

Ratas!

It was a great dogfight. Up, down, left, right: so it went for almost fifteen minutes, yet none of us fired a single shot.

The enemy had obviously devised a plan to repeatedly climb back into the sun and then dive at us out of the sun like crows. Then, suddenly, an aircraft appeared beside me,

Bf 109 E-3 6 • 87 at La Sénia with 6 • 89 in the background, photographed soon after their arrival. Both are cannon-armed E-3s. Note that the front sides of the propeller blades are natural metal while the backs are painted black-green. Also note the black areas around the exhausts and wing root. The oval marking on the propeller blade is the early-style VDM logo. The aircraft have no unit emblems, and the absence of mast antennas suggests that radios have not yet been installed. *Private Collection*

a black monster filling my view. I could have seen the pilot looking across at me from his seat had not everything been moving so incredibly fast.

Just don't let rage cloud your judgment!

Too bad he appeared where I couldn't reach him with my guns. But I? I had dived right into his line of fire. He had me!

I saw the trails left by his tracing ammunition; for a brief moment they streaked toward me by the dozen.

Just don't catch fire, old heart of my engine. No, only a linkage was hit.

I quickly turn my head as I hear bullets striking just behind my shoulder. The rogue is clinging to my tail. Out of everyone he picked me. I appear to be his type.

Don't settle up yet, my lad! It's still far from over. Watch and see how a German fighter pilot can scamper away—if he has to.

I put my machine's nose down and go down in a steep, descending turn. Near the ground I pull up, while thinking: "You're going to pull the wings off the fuselage!"

No, it stays together. The Rata swept past me and pulled up too late. I am already back at altitude. Time to rejoin my comrades.

Sweat beads on my upper lip; big drops cover my face, as if I were under a brutal equatorial sun.

Children, this time it was a close call, damned Russian! For half a second I even thought of home, of my parents, and of Rosi. They say that means the end is near.

I rejoin the others. The dogfight is over and the enemy machines all have disappeared. We can sneak home. But at least they didn't get us. The year has begun well.

Two Bf 109s on an unidentified Spanish airfield. The aircraft in the background is Bf 109 E 6 • 88. The presence of the antenna mast just aft of the cockpit suggests that radios had been installed by this time. The aircraft in the foreground is a mystery. It is finished in the late-war RLM 63/65 camouflage scheme and has ten victory bars marked on its fin. The last digit of the aircraft code is "9." *Private Collection*

Aircraft 6 • 89, a Bf 109 E-3 in the colors of the Legion Condor, possibly at León after reassembly. Note the black-painted area around the exhausts, extending back to the wing root. As of yet, no unit markings have been applied. *Private Collection*

6 • 89 again, this time at La Senia. The aircraft still has no unit emblem or antenna mast. *Private Collection*

Lacking air support, the Nationalist offensive made little progress. Then on January 5, the Republicans launched a relief offensive in Estramadura in the direction of Seville. The situation appeared threatening, but by January 7 the attack began to falter. Little air support was available, since most Nationalist resources had been moved north for the attack in Catalonia. On January 15, Nationalist forces encircled the Republican Catalonian army. What followed was a pursuit of the shattered Republican divisions toward the north.

J/88 followed the advance, moving to Valls airfield on January 21. *Lt.* Böttcher's Bf 109 was shot down by ground fire on the 29th, and he was killed. There was fighting in the air over Barcelona, and between January 17 and 22, *Jagdgruppe* 88 claimed seven enemy aircraft shot down, including four on the seventeenth by *Oblt.* von Bonin, *Lt.* Fözö, *Obfw.* Müller, and *Fhr.* Tornow. *Lt.* Fözö described the action:[95]

"Events are coming to a head again!" So went our blithe self-mockery when, day after day, nothing happened. This time, however, events really were coming to a head, since at noon the next day we were patrolling the area close around Barcelona. We closed with the aircraft of our bomber group, which as always rendezvoused with us right on time. I was leader of the flight of four fighters assigned to provide escort.

Below, on the gently sloping terrain, the Nationalists have been halted by enemy troops holding the chain of hills there. Less than 300 feet of no man's land separates the lines. Here, bombing accuracy is paramount if we are to avoid hitting our own troops. That is a feat from the altitude at which we're flying. The bombers drop their loads; the bombs tumble earthward. There! A rising cloud of smoke; a second forms beside it. Four then six pillars of smoke rise up from just behind the enemy's fortified hill line. That was right on the money! The bombs destroy dugouts and trenches, camps and depots. That was what Mölders called "German precision work." Well done.

The Bolsheviks have been alerted. Their nearest forward airfield can't be far from here. I thought I spotted it yesterday while flying escort for the reconnaissance aircraft around Barcelona.

In any event, now I'm waiting. In my mind I count the minutes that an enemy fighter squadron might require from first alert until its arrival. I take into account our speed, and I will be disappointed if nothing shows up. But then I see several fighters spiraling upward toward us.

I give the signal to attack: "Attention Buzzard, eight enemy fighters, below and to my right."

We turn a little to the side as they approach. This forces them to split up. Then begins a hunt, which, in terms of conciseness, I have not experienced since . . .

Can I hope to bring one of these fellows down?

I select the second from the right. The biplane worms its way toward me in two shallow turns. But one of my comrades is quicker and, before I can get into position, puts several bursts into him. His fire is on target.

Is he burning? Yes! He's finished. We worry no more about him.

"Congratulations!" I call through my throat microphone. I have enough time for that but no more: to my left I see a second enemy fighter, a Rata, on fire and going down between us in a steep turn. Two victories in less than a minute?

I am in a frenzy of victory certainty: I must get it, the first of the new year. Then one passes beneath me.

"Don't take him from the side; that reduces your chances. The enemy will pass by much too quickly."

I throttle back and drop beneath him. Now, press the button. Fire! Then I fire a second burst, just to be sure. It's not necessary; the first must have been on target. Three seconds later I see the despicable kite on fire and falling away into a spin. Finally it begins to tumble: it somersaults over and over.

It's not going to recover. By the time it strikes the ground it will be no more than burning wreckage. I watch the doomed machine's descent, enthused and aghast, since one cannot tear oneself away from a terrific natural spectacle.

Nearby, another enemy machine is on fire. The two aircraft collide, the fuselage of one striking the wing of the other. Pieces whirl about. A fourth must have fallen from the sky, for the first two victories must—if time hasn't lied—gone down at least half a minute earlier.

Four fighters, four victories! I thirst for more.

"I feel like dancing," says the mouse, "where's the cat?"

I would like the opportunity to use my guns again, but the remaining four Ratas have had enough and make off like freshly greased lightning. They zigzag away—like hares across a field—from my guns and are soon out of range.

I assemble my people. Four voices have reported victories. The distribution was thus equitable. We congratulate each other on the air. An action lasting less than three minutes has cost the enemy four valuable fighter aircraft, and an entire flight of fighters returns victoriously.

The new *Gruppenkommandeur* congratulates us warmly. *Hauptmann* Grabmann, our new chief, who only a few days ago replaced Handrick, can barely grasp it.

The Messerschmitts of J/88 escorted bombers attacking targets in Barcelona, whose seaport was of vital importance to the Republicans. *Lt.* Fözö described one such escort mission in support of Do 17s of A/88, during which he recorded his third and last victory in Spain:[96]

We are slowly turning from hunters to governesses, because the escort missions in support of our Do 17s are

Aircraft 6 • 90, a Bf 109 E-1 armed with four MG 17 machine guns, after a forced landing. No unit markings have as yet been applied to the aircraft. Note the shape of the black area from in front of the exhausts, extending to the lower fuselage aft of the wing root. This was obviously designed to conceal exhaust staining from the aircraft's DB 601 engine. *Private Collection*

Bf 109 E 6 • 91 in flight, photographed from the cockpit of another Messerschmitt. *Private Collection*

multiplying like rabbits. Our comrades of the bomber group are grateful for our support, however. One evening they came over from their base and brought us all sorts of gifts.

A few days later we have the opportunity to give our firm friendship a solid test: mission to Barcelona.

The head of the Bolshevik dragon must fall. For weeks our army has been pressing toward the city. A hundred times already the enemy has had to withdraw his defense line as a fresh attack by Franco's troops forced him to abandon his positions. Now we are at the gates of the city.

We make our way between the coast and the sea. Fog shrouds the rugged coastal landscape, blurring the boundary between sea and land.

There is the spot over which a dense cloud hangs, a mixture of big-city pollution and a thousand fires from the throats of cannon; that is Barcelona, home to millions. We approach the city as if on a sightseeing excursion.

We leave the city to our left and pass over the suburbs on the way to the target. There are explosions everywhere. That is Franco's artillery in a singing match with the enemy's gun positions, which are putting up the last resistance among the suburbs. It is a display of irresistible, alluring force.

Then a forest of flak clouds springs up before us and is blown away only slowly by a placid wind. The people down there are blazing away madly, trying to create a true wall of fire between us and the port.

In vain! . . . I clench my teeth and grip the stick firmly, pressed low in my seat as if this were a defense against the shower of steel filling the sky. Flashes and clouds, that's how it goes again and again; there is no stopping.

Then we are through the outer belt. Those were the heavy-caliber guns, but they still pursue us with light-caliber weapons, trying to make our job as unpleasant as

Two armorers at work on the MG 17 machine guns of Bf 109 E-3 6 • 107. Note 2.J/88's "Top Hat" emblem and the yellow fuel triangle beneath the open fuel filler point access hatch. The brown oil triangle on the forward fuselage is partially hidden by the belt of ammunition. Note the antenna mast and wire. *Private Collection*

possible. But we have the port. Our Dorniers glide over the black bustle of the broad basin and unload the cargoes hidden in their bellies.

Following behind the bombers, we drop low and fire our guns in short bursts. Perhaps the fires we start are small, but is not the biggest fire an army of thousands of tongues of flame?

So it kindles below. A big barge sinks under the force of the greedy flames. Water rushes into the holed sides of ships and slowly pulls the heavy vessels to the bottom. How many transports and warships will never serve the Bolsheviks again—five, ten, forty . . .? We don't know; it is impossible to count them. We simply stare into a sea of flames, into a jumble of death and destruction; incredible to see, incredible to think about the consequences.

Again and again we turn back for another pass over Barcelona's harbor. There is no end to the explosions. These are bitter days, and the victories we are winning come at a cost. But the enemy is suffering heavy losses: every hit, every fire in the harbor brings us closer to our goal. As difficult as it may sometimes be, the enemy will no longer escape, neither on land nor on the sea.

I return with my third victory. It was an easy piece of work, and the fellow casually circling over the city must have been struck by blindness if he didn't see me moving closer and closer. I had been on his tail for some time by the time he finally saw me. He increased power in an effort to escape, but my machine was faster and I stayed on his tail.

Now he is square in my sights, and the rest is like target practice. And yet my heart is beating so hard against my ribs that I feel as if my chest must burst.

The bullets leave my guns. My eyes follow the tracer's smoke trails to the enemy aircraft, which turns desperately in an effort to escape. But it is too late; my first burst has set him on fire.

"Save your ammunition, Joschko," I tell myself, "he's finished!"

Heavy smoke spews from his nose. Once again he tries to escape, putting his machine into a dive. At least that's what it looks like, for the machine is obviously still under control. But then it staggers and goes down, down, down.

My gaze follows the fiery dot as it falls to earth, fresh air feeding the flames. But then it is extinguished as it crashes in the midst of the city.

My black boys leap for joy when I return with my third victory.

Barcelona, the last bastion of Republican Spain, fell on January 26. The units of the Legion Condor now took up the pursuit of the beaten enemy units fleeing toward the Pyrenees. Sabadell airport was prepared for use by J/88 and A/88. J/88 moved to Sabadell on February 1. The Bf 109s continued to fly escort

Lineup of Bf 109 Es on an unidentified Spanish airfield. In the foreground is 6 • 104, a cannon-armed Bf 109 E-3. These appear to be aircraft of 1.J/88, since the circular outline of that unit's *Holzauge* emblem can be seen just above the wingtip of aircraft 6 • 104. *Private Collection*

Ground personnel at work raising 6 • 107, a Bf 109 E-3, after undercarriage failure. One group is pulling down on the port wingtip, while another lifts the starboard wing. Note the words "*Mors Mors!*," part of a traditional Hamburg greeting, on the engine cowling above the exhaust on the port side, and the later triangular VDM logos on the RLM 70 black-green propeller blades. *Private Collection*

for bombers attacking targets in Gerona and Figueras and occasionally strafed ground targets as well.

On February 4, while escorting Do 17 reconnaissance aircraft of A/88, fighters of the *Jagdgruppe* engaged Chatos and Ratas in the Figueras-Rosas area. *Lt.* Schumann of 2nd *Staffel* claimed to have shot down a Curtiss.

The Nationalist air force and the Legion Condor turned their attention to the remaining Republican airfields. Figueras was attacked and several Chatos were shot down, while four

Aircraft 6 • 111, a Bf 109 E-3 of 2.J/88 flown by *Lt*. Werner Ursinus, after suffering undercarriage failure on an unidentified Spanish airfield. Beneath the windscreen is the name "*Bärchen*" (Little Bear), possibly a reference to the pilot's name, which in Latin refers to a bear. *Private Collection*

Bf 109 E-3 6 • 116, an aircraft of 1.J/88, after suffering undercarriage failure, something that was to plague the Bf 109 throughout its career. Note that most of the RLM 70 black-green paint has worn off the propeller blades. *Private Collection*

Bf 109 E fighters at Barcience-Toledo. The aircraft in the foreground is 6 • 128. Part of 3.J/88's "Mickey Mouse" emblem (the ears) can be seen just to the left of the MG FF cannon muzzle in the port wing. The two nearest aircraft are both cannon-armed E-3s. By this time radio equipment had been installed, as evidenced by the mast antennas. *Private Collection*

Bf 109 E-3 6 • 128 at Barcience-Toledo. The aircraft's unit emblem cannot be seen. Behind it is 6 • 108 of 3.J/88. The radio mast and antenna wire are clearly visible on aircraft 6 • 128. *Private Collection*

Ratas were destroyed on the ground. On February 5, reconnaissance aircraft determined that the airfield at Vilajuiga was occupied by Red aircraft, and an attack was ordered for the next day. *Lt.* Fözö described the attack:[97]

The Bolshevik army has been forced against the wall. With each day, Franco herds its remnants closer together and flattens them. Will they surrender, here in the midst of the mountains, squeezed into the tiniest area, with Franco's iron shield before them and the French border behind them? Or will they cross over into the neighboring zone? That has to be prevented at all costs.

We are now flying escort day after day. Our bombers are in the air constantly, striking the Bolsheviks' rear; they strike the crossings and destroy bridges and passes leading to France. The mushroom clouds produced by the bombs number in the hundreds, rising up the sides of the gorges and sending a hail of shrapnel into the pitiful assembled remnants of the enemy columns.

Antiaircraft fire? What is that? We haven't encountered any for quite some time. Occasionally a machine gun is raised against us in desperation, but in vain. We are victorious wherever we go.

The enemy has assembled the remnants of his northern air fleet. We know the base from which he is conducting his final feeble operations. Today we are paying it a visit, and it will not be a courtesy visit. We must approach stealthily, to avoid alerting the enemy to our attack. We therefore fly far out over the sea and climb to 20,000 [feet]. But then: descend, descend! There is the airfield!

We make out twenty aircraft, lined up neatly one beside the other, aircraft after aircraft, half an airfield full—and there is no antiaircraft fire.

Our hands are constantly on the firing button. We make diving pass after diving pass and climb back up before pushing the stick forward again. And each time we climb away, we see the results of our work: our guns inflict devastation on the parked Ratas and Curtisses.

There a fuselage splinters, and there a torn wing falls to the ground; rounds strike the engines and cause the cold noses of the Bolshevik machines to spurt fire. Here a tail section is in pieces, and there a bird lies on its side, its undercarriage shot up, one wing pointing accusingly into the sky.

We counted twenty aircraft as we approached. Minutes later, twenty wrecks lie on the ground, never to rise again. We have done a thorough job . . .

Now, with our work almost done, the enemy's antiaircraft guns finally make their presence felt. Tracer fills the sky around us, shells doing a violent dance.

We climb away. But then one of our own machines becomes the twenty-first wrecked machine down below on the airfield. An *Unteroffizier* from the 2nd *Staffel*, a bright young fellow, goes down. His engine doesn't burn; he must have been hit himself. Uncontrolled, the aircraft falls from the sky.

Three days later Franco's troops capture the airfield. We drive over to pay a visit to the place where Windemuth was killed. The airfield is still as we left it. Only now do the cleanup columns arrive to begin their work.

We find the fighter aircraft lying shattered on the ground. We also find our comrade: his body lies 65 feet from his machine. His chest is flat and narrow.

"Shot through the heart," says our medical officer.

He had it easy. He was dead long before he struck the ground. We take the sad remains of our comrade home.

The German side admitted the loss of *Uffz.* Heinrich Windemuth; however, the Spanish pilot who shot him down, José Falco, claimed that he had in fact brought down two Messerschmitt fighters. The following is his account of the action on that day:[98]

Most of the personnel had been evacuated after the attack by the Italians on the afternoon of the 5th, in which they did not destroy as many aircraft as they had claimed. Only those needed to start the engines the following day remained. I stayed awake all night because I was on guard in case of a night attack. Dawn had just broken, with its usual mist, and I was in the cockpit of my CA-205 surrounded by the other pilots. The engine was running as I was waiting for the Moscas from Figueras, which were supposed to accompany us to France, to pass by. All of a sudden I saw six aircraft approaching from over the sea. Someone shouted, "It's the Moscas!"; others, "It's the Messers!" After several minutes of doubt it turned out that it was the Germans. I didn't wait for the order to take off. I applied full power and climbed to intercept them. I attacked the formation of six Bf 109s, passing right through the middle while firing my four guns. I saw that I had scored a bull's-eye on one of them, hitting it in the side. I continued climbing while looking around, and I saw a Bf 109 attacking a Grumman that was turning toward the sea. In doing so, it passed in front of a fog bank, making it stand out like a fly in a glass of milk. I went after the ME and positioned myself on its tail, ready to fire my four guns, while at the same time reducing power to avoid a collision. Blinded by his desire to shoot down the Grumman, the German pilot failed to see that I was behind him. Before I could intervene,

The burnt-out remains of an I-16 discovered on a former Republican airfield. The aircraft is still attached to its Hucks-type starter truck. *Private Collection*

113

A variety of aircraft, still in Republican colors, on a captured airfield. In the foreground are two SB bombers, while two I-15 Chatos can be seen on the right. In the center is a Polikarpov R-Z Natacha. This type served in large numbers with the Republican side (93 or 124 depending on the source), and it is therefore rather surprising that none were claimed by pilots of J/88. *Author's Collection*

however, the bursts from his cannon hit the Grumman's top wing and it went down in flames. It was AD-010, flown by Diego Sanchez. Immediately after the Grumman crashed, the Messer turned to its left and I took advantage of this to fire again. We closed head on and I had to pull back on the stick to avoid a collision. I then turned inside him to the right, and I was able to hit him again while he was in a turn to his left. I saw him losing altitude and heading toward the airfield. Then, because of the very abrupt maneuver I had just made, my engine began to fail. Finding myself at very low altitude, I was forced to make an emergency landing in a sown field near the road from Rosas to Vilajuiga. I abandoned my faithful Chato and climbed onto one of two horses being led by a soldier, who directed me to the village of Vilajuiga, from where a motorcycle took me back to the aerodrome. I arrived there several hours after my forced landing, and I found it deserted with, to my surprise, the wreck of Bf 109 6-96, against which I had fought a short time before. I walked over to it and saw that it had broken in two at the engine

block, with no trace of fire, but many bullet holes from my guns. The parachute was still in the seat, and I removed the inspection card, the collimator [gunsight], the first-aid kit, and a notebook bearing the name Nirminger. I later handed these over to a member of the headquarters staff and made a claim for my two victories. This was reduced to one pending the discovery of the remains of the second aircraft. Years later, when I returned to Spain in 1963, I made my way to Vilajuiga to search the area and look for some indication of where the first aircraft I had shot down had fallen. I questioned several people without result, but then I met a gentleman of the right age and asked him if he had been there at the end of the war. He said that he had, and he recalled that an aircraft had crashed not far from where we were. And by chance he told me precisely where, a little farther away, I could find a small monolith beside the road from Figueras to Llanca. Indeed I found a stone dedicated to Windemuth, my first victory on that day.

Concerning the question of Falco's two victory claims, after interviewing surviving Republican pilots who were at Vilajuiga that day, author Juan Arraez Cerda wrote the following:[99]

The loss of Windemuth is confirmed and there has never been any doubt about it. As for Nirminger, it is clear that he crashed badly wounded onto the aerodrome at Vilajuiga. When Antonio Arias, commander of the 2nd Escuadrilla de Moscas, reached his aircraft and saw the condition the pilot was in, he put a bullet in his head to end his suffering. His body was subsequently taken by truck to the nearby cemetery in Vilajuiga. The Germans never admitted the loss of Nirminger at Vilajuiga, but they announced that he had died in an accident at León on May 13, 1939, and had placed a commemorative stone by the road that leads past the base of the l'Ermitage de la Virgen del Camino, where it perhaps remains to this day. The German archives verify that it was Nirminger who shot down Sanchez's Grumman, effectively confirming that he was shot down by Falco. A photograph of the wreckage of a Bf 109 E with the code 6-98 at Vilajuiga was later published with a claim that it was Windemuth's aircraft. All the pilots with whom I have spoken, without exception, have assured me that the photo really was taken at Vilajuiga, but that the aircraft in it is not the one they saw crash there, because it had suffered far worse damage. The one in the photo gives the impression of having been transported there afterward from somewhere else. The aircraft appears to have crashed onto the aerodrome virtually intact, with the exception of the engine compartment between the nose and the cockpit. Recently, while visiting the French Air Force Museum, I found a typed casualty list made by the Legion Condor of its 174 men killed in action and ninety-seven killed in accidents. To my great surprise I found an entry showing Hans Nirminger killed in action on May 11, 1939, which is incomprehensible and, in my opinion, confirms his death at Vilajuiga. The question remains: Why did the Germans take such steps to conceal the truth? Were they loath to admit that two of their most modern monoplanes had been shot down by an outmoded biplane in a matter of minutes? Perhaps one day we will know.

There was almost no further combat in the air, although on March 6, *Sargento* Augustín Maestro Romerales of the 2nd *Escuadrilla de Chatos*, who had just taken off from the field at La Rabasa, was shot down and killed by *Oberleutnant* Hubertus von Bonin, who was on a sortie over d'Alicante in his Bf 109 E. Romerales was the last pilot killed in aerial combat during the Spanish Civil War.

PART II
MESSERSCHMITT BF 109 VARIANTS IN SPAIN

BF 109 PROTOTYPES

Three prototypes—the V3, V4, and V6—were the first Bf 109s sent to Spain, arriving in December 1936. The oldest of the three, the V3, had been flying since April, and the V4 since September, while the V6 was essentially brand new and had flown but little before leaving Germany for Spain.

Bf 109 V3

The Bf 109 V3, *Werknummer* 760, registration D-IOQY, first flew on April 8, 1936.[1] It was the first armed Bf 109, carrying two mechanically operated MG 17 machine guns above the engine. Plans to mount the MG C/30 L cannon as an engine-mounted weapon were delayed because of ongoing difficulties with the weapon. It has been claimed that the V3 was the prototype for the A-series, but it differed from that variant in a number of respects. The aircraft was fitted with low-pressure tires, which required bulges on the upper surface of the wing. The windscreen and folding canopy also differed from that of the Bf 109 A, as may be seen in the accompanying photos. The rectangular spark plug access panels above the exhausts, a feature of the Bf 109 A, were also absent from the V3. At the end of October 1936, the V3 was crated and sent to VK/88 at Seville. The Bf 109 V3 was actually the last of the three Bf 109 prototypes to reach Spain, arriving by ship on December 15, 1936. Once there, it was unloaded and shipped to Seville-Tablada for assembly. Engine test runs began on December 21. The V3 was given the code 6 ● 2 and began operational testing

on December 28. On January 3, 1937, it took part in a scramble to intercept an incoming raid, which proved to be a false alarm. The V3 was delivered with a Jumo 210 C engine driving a Schwarz twin-blade metal propeller,[2] but on January 5, 1937, that engine had to be replaced with a Jumo 210 B, and a twin-blade wooden propeller was fitted. The Bf 109 V3's career in Spain was a brief one, since it was destroyed in a crash at Caceres on February 11, 1937. The following is the official accident report:[3]

Report on the Crash of the Bf 109 V3 with *Leutnant* Rehahn in Cacares on February 11, 1937

General

(1) a. Aircraft Information:
Bf 109 V3 No. 6-2 with Jumo 210 B engine, local flying time approximately 40 hours.

b. Pilot:
Leutnant Paul Rehahn
Born Dec. 18, 1910
Pilot with VK/88 since January 1937

(2) Description of Accident: (reconstructed from witness statements and examination of the crash site)
On February 11, 1937, the He 112 No. 5-1 flown by *Oberleutnant* Radusch and the Bf 109 No. 6-2 flown by *Leutnant* Rehahn took off from Seville at 0930 to fly to Villa del Prado, with a planned stop in Caceres. Prior to takeoff, both aircraft were checked over by the responsible fitters, run up, and reported in order to the technical director, who gave approval for takeoff. The aircraft landed at Caceres at approximately 1040 and refueled there, during which time the pilots remained with their machines. The He 112 took off first, at 1126, followed by the Bf 109 one minute later. Both aircraft made a wide 270-degree turn before taking up a roughly northeast heading. When the He 112 had just about reached the line of hills that lay in the direction of flight (see map 1), the Bf 109 had just turned on course and was in normal cruising attitude at a height of about 1,100 feet. The undercarriage had been retracted during the climb. At that moment the aircraft pitched forward into a nose-down attitude and, in an almost vertical dive, crashed propeller-first into the ground. The ignition switch was apparently turned off, since no engine noise was heard during the dive and the switch was found in position M 1—next to the OFF position and probably moved there only on impact. On initial impact the left wing scraped the ground (see map 2); the aircraft was then turned 90 degrees and bounced approximately 65 feet to the next impact point, where the left wing broke off. The fuselage slid another 65 feet down a slope with a height difference of about 20 feet,

tearing off the right wing in the process. Just before the fuselage came to rest, the engine was torn from its mounts.

The pilot was killed instantly.

WITNESS STATEMENTS (in appendix)

(4) Report of Findings:
The aircraft was completely destroyed. Only the fuselage partly retained its original shape; the wings were partially broken through. The engine also broke apart in many places. The force of the impact must have been great because parts such as the camshaft were bent as much as 30 degrees.

Examination of the control cables revealed no breaks, jams, or blockages. There also could not have been engine trouble, since the aircraft's engine was turned off suddenly before it struck the ground.

The wreckage was transported by truck back to Seville and completely scrapped, so that no further details can be found. The engine was sent back to Germany.

(5) Cause of the Accident:
No cause for the accident was found. No mechanical breakdown was discovered.

Knüppel, *Oberleutnant* and
Detachment Leader
Caceres, 11 February 1937

The flight director, interpreter Paul Hoster, appeared and, after swearing to tell the truth, gave the following statement concerning the matter at hand:

Personal Information:
My name is Paul Hoster, born in Odenkirchen in the München Gladbach/Rhineland District on June 21, 1894, joined the "Legion Condor" from Hisma[4] on January 15, 1937.

As to the matter at hand:
Arrival of the aircraft, 1 Messerschmitt No. . . . and a He 112 No. . . . at . . . hours. After they had refueled, during which I would like to point out the pilots did not leave their aircraft, the aircraft took off at 1125 (He) and 1126 (Messerschmitt). I watched both aircraft carry out normal takeoffs. The aircraft took off from the airfield from south to north and then circled the airfield in a shallow left turn, during which they gained altitude in a normal way.

After about 270 degrees of turn, both aircraft headed northeast. The first aircraft had a lead of about one minute and had almost reached the line of hills about 0.6 miles away. At that moment the second aircraft had reached a height of about 1,000 to 1,300 feet and had also set course to the northeast. Immediately after completing the turn, after the aircraft was again in level flight, it went into a steep dive. Until it turned onto the northeast heading, the aircraft's engine had been running normally, but during the dive it stopped completely. I would like to stress that I paid particular attention to the engine and heard no further engine sounds during the dive. The aircraft went down vertically like an arrow and struck the ground, and I was able to see that it apparently bounced once. I immediately proceeded on foot to the site, which was approximately a quarter of a mile away (to the southwest) to render assistance. When I arrived, I saw that the aircraft was completely destroyed and then went to recover the body [of the pilot].

Bf 109 V4

The Bf 109 V4, *Werknummer* 878, registration D-IALY, made its first flight on September 23, 1936.[5] The V4 was similar in almost every respect to the production Bf 109 A. One difference was the location of a pitot-venturi tube on the starboard side

The Bf 109 V4, wearing the aircraft number 6 • 3, while attached to 2.J/88, possibly at Almorox. It had previously been flown by Hannes Trautloft until his return to Germany in February 1937. On March 14, 1937, it became one of the first three Bf 109s to join 2.J/88 at Almorox, along with 6 • 3 and 6 • 4, both Bf 109 As. Note the light-colored panel beneath the cockpit where Trautloft's Green Heart had been. *Private Collection*

The aft fuselage and wings of the Bf 109 V4 after it was written off in a crash while serving with 1.J/88, probably in the summer or autumn of 1937. Since this was during the period when aircraft of 1.J/88 were finished in the RLM 70/71/65 camouflage scheme, it may have been painted a single shade of green on its upper surfaces and pale blue on its undersurfaces. The aircraft code 6 • 1 and the 1st *Staffel* emblem can be seen in this photo. Also note the position of the aircraft's oil cooler near the root of the port wing. *Private Collection*

The underside of 6 • 1's aft fuselage after its crash. The tailwheel, which had originally been retractable, has obviously been locked in the DOWN position, and a metal panel has been riveted over the wheel well. Trautloft reported several instances of the tailwheel failing to extend before landing, resulting in damage to the aircraft. Also note the bumper just aft of the tailwheel well cover. *Private Collection*

of the fuselage in front of the cockpit (this was later replaced by a pitot tube beneath the port wing).

The V4 apparently flew little before shipment to Spain. It arrived there on December 4, 1936, and made its first test flight on the 14th. The aircraft was assigned to Hannes Trautloft, who flew it from December 11, 1936, until February 19, 1937. The V4 bore the code 6 ● 1 and while in the hands of Trautloft wore a "Green Heart" emblem on both sides of the fuselage. On March 14, 1937, 6 ● 1 was part of the first flight of three Bf 109s to leave for the northern front, taking off from Seville-Tablada for Almorox with aircraft 6 ● 3 and 6 ● 4. Photographs reveal that the V4 went on to serve with 2.J/88 and later 1.J/88 and was written off in a crash landing.

Bf 109 V6

The Messerschmitt 109 V6, *Werknummer* 880, first flew on November 11, 1936.[6] Little is known about the aircraft, but it appears to have been largely similar to the V4. On December 5, 1936, it arrived in Spain, where it was supposed to be used by VJ/88 for operational trials alongside the other two prototypes. Of the three Bf 109 prototypes to arrive at Seville, it was the first one ready to fly. After assembly and checks, it was cleared for flight. On December 9, 1936, pilot Richard Koch attempted to take off, but the aircraft stalled and crashed.[7] It was declared beyond repair and was subsequently used as a source of spare parts. Since it was written off just four days after its arrival in Spain, the aircraft does not appear to have been assigned a code number.

BF 109 A

The first production variant of the Bf 109, the A series has been largely overlooked by aviation historians. In fact, Messerschmitt documents[8] reveal that a total of twenty-two aircraft was built at Augsburg. Fourteen of these aircraft were sent to the Legion Condor in Spain, where they were assigned the codes 6 ● 3 to 6 ● 16.

While aircraft handbooks, technical descriptions, and spare-parts lists exist for the other variants of the Bf 109 used in Spain, none have as yet surfaced for the Bf 109 A. Until now, one has had to rely on photographic evidence to reconstruct the history of these machines, but happily, daily and weekly reports by VK/88 covering the period in which the Bf 109 As arrived in Spain have been discovered, revealing the initial histories of these aircraft.[9] As delivered, the Bf 109 A differed from the subsequent B variant in a number of respects. Over the course of the next two years, however, the survivors underwent a modification process that rendered them almost indistinguishable from the Bf 109 B.

As delivered to the Legion Condor, the Bf 109 A differed from the subsequent B variant in a number of respects:

Close-up of the nose section of Bf 109 A 6 ● 15 in Soviet hands. Features visible in this photo include the capped spinner and wooden propeller, as well as the open hatch over the filler point for the fuselage-mounted oil tank. This aircraft left for the front before the new oil tanks arrived at Seville, and was retrofitted in the field. *moskittech.ru*

Propeller and Spinner: All Bf 109 As were equipped with a fixed-pitch wooden propeller with a capped spinner. The cap was initially removed from the spinner of aircraft 6 ● 3, which was fitted with a 20 mm engine-mounted MG C 30 cannon. As well, at least one aircraft was fitted with a ducted spinner.

Armament: Two MG 17 machine guns were mounted above the engine, with mechanical cocking. There is no evidence to suggest the presence of a third, engine-mounted machine gun; however, one aircraft, 6 ● 3, was fitted with an engine-mounted MG C 30 cannon for a time.

In this photo can be seen the Bf 109 A's fixed armament of two 7.9 mm MG 17 machine guns synchronized to fire through the propeller arc. Also visible are the access hatch over the fuselage-mounted oil tank's filler point, the canvas cover with zipper over the cockpit instruments, the panel covering the opening in the windscreen originally present for the external elements of the Revi 3a/b gunsight, and the long leading-edge slat on the starboard wing. *moskittech.ru*

Front view of the Bf 109 A's fuselage with engine and armament removed. The object between the rudder pedals, visible through the cutout in the fuselage bulkhead, is the retrofitted oil tank, which was introduced in response to flow problems caused by the original flat oil tank mounted in the port wing. Also visible are the machine gun mounts and the undercarriage attachment points. *moskittech.ru*

Close-up of the oil cooler of Bf 109 A 6 • 15. *moskittech.ru*

Oil Tank and Filler Hatch: As delivered to Spain, the Bf 109 A had its oil tank installed in the port wing, with the filler hatch located on the upper surface of the port wing near the wing root. Problems with this flat, wing-mounted oil tank contributed to engine-overheating problems and piston seizures, and it was replaced by a deeper oil tank mounted in the forward fuselage. Aircraft so modified can be identified by the presence of a circular filler hatch on the left side of the fuselage, forward of the cockpit. One such aircraft was Polenz's 6 • 15, which had the new oil tank mounted in the fuselage just forward of the cockpit, with the filler hatch located on the port side of the fuselage, forward of the cockpit above the leading edge of the wing.

Oil Cooler: This was located beneath the wing near the wing-fuselage join at about the two-thirds chord position, farther inboard than the oil cooler of the Bf 109 B.

This photo graphically illustrates the relative locations of the underwing oil coolers of the Bf 109 A and the Bf 109 B. The first wing in this wooden wing rack is from a Bf 109 B, with the oil cooler mounted behind the undercarriage leg well. The second wing is that of a Bf 109 A, with the oil cooler positioned farther aft near the wing-fuselage join. The Bf 109 V3 and V4 prototypes sent to Spain had their oil coolers in the same position. *Private Collection*

A Bf 109 A on an unidentified Spanish airfield. The modification process that would ultimately produce an aircraft largely similar to the Bf 109 B had already begun when this photo was taken. While it has a metal variable-pitch propeller and spinner like those of the Bf 109 B, it still has the smooth forward engine cowling with no cooling vents. The silhouette of the oil cooler can barely be seen aft of the port undercarriage leg. *Private Collection*

Engine Cowling: The cowling of the A variant tapered smoothly from just forward of the gun troughs to where it met the spinner. Also, no cooling vents of any kind were present.

Cockpit: Apart from the presence of two gun-cocking handles, the Bf 109 A's instrument panel was identical to that of the B. The control stick was fitted with a "spade handle" grip similar to that seen in British aircraft. The arrangement of the throttle and supercharger levers, fuel cock lever, and cooling-flap control was essentially the same as that of the Bf 109 B.

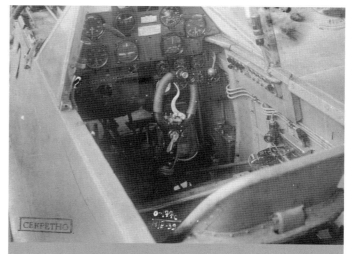

The cockpit of Bf 109 A 6 • 15 photographed while in Soviet hands. The most-obvious differences from the cockpit of the Bf 109 B are the presence of two cocking handles for the aircraft's MG 17 machine guns on the instrument panel and the "spade grip" on the aircraft's control stick, similar to that used by the British Spitfire and Hurricane fighters. *moskittech.ru*

Close-up of the grip on the aircraft's control stick. *moskittech.ru*

Gunsight: Unlike subsequent versions of the Bf 109, the A variant was initially equipped with a Revi 3a/b gunsight. This predecessor to the Revi C12 was installed in such a way that the reflector glass and tinted shield sat in a cutout in the windscreen. A backup ring-and-bead sight was also fitted, with the ring in front of the windscreen and the bead inside the cockpit behind the reflector glass. The ring-and-bead sight was normally folded to the side, but it could be raised by means of a lever on the gunsight.[10] During the upgrading process that followed the arrival in Spain of the Bf 109 B, the Revi 3a/b appears to have been replaced by the improved C12 gunsight.

Leading Edge Slats: The slats on the Bf 109 A were longer than those of subsequent versions, extending from just outboard of the wheel well to the wingtip. When the Bf 109 As were delivered to Spain, their slats were locked shut. The VK 88 records do not reveal what the nature of the problem was, but on March 17, 1937, a memorandum to VS 88's operations officer directed that the slats be "released in such a way as to not hinder their soonest possible use at the front."

The three Bf 109 prototypes that were sent to Spain in December 1936 were very new indeed, and none had flown many hours before leaving Germany. The Bf 109 As that followed them, arriving in February and March 1937, had left the production line only in January and February. It is not surprising, therefore, that VK/88 and VJ/88 had to address a number of issues before the aircraft could enter service. The following is a brief summary of these problems, compiled from VK/88's daily and weekly reports.

On arrival in Spain the aircraft's S.O. 3 system, radio equipment, and heated flying-suit plug were removed, resulting in a weight saving of about 125 pounds.

The first Jumo 210 engines sent to Spain had a compression ratio of 1:6, while the last twelve Bf 109 As delivered to Seville in early March 1937 had engines with a higher compression ratio of 1:7.3. It was found that the latter were not "in a fully developed state, and in several cases engines have seized." Two Junkers engine fitters were dispatched to Spain to convert these engines to the lower compression ratio. Since the Bf 109s were urgently needed at the front, in the interim pilots were ordered to remain within gliding distance of "White" (Nationalist) territory. On March 20, the Legion Condor was advised that *Dipl.Ing.* Jodlbauer of the *E-Stelle Travemünde* was en route to Spain and that the aircraft were not to be flown until his arrival. This order was rescinded, however, on the basis of experience to date and the urgent need for the aircraft to participate in the northern campaign. Ultimately, it was discovered that the problem was not the compression ratio, but rather the poor quality of Jumo engines produced at the company's Magdeburg facility and inadequate oil flow from the wing-mounted oil tank.

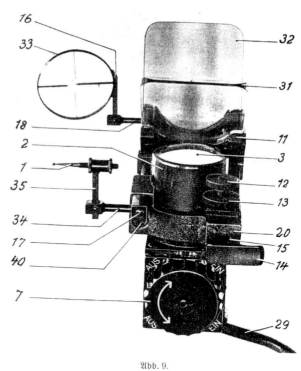

2lbb. 9.

Vorderansicht des Revi 3 a mit seitlich weggeklapptem mechanischem Visier.

1 = Korn	17 = Achse des mechanischen Visiers
2 = Fassung für Objektiv	18 = Visierstrebe
3 = Objektiv	20 = Visierträger
7 = Einstellknopf für Widerstand	29 = Kabel
11 = Reflexscheibenhalter	31 = Reflexscheibe
12 = Rändelmutter	32 = Filter
13 = Gegenmutter	33 = Kreiskimme
14 = Griffknopf	34 = Kornstrebe
15 = Schubstange	35 = Kornarm
16 = Visierarm	40 = Schraube

Pilot's view of the Revi 3a gunsight, here with the auxiliary ring and bead sight folded away. *Hafner Archiv*

The Revi 3a gunsight installed in the windscreen of an unidentified fighter, possibly a He 51. The elements of the gunsight outside the cockpit are clearly visible in this handbook illustration. *Hafner Archiv*

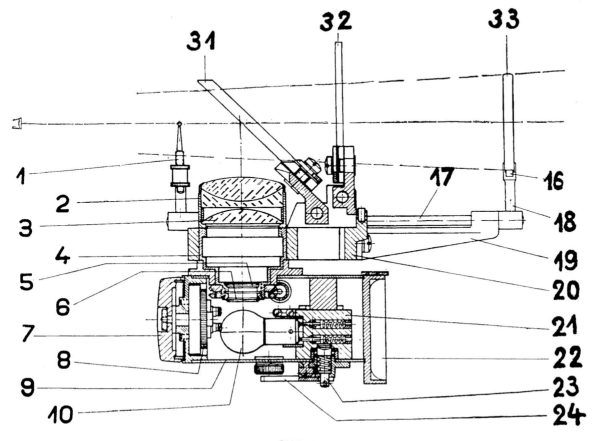

Abb. 1.

Längsschnitt des Revi 3 a.

1 =	Korn	17 =	Achse des mechanischen Visiers
2 =	Fassung für Objektiv		
3 =	Objektiv	18 =	Visierstrebe
4 =	Projektor	19 =	Trägerarm
5 =	Abkommen	20 =	Visierträger
6 =	Mattscheibe	21 =	Kontaktkörper
7 =	Einstellknopf für Widerstand	22 =	Schwalbe am Traggehäuse
8 =	Widerstand zur Regulierung der Lampe	23 =	Rastung für Kontaktkörper
		24 =	Hebel
9 =	Traggehäuse	31 =	Reflexscheibe
10 =	Lampe	32 =	Filter
16 =	Visierarm	33 =	Kreiskimme

Cutaway side view of the Revi 3a gunsight from the handbook. The numbered components include the ring and bead of the mechanical sight (33 and 1), the gunsight glass (31), the tinted shield, which was located forward of the windscreen (32), and the mechanical sight's axis (17) and bearer arm (19), also forward of the windscreen. *Hafner Archiv*

An unidentified pilot in the cockpit of a Bf 109 A fighter of 2.J/88. The Revi 3a gunsight's auxiliary sight is in the raised position. Also visible in front of the windscreen are the frame supporting the tinted filter and the sight bearer arm. This aircraft had not yet been fitted with the fuselage-mounted oil tank, since the circular access hatch is not present. *Private Collection*

The original shallow oil tank located in the port wing was found to be the main cause of the Jumo 210 engine seizures. After about half an hour of operation, the tank failed to deliver sufficient oil to the engine, resulting in piston seizure. The pressure relief valve in the engine's oil pump was another source of problems. A new type of oil tank, to be mounted in the fuselage, was sent to Spain to address this problem. In the interim, the pressure relief valves were removed and ground crews were instructed to top off the engine oil after every flight. Some aircraft had the new oil tank installed at Seville, while others had already been dispatched to Almorox by the time they arrived, and the new tanks had to be fitted in the field.

It was also found that the radiator had inadequate cooling capacity for conditions in Spain. The report states that "It must, however, be assumed that the testing stations at home have seen to the installation of a radiator that is adequate even for frontline conditions [in Spain]."

When the Bf 109 As were delivered to Spain, their leading-edge slats were locked shut, but the VK/88 reports

Two views of the engine running-in bed created using the airframe of a Bf 109 A that had been written off. This apparatus was used to run in engines before they were installed in the airframes of operational fighters. The 2.J/88's "Top Hat" emblem can be made out, but unfortunately the aircraft number cannot. *Private Collection*

do not identify the nature of the problem that was responsible. This restriction was later lifted.

Other less serious problems included the absence of a tailwheel position indicator light, fouling of pistons caused by dust, and poor-quality fuel. Gauze filters were installed to help with piston fouling, and pilots were ordered to take off from grass surfaces wherever possible, since grit from the concrete runway at Vitoria was thought to be responsible for the piston fouling. To facilitate piston changes and partial overhauls, a BMW VI assembly trestle was modified to accept the Jumo 210, and a running-in bed was fashioned from a wrecked airframe. The engines were then run for four to five hours, including ten minutes at maximum rpm (2,700) and 18.7 psi of boost pressure.

Recommendations by VK/88 included an improved radiator, a variable-pitch propeller, a dipstick for the new oil tank, and a redesigned throttle lever for simpler operation.

As operational experience was gained, other complaints emerged: high wastage of tailwheel tires, cracks in engine manifold welds, securing of the starter crank in the compartment behind the pilot (inadvertent opening of the hatch and contents falling on the pilot's neck were thought to have contributed to the crash of the Bf 109 V3), and poor reliability of the electric gun-firing mechanism.

At some point after the arrival of the Bf 109 B in Spain, a process was begun that saw the surviving Bf 109 As brought up to a standard approaching that of the later variant. The modifications probably began in the autumn of 1937, when J/88 was sent to León, where the Legion Condor's maintenance facility was located, to rest. At León the unit's aircraft underwent a complete overhaul, a perfect opportunity to carry out modifications. The most-significant changes were the installation of a metal, variable-pitch propeller in place of the A's fixed-pitch wooden unit and the replacement of the removable cowling sections with B-type units incorporating cooling vents. As well, the Revi 3a was replaced with a later C12 sight. It appears, however, that there were insufficient spares to allow all of the Bf 109 As to be fully modified at that time. As a result, aircraft could later be seen with various combinations of cowlings and propellers. Otto Polenz's 6 ● 15 provides a perfect example. Photos taken after the aircraft's capture on December 4, 1937, reveal that it had been fitted with a full suite of vented cowling panels but retained the original wooden propeller. Polenz's machine had also been fitted with a Revi C12 gunsight.

The upgrade program continued, and by early 1938, surviving examples of the Bf 109 A were virtually indistinguishable from the Bf 109 B. The last three examples of the Bf 109 A still in service were aircraft 6 ● 6, 6 ● 10, and 6 ● 16. Aircraft 6 ● 6 survived until July 29, 1938, when it was written off in a crash, while the other two machines were eventually handed over to the Nationalist air force following the arrival in Spain of the Bf 109 E.

6–10 in its original configuration and *silberweiss* finish after assembly at Seville-Tablada. Note the dark tips of the fixed-pitch wooden propeller's blades and the black-painted areas on the engine cowling, including the flap which provided access to the Jumo 210's spark plugs, the panel containing the engine exhausts tubs and the one around the radiator bath. Also note the gust lock on the aircraft's rudder and the inertia starter crank. The absence of the circular hatch forward of the windscreen indicates that this photo was taken prior to installation of the replacement oil tank, which was mounted in the fuselage. *Private Collection*

Still in its original configuration and markings, here 6–10 has been positioned tail-up for boresighting of its guns. The aircraft is wearing 2.J/88's "Top Hat" emblem and the aircraft number 6–10 is in small characters aft of the fuselage disc. By the time this photo was taken the fuselage oil tank had been installed, as the circular filler hatch can be seen just behind the leg of the man standing on the wing root. *Private Collection*

6–10 parked on a barren Spanish airfield, still in its original *silberweiss* finish. Beneath the cockpit is the special marking commemorating Günther Lützow's first victory, the first ever by the pilot of a Bf 109. It consists of a number "1" inside a laurel wreath, flanked by the dates 1937 and 1938. Aft of the 2.J/88 emblem is another special marking, a bearded figure drinking from a foaming mug of beer with the legend "*Pass uff!*" ("Watch out!"). Note that the outer portions of the wooden propeller blades have been painted black. Ironically this was not the aircraft in which Lützow achieved his first victory on April 6, 1937, because 6-10 was not flown from Seville to Vitoria on the northern front until April 29. *Private Collection*

6–10 in a hangar, possibly at Burgos during overhaul. It is still has the early *silberweiss* finish and markings, including the original versions of the laurel wreath and "*Pass uff*" markings. On the upturned crate beneath the open radio compartment hatch is the fuselage-mounted oil tank. *Private Collection*

An unidentified pilot poses in front of 6 • 10 wearing his parachute. By the time this photo was taken, the aircraft had undergone a number of changes. The original wooden propeller had been replaced by a metal variable-pitch propeller unit and it had a full suite of vented cowling panels. The machine also exhibits the revised style of aircraft code, with the number "6," the aircraft type designator, forward of the black disc, and the aircraft number "10" aft. A smaller rendition of the laurel wreath and "1" emblem appears beneath the cockpit, while a simplified version of the "*Pass uff*!" marking appears on the smaller fuselage disc. The original bearded figure has given way to a head wearing a top hat in a foaming mug of beer. By this time the aircraft's original *silberweiss* finish had become severely worn with evidence of much repainting. *Private Collection*

Another photo of 6–10 during overhaul at Burgos. This view of the starboard side of the aircraft reveals that the special markings were applied to the port side of the fuselage only. With the cowling removed it is possible to see the coolant tank (pale object beneath the propeller shaft), radiator, engine mounts and other engine accessories. By the time this photo was taken the wings had been removed, revealing the wing attachment points. *Private Collection*

Another image of 6 • 10, this time at La Senia. When this shot was taken the aircraft was still finished in *silberweiss* with the black section around the radiator bath. The second renditions of the laurel wreath and "*Pass uff*" markings are also still present. The aircraft had been fitted with Bf 109 B wings by this point, as indicated by the position of the oil cooler beneath the wing. Note the dark-painted tips of the propeller blades and white spinner. *Private Collection*

6 • 10, again at La Senia. The aircraft now bears the name *Altertum* (antiquity) on the radiator bath, obviously a reference to its age. By this time the aircraft has been refinished in the RLM 63/65 scheme, while the area of the wing root and inner wing appear to be in a slightly darker color. The laurel wreath and number "1" marking are still present beneath the cockpit. Note the rag stuffed into the mouth of the oil cooler beneath the wing. By this time the aircraft had been fitted with Bf 109 B wings, as evidenced by the position of the oil cooler beneath the wing. About the only remaining feature that distinguished it from a Bf 109 B was the circular oil filler hatch visible here beneath the aircraft's windscreen. *Private Collection*

An unidentified man poses with a pristine 6 • 10, probably at Leon after an overhaul and repainting. The *Altertum* legend is now on the aircraft's engine cowling above the exhaust and it is finished in RLM 65 on the undersides and RLM 63 on the uppers. The laurel wreath and "*Pass uff*" markings apparently disappeared during repainting. By this time 6 • 10 had also been fitted with the more vertical windscreen. There is a total of fifteen victory bars on the fin. Note the unusual finish on the Bf 109 in the background, apparently prior to repainting. *Private Collection*

A view of 6 • 10's starboard side at La Senia. The fifteen victory bars are on the vertical tail, but unlike the other side the top row has seven and the bottom row eight victory bars. This victory tally was a popular subject for photographers. This impressive victory tally made 6 • 10 the top-scoring Messerschmitt of the Spanish Civil War. *Private Collection*

BF 109 B

The Bf 109 B was the first major production variant of the Messerschmitt fighter, with a total of 341 aircraft constructed by BFW in Augsburg, Erla Maschinenwerk in Leipzig, and Fieseler-Werke in Kassel.[11] Various figures have been offered for the number of Bf 109 Bs sent to the Legion Condor in Spain, but photographic evidence suggests a total of forty-two aircraft (6 ● 17 to 6 ● 58). The first twenty-two examples of the Bf 109 B arrived in Spain in mid-July 1937, but delivery dates for the rest are not known.

Despite claims to the contrary, there was only one production version of the Bf 109 B. For many years the designations Bf 109 B-1 and B-2 have been used to differentiate between aircraft with wooden and metal propellers, respectively. These are entirely fictitious, however, since there are no subtypes identified in the Bf 109 B handbook. This error is probably attributable in part to ignorance of the existence of the Bf 109 A, and to the fact that some early Bf 109 Bs were equipped with fixed-pitch wooden propellers.[12] Although the B version was designed for a metal propeller and vented cowling

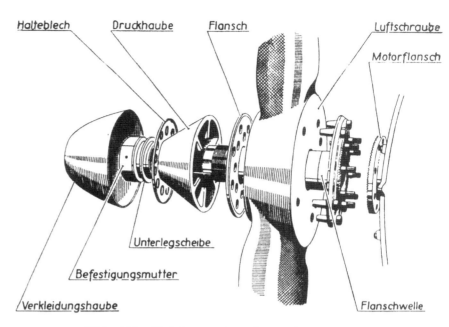

Halteblech Druckhaube Flansch Luftschraube Motorflansch Unterlegscheibe Befestigungsmutter Verkleidungshaube Flanschwelle

Abb. 129: Anbringen einer festen Luftschraube.

From the Bf 109 B handbook, an illustration showing how the fixed-pitch wooden propeller was fitted. All Jumo-engined variants could be fitted with a wooden propeller, which required removal of the tail ballast weight. *Hafner Archiv*

2) Schmierstoffbehälter
Am Schmierstoffbehälter oberhalb des Anschlußstutzens für die Entnahmeleitung den Schraubstutzen für den Anbau der Schmierstoff-Rücklaufleitung und dahinter,

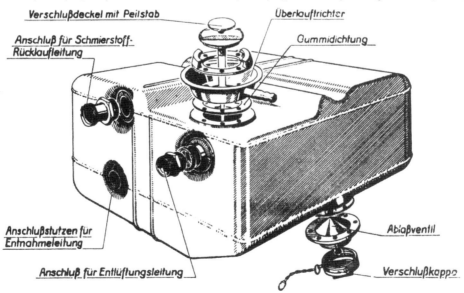

Verschlußdeckel mit Peilstab Überlaufrichter Anschluß für Schmierstoff-Rücklaufleitung Gummidichtung Anschlußstutzen für Entnahmeleitung Anschluß für Entlüftungsleitung Abiaßventil Verschlußkappe

Abb. 92: Schmierstoffbehälter.

Illustration from the Bf 109 B handbook, showing the aircraft's oil tank, which was installed in the aircraft's port wing. Atop the tank is the filler point with cap and dipstick and the overflow funnel. On the bottom is the drain valve and cap, while on the front of the tank are fittings for the oil return and ventilation lines. *Hafner Archiv*

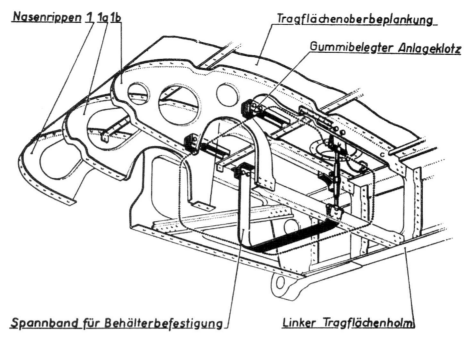

Nasenrippen 1, 1a, 1b

Tragflächenoberbeplankung

Gummibelegter Anlageklotz

Spannband für Behälterbefestigung

Linker Tragflächenholm

Abb. 93: Anbauvorrichtung für Schmierstoffbehälter.

Quelle: Luftfahrt-Archiv Hafner

Another illustration from the Bf 109 B handbook, showing where and how the oil tank was fitted inside the port wing. The tank was held in place by rubber-coated mounts and a tension strap. *Hafner Archiv*

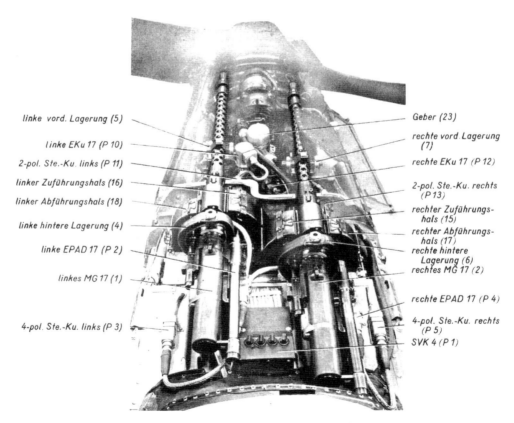

linke vord. Lagerung (5)

linke EKu 17 (P 10)

2-pol. Ste.-Ku. links (P 11)

linker Zuführungshals (16)

linker Abführungshals (18)

linke hintere Lagerung (4)

linke EPAD 17 (P 2)

linkes MG 17 (1)

4-pol. Ste.-Ku. links (P 3)

Geber (23)

rechte vord. Lagerung (7)

rechte EKu 17 (P 12)

2-pol. Ste.-Ku. rechts (P 13)

rechter Zuführungshals (15)

rechter Abführungshals (17)

rechte hintere Lagerung (6)

rechtes MG 17 (2)

rechte EPAD 17 (P 4)

4-pol. Ste.-Ku. rechts (P 5)

SVK 4 (P 1)

Abb. 2: Die gesteuert schießenden MG.

Handbook illustration showing the two MG 17 machine guns mounted in the forward fuselage, ammunition feeds, gun-cocking and firing system (EPAD 17), and gun mounts of the Bf 109 B. *Hafner Archiv*

The two fuselage-mounted MG 17 machine guns of a Bf 109 B. *Private Collection*

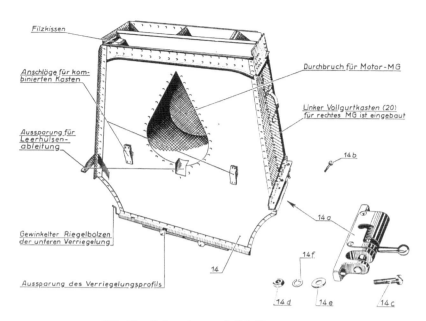

Filzkissen

Anschläge für kombinierten Kasten

Aussparung für Leerhülsenableitung

Gewinkelter Riegelbolzen der unteren Verriegelung

Aussparung des Verriegelungsprofils

Durchbruch für Motor-MG

Linker Vollgurtkasten (20) für rechtes MG ist eingebaut

14b

14a

14f

14

14d   14e   14c

Abb. 11: Kastenrahmen mit Zubehör, von vorne.

Handbook illustration depicting the structure that housed the ammunition boxes of the Bf 109 B. The teardrop-shaped cutout in the structure accommodated the breech of the engine-mounted MG 17 machine gun. On the front of the structure are fittings for adding the ammunition box for the engine-mounted machine gun. *Hafner Archiv*

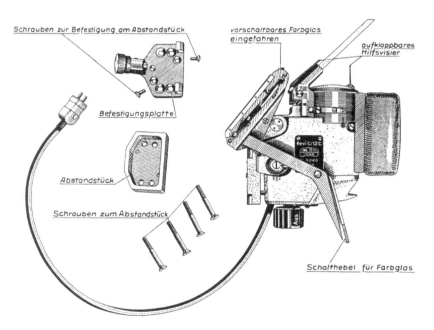

Schrauben zur Befestigung am Abstandstück

vorschaltbares Farbglas eingefahren

aufklappbares Hilfsvisier

Befestigungsplatte

Abstandstück

Schrauben zum Abstandstück

Schalthebel für Farbglas

Abb. 31a: Revi C/12 C mit Zubehör.

Handbook illustration of the Revi C/12 C gunsight installed in the Bf 109 B. *Hafner Archiv*

panels, these features were absent from some early-production aircraft. Also, the wooden propeller fitted to the Bf 109 B differed from that of the A variant: its spinner matched the diameter of the forward fuselage, and there was a firing tube through the axis of the propeller for the engine-mounted MG 17. All Bf 109 Bs sent to the Legion Condor were equipped with metal propellers and vented cowling panels on delivery.

The oil tank was located in the port wing on all B-series aircraft. The circular filler cap access hatch was positioned near the port wing root and was usually accompanied by a brown servicing triangle indicating the type of oil to be used. The oil cooler of the Bf 109 B was relocated to a position just inboard and aft of the port wheel well.

Another change affected the leading-edge slats, which were reduced in span compared to those of the Bf 109 A.

The armament of the Bf 109 B consisted of three MG 17s, two above the engine and one mounted between the engine cylinder banks. It has been claimed that the engine-mounted weapon proved troublesome and was removed, but personal accounts and photographs reveal that all three weapons were retained for a time.

The first Bf 109 Bs sent to Spain had a windscreen with the gunsight glass set into it. Later aircraft had a more vertical windscreen with an angle of 53 degrees and the gunsight glass completely inside. The early upper windscreen frame was shorter, with just three rivets, while the later model's upper frame had four rivets.

BF 109 C

Production of the Bf 109 C began in the spring of 1938, and one small batch of just fifty-eight examples was built by BFW at Augsburg, including a handful of the cannon-armed C-3.[13] The C variant was powered by a fuel-injected Jumo 210 G engine, which gave a slight increase in performance at heights greater than 10,000 feet. The Bf 109 C also carried a more powerful armament. The engine-mounted machine gun of the Bf 109 B was deleted, and two additional MG 17s were installed in the outer wings. Access hatches for these were installed on the upper surface of the wing.

The addition of the wing-mounted weapons resulted in a number of changes compared to the Bf 109 B. The oil tank was moved to the fuselage, and the oil filler hatch was relocated to a position high up on the panel in front of the cockpit, on the port side of the fuselage, and was accompanied by a brown servicing triangle.

The oxygen filler hatch and electrical socket on the starboard side of the fuselage were moved farther aft, and the oxygen filler hatch was placed higher on the fuselage.

Externally the Bf 109 C was identical to the D variant. The differences between the two were restricted to the engine, engine accessories, fuel system, and engine controls. Unfortunately, these areas were rarely photographed. To date, the author has been unable to conclusively identify any of the Bf 109 Cs claimed to have been used by the Legion Condor.

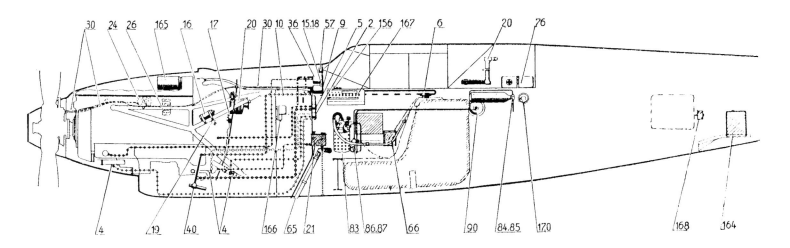

Die Zahlen entsprechen den laufenden Nummern der Ausrüstungsgeräte (Anlage 9)

Betriebsgeräte BF 109 C

Handbook illustration of operating systems installed in the fuselage of the Bf 109 C: external power socket (170), oxygen filler hatch (90), and oxygen cylinder and remote filling point (84, 85). *Hafner Archiv*

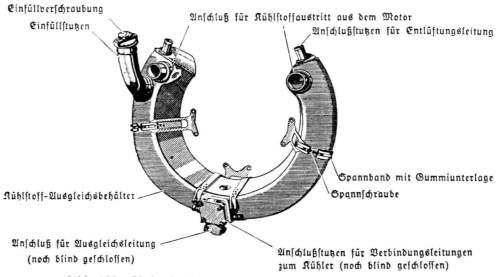

Einfüllverſchraubung
Einfüllſtutzen

Anſchluß für Kühlſtoffaustritt aus dem Motor
Anſchlußſtutzen für Entlüftungsleitung

Spannband mit Gummiunterlage
Spannſchraube

Kühlſtoff-Ausgleichsbehälter

Anſchluß für Ausgleichsleitung
(noch blind geſchloſſen)

Anſchlußſtutzen für Verbindungsleitungen
zum Kühler (noch blind geſchloſſen)

Abb. 103: Einbaufertiger Kühlſtoff-Ausgleichsbehälter (BF 109 C)

Handbook illustration of the Bf 109 C's coolant header tank, which was considerably larger than that of the Bf 109 D (see next illustration). *Hafner Archiv*

If five or six Bf 109 Cs with their fuel-injected engines had been sent to Spain, they would surely have become a maintenance and spare-parts nightmare, having a number of systems not found in other Jumo-engined Messerschmitts. The earliest reference the author could find to the Bf 109 C being used by the Legion Condor was in William Green's *War Planes of the Second World War: Fighters; Volume 1*, first published in 1960, in which he wrote:

> Twelve Bf 109 C-1 fighters reached Spain early in 1938 to re-equip *Jagdgruppe* 88's 3rd *Staffel*.

And regarding the Bf 109 D, Green wrote:

> . . . these were followed by the Bf 109 D-1, which carried an armament of one engine-mounted MG-FF cannon and two MG 17 machine guns mounted over the engine and, powered by the DB 600Aa, attained a speed of 323 mph at rated altitude.

At the time, therefore, it was thought that the Bf 109 C was the only Jumo-powered variant of the Bf 109 armed with four machine guns, and all the aircraft that we now know to have been Bf 109 Ds would have been identified as Cs. This inaccurate information has, I believe, been repeated

so often that it has become accepted as fact. Unfortunately, I have been unable to positively prove this theory, but until evidence confirming the presence of the Bf 109 C in Spain is found, I will continue to doubt the oft-repeated claims that the Legion Condor operated that type in Spain.

BF 109 D

The D series was the second major production variant of the Bf 109.[14] It was built almost exclusively under license by Erla, Fieseler, Focke-Wulf, AGO, and Arado. Altogether, 647 examples were completed. The Bf 109 D was powered by a Jumo 210 D carburetor engine but otherwise was identical to the C version. Like the Bf 109 C, which entered production at about the same time, the Bf 109 D was armed with four MG 17 machine guns, two above the engine and two in the wings. It also had the relocated oil tank (in the forward fuselage), oxygen filler point, and external electrical socket.

Another feature that differentiated the Bf 109 C/D from the earlier B was longer, curved exhaust stubs.

Analysis of photographs indicates that twenty-eight Bf 109 Ds were delivered to the Legion Condor, bearing the codes 6 ● 59 to 6 ● 86.

Rumpffeite.

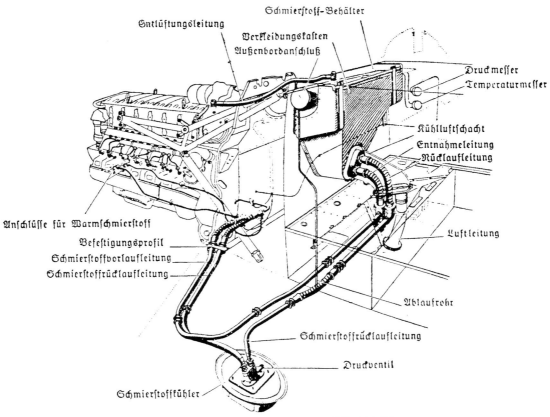

Entlüftungsöleitung
Schmierstoff-Behälter
Verkleidungskasten
Außenbordanschluß
Druckmesser
Temperaturmesser
Kühlluftschacht
Entnahmeleitung
Rücklaufleitung
Anschlüsse für Warmschmierstoff
Befestigungsprofil
Schmierstoffvorlaufleitung
Schmierstoffrücklaufleitung
Luftleitung
Ablaufrohr
Schmierstoffrücklaufleitung
Druckventil
Schmierstoffkühler

Abb. 15: Schmierstoffanlage (BF 109 D)

An illustration from the Bf 109 C and D handbook, showing the oil tank mounted in the forward fuselage of the Bf 109 D, the oil temperature and pressure gauges on the instrument panel, and the associated plumbing from the tank to the oil cooler and engine. *Hafner Archiv*

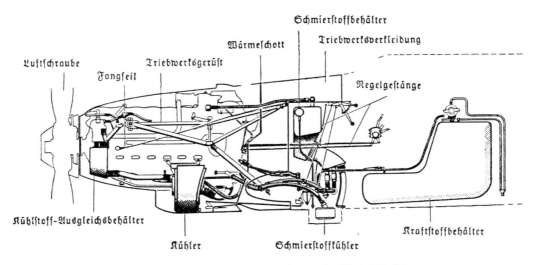

Schmierstoffbehälter
Wärmeschott
Triebwerksverkleidung
Luftschraube
Fangseil
Triebwerksgerüst
Regelgestänge
Kühlstoff-Ausgleichsbehälter
Kühler
Schmierstoffkühler
Kraftstoffbehälter

Abb. 7: Anordnung des Triebwerks (BF 109 D)

Handbook illustration showing the arrangement of the Bf 109 D's engine and engine accessories in the Bf 109 D. Note the smaller coolant header tank compared to the one in the Bf 109 C. *Hafner Archiv*

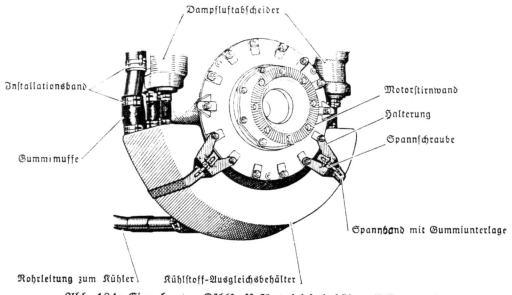

Dampfluftabscheider

Installationsband

Motorstirnwand

Halterung

Spannschraube

Gummimuffe

Spannband mit Gummiunterlage

Rohrleitung zum Kühler

Kühlstoff-Ausgleichsbehälter

Abb. 104: Eingebauter Kühlstoff-Ausgleichsbehälter (BF 109 D)

The Bf 109 D's coolant header tank installed on the front of the Jumo 210 engine. *Hafner Archiv*

Bf 109 D 6 • 60, the aircraft flown by *Uffz*. Herbert Schob. Several of the features that distinguished the Bf 109 D from the earlier A and B variants can be seen in this photo. Just forward of the numeral "0" on the fuselage is the external power socket, and just forward of it is the oxygen filler point, both of which were farther aft than those of the Bf 109 A and B. Also note the port in the leading edge of the starboard wing for the wing-mounted MG 17 machine gun. Just behind the propeller spinner can be seen one of the steam separators, which sat atop the coolant header tank. This feature confirms that the aircraft is a Bf 109 D and not a C, which had a larger coolant tank and no steam separators. *Private Collection*

Another Bf 109 D undergoing maintenance. In this view the coolant header tank (the pale object just behind and below the spinner) can be seen clearly, as can the steam separator above it. *Private Collection*

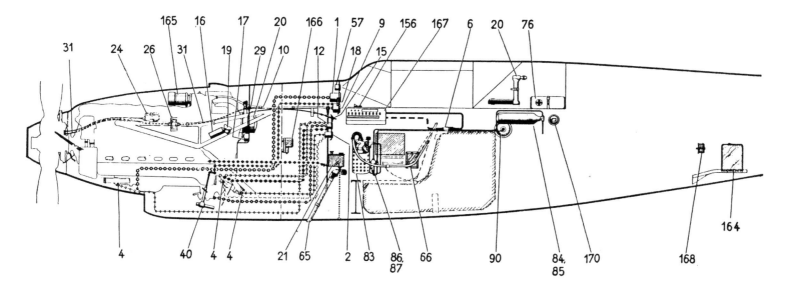

Die Zahlen entſprechen den laufenden Nummern der Ausrüſtungsgerätelifte
(Anlage 9)

Betriebsgeräte BF 109 D

Handbook illustration of operating systems installed in the fuselage of the Bf 109 D: external power socket (170), oxygen filler hatch (90), and oxygen cylinder and remote filling point (84, 85). Note the positions of the external power socket and oxygen filler point compared to those in the illustration of the Bf 109 B's fuselage systems. *Hafner Archiv*

An unidentified Bf 109 D at La Sénia. Note the long, curved exhaust stubs and the wing-mounted machine gun, both features of the Bf 109 C/D. Hanging from the leading-edge slat is the zippered wheel well cover, which was held in place by snap fasteners. *Private Collection*

Close-up of the Bf 109 E's DB 601 A engine. This power plant delivered 1,050 hp, almost 400 hp more than the Jumo 210, and transformed the Bf 109's performance. The E version remained the Luftwaffe's primary day fighter until early 1941, when it was superseded by the Bf 109 F. *Private Collection*

Two Bf 109 Es undergoing maintenance. The aircraft on the left is 6 • 92, a cannon-armed E-3, while the one on the right is an E-1, which was armed with four MG 17 machine guns. Both aircraft have propellers painted RLM 70 black-green. Note the triangular VDM logo on the propeller blades of the E-3 and the earlier oval version on those of the E-1. *Private Collection*

BF 109 E

In mid-1937, Messerschmitt initiated development of a version of the Bf 109 powered by the Daimler-Benz DB 601 A engine. Compared to the 730 horsepower of the Jumo 210 G, the DB 601 A produced 1,100 horsepower, and the new engine radically transformed the fighter's performance. The Bf 109 E-1 entered production in the autumn of 1938, followed closely by the Messerschmitt 109 E-3. The two variants differed solely in the armament they carried: while the E-1 retained the four MG 17s of the D series, the E-3 was armed with two MG 17 machine guns above the engine and two 20 mm MG FF cannon in the wings. A total of forty-four examples of the Bf 109 E-1 and E-3 were delivered to the Legion Condor, beginning in early 1939, bearing the codes 6 • 87 to 6 • 130.

PART III

CAMOUFLAGE SCHEMES APPLIED TO BF 109S OF THE LEGION CONDOR

Bf 109s of 2.J/88 on an unidentified airfield. Aircraft 6 • 29 and 6 • 45 are new Bf 109 Bs repainted in *silberweiss*, while 6 • 6 (second machine from left) is one of the *Staffel*'s original Bf 109 As. *Private Collection*

SILBERWEISS (SILVER-WHITE)

The first seventeen Bf 109s delivered to the Legion Condor (three prototypes and fourteen Bf 109 As)[1] were finished in a color that is called *silberweiss*[2] (silver-white) in VK/88

Bf 109 A 6 • 5 at Vitoria, tied down with a canvas cover over the engine and cockpit. The brightness of the fresh *silberweiss* scheme is readily apparent. *Author's Collection*

This photograph is of interest because it illustrates four of the finishes sported by Bf 109s of the Legion Condor. In the foreground is Bf 109 B 6 • 32, the aircraft flown by Reinhard Seiler. It is finished in the RLM 63 grey and RLM 65 pale blue scheme (note the color separation line on the radiator bath). The next aircraft is Bf 109 A 6 • 10, still in its original *silberweiss* finish (note the black areas around the exhausts and radiator bath). The next two machines are Bf 109 Bs, 6 • 46, and 6 • 45, which had their original RLM 70/71/65 schemes overpainted in *silberweiss*. The fifth aircraft is an unidentified Bf 109 B finished in the delivery scheme of European greens with pale blue undersides. *Author's Collection*

Lineup of Bf 109 As of 2.J/88 on an unidentified airfield in northern Spain. In the foreground is 6 • 4, while 6 • 6 and 6 • 12 can be made out in the background. At the end of the line is an unidentified Ju 86. The *silberweiss* finish worn by the Messerschmitt fighters looks very light in the bright sunshine. *Private Collection*

An unidentified Bf 109 A near the hangars at Seville-Tablada, probably soon after reassembly. The aircraft's clean lines are marred only by the Jumo 210's prominent radiator housing. Note the emblem of the Schwarz Propellerwerke on the blades of the wooden fixed-pitch propeller. The aircraft's *silberweiss* finish appears to be in mint condition. *Private Collection*

Still smiling, the pilot of 6 • 29 poses with his aircraft at Avila. Landing in a crosswind resulted in the port undercarriage leg shearing off. This was one of the Bf 109 B fighters assigned to 2.J/88 and repainted in *silberweiss*. *Private Collection*

Aircraft of 2.J/88 at Burgo de Osma. The first batch of twenty-two Bf 109 B fighters arrived in Spain in mid-July 1937. These were used to replace 1.J/88's He 51s and also to bring 2.J/88 up to strength. It was decided that the 1st *Staffel*'s aircraft would retain their European dark-green camouflage, while the 2nd *Staffel* would have its new aircraft finished in *silberweiss* to match its Bf 109 As and to evaluate the relative merits of the two schemes. This meant that the Bf 109 Bs assigned to 2nd *Staffel* had to be repainted. Aircraft 6 • 23 on the left of the photo is one such machine. Once again the contrast between the local transport, here carts pulled by mules, and that of the Legion Condor, in this case a motorcycle-sidecar on the left of the photo, is marked. *Private Collection*

documents. In the summer of 1937, following the arrival of the first batch of Bf 109 B fighters finished in the European scheme of 70/71/65, a second *Staffel* (1st J/88) was equipped with Messerschmitt fighters, and it was decided that one (2nd J/88) should retain the *silberweiss* finish, while the other's aircraft would be in the European scheme, in order to assess their relative merits. There is photographic evidence to verify this, since Bf 109 Bs can be seen repainted in the comparatively bright *silberweiss* (aircraft 6 ● 23, 6 ● 26, and 6 ● 32, for example). There is anecdotal evidence to suggest that the *silberweiss* scheme was, in some cases, retained well into 1938. Josef Fözö, who joined J/88 in the summer of 1938, described his aircraft (6 ● 16) as being "*silbergrau*"[3] or silver-gray. The three Bf 109 A fighters that were still in service in 1938 (6 ● 6, 6 ● 10, and 6 ● 16) appear to have remained in *silberweiss* until repainted in the definitive 63/65 scheme.

BF 109 B 6 ● 29, the aircraft seen in the photo at the top of the previous page, at León while still in its delivery scheme of RLM 70/71/65. No unit marking is visible. *Private Collection*

RLM 70/71/65 (BLACK-GREEN, DARK GREEN, PALE BLUE)

Photographic evidence suggests that all Bf 109 B and at least some, if not all, Bf 109 D and E fighters arrived in Spain still wearing the RLM 70/71/65 camouflage scheme then in use in Europe. Many Bf 109 Bs retained the dark-green upper-surface colors for quite some time, while the Ds and Es appear to have been painted in the new RLM 63/65 (medium gray and pale blue) scheme before they were issued to the units.

Bf 109 B 6 ● 22 at León in the markings of 1.J/88. Other 1st *Staffel* aircraft can be seen in the background. On the right is a Bf 108 *Taifun*, one of four operated by the Legion Condor. *Private Collection*

Bf 109 B 6 • 21, the aircraft of Oblt. Rolf Pingel, while undergoing servicing at Santander-West airfield. The aircraft is finished in the delivery scheme of RLM 70/71/65. The aircraft's pristine finish suggests that it was photographed soon after it arrived in Spain in July 1937. *Author's Collection*

Taken at Gallur, this photo shows Wolfgang Schellmann's 6 • 51 in its original RLM 70/71/65 scheme. The aircraft number is repeated on the canvas cover over the engine. There are two victory bars on the fin, indicating that the photo was taken sometime between March 8, 1938, when he shot down a Curtiss for his second victory, and the 24th, when he downed another Curtiss for his third. *Private Collection*

Bf 109 Bs in their delivery scheme of RLM 70/71/65 during reassembly at León. The aircraft in the background appears to be virtually complete, while the one in the foreground awaits its wings, which are lying on the floor of the hangar in front of it, and propeller. *Private Collection*

A Bf 109 D in a hangar at León after reassembly. This Bf 109 D arrived in Spain in the European camouflage scheme of RLM 70/71/65. The presence of steam separators above the coolant tank clearly identifies this aircraft as a Bf 109 D, the C having a larger horseshoe-shaped coolant tank that eliminated the separators. Also note the positions of the external power socket and oxygen filler point on the fuselage side and the curved exhaust ejector stubs. *Private Collection*

Five Bf 109s parked at León. The aircraft in the foreground is a Bf 109 B, while just beyond it is an unidentified Bf 109 E. This aircraft is particularly interesting because it appears to be wearing the European color scheme of RLM 70/71/65. The area of the fuselage where the *Balkenkreuz* would have been has been overpainted in a lighter color, possibly RLM gray 02. Nationalist markings are already present on the rudder and beneath the starboard wing. *Private Collection*

Another photo from the series taken by Adolf Galland, in which Schellmann is leading a Schwarm of Bf 109s of 1.J/88. Schellmann's machine is wearing the modified delivery scheme introduced by 1.J/88. The second aircraft, 6 • 38, appears to have been repainted in a style similar to Schellmann's machine and has two victory bars on its tail. It may have been flown by *Uffz.* Kuhlmann, who scored his second victory on June 13. The third aircraft is still finished in the dark 70/71/65 scheme and obviously stands out more clearly against the local terrain. There is a single victory bar on the fin. The fourth Bf 109, 6 • 42, was being flown by Werner Mölders and also wears a modified 70/71/65 scheme. *Author's Collection*

MODIFIED RLM 70/71/65 CAMOUFLAGE SCHEME

It appears that in 1938, after a period during which both the 70/71/65 and the *silberweiss* schemes were retained for evaluation, 1.J/88 began modifying the dark-green upper-surface finish to better reflect the environment in which the aircraft were being operated. Photographic evidence shows that the black-green segments on the wings and tailplane were overpainted in lighter colors. Schellmann's Bf 109 B

Schellmann's 6 • 51 photographed on an unidentified airfield. The aircraft still has remnants of its original RLM 70/71/65 scheme on its wings and tailplane. By this time there are eight victory bars on the tail, indicating that the photo was taken sometime after July 20, 1938, when Schellmann scored his seventh and eighth victories. The light band on the undercarriage leg is still present. Also note the dark-painted tips of the propeller blades. *Private Collection*

Aircraft 6 • 38, a Bf 109 B of 1st *Staffel J/88* with modified 70/71/65 camouflage scheme. Fuselage appears to be RLM 63 gray, while the 70/71 finish on the wings and tailplane has been partly overpainted. In the background is an *Ah.447 Navigations-Funkpeilanhänger (2. achs)*, a trailer on which was mounted a radio direction finder, which served as a navigation aid for use at forward airfields. *Private Collection*

Bf 109 B 6 • 44 being ferried across a body of water by small boats. This is another 2nd *Staffel* aircraft with a modified 70/71/65 finish. There are four colors visible on the upper wing—RLM 70 and 71 and two others, one lighter and one very much lighter (possibly RLM 62 green and RLM 63 gray). The fuselage is RLM 63. *Private Collection*

6 ● 51 is a perfect example. In the photos on pages 59 and 148, 6 ● 51 is seen at Gallur wearing the 70/71/65 scheme with two victory bars on its fin. This suggests that the photos were taken in March 1938. The photo on page 76, taken at La Sénia, shows the aircraft with the fuselage painted 63/65 and the wings and tailplane partly repainted, sometime after June 13, when Schellmann claimed his fourth victory. The photo on page 150 shows the machine with five victory bars on the tail, meaning that it was photographed after June 25 but prior to July 18, when he scored his sixth victory. The photos of aircraft 6 ● 44 being recovered after a forced landing show a somewhat more involved repainting of the wings and horizontal tail. At least four different colors can be made out on the aircraft's wing surfaces, probably the original RLM 70 and 71 plus two lighter colors, possibly RLM 62 and 63. It appears that the modified green scheme was in use for only a short time during the spring and summer of 1938. Other aircraft so painted include 6 ● 38, 6 ● 42, 6 ● 44, and 6 ● 50 (all Bf 109 B).

RLM 61/62/63/65 (BROWN, GREEN, GRAY, PALE BLUE)

Used on the Legion Condor's bomber and reconnaissance aircraft, this scheme appears to have been tried out on at least one Bf 109 B (6 ● 55). Curiously, the upper surfaces of the aircraft's fuselage were finished in RLM 63 (gray) only. This paint scheme, apparently applied at the legion's maintenance base in León, may have been a formalized application of the modified 70/71/65 scheme used by 1.J/88 (Bf 109 B).

Bf 109 B 6 ● 55 in the brilliant Spanish sunshine at León. It appears to have been freshly painted. While the wings appear to be finished in the three-color scheme of RLM 61/62/63, the fuselage, wing root, and tail are in a very pale color. Because there is no obvious color separation line on the fuselage, this may be RLM 65 pale blue. *Private Collection*

Bf 109 B 6 • 55 undergoing maintenance at La Sénia. The unusual splinter scheme on the aircraft's wings and tailplane is clearly visible. The aircraft's fuselage is painted RLM 63 gray, with RLM 65 pale-blue undersides. There are three victory bars on the aircraft's fin. Close examination of the photo reveals that one of the ground crewmen has removed the hatch covering the aircraft's oil tank filler point. The Bf 109 B's oil tank was in the port wing, while the later C and D versions had a fuselage-mounted oil tank forward of the cockpit. *Private Collection*

At La Sénia, a young member of the Legion Condor poses for a photo on the wing of Bf 109 B, finished in a color scheme similar to the one worn by 6 • 55 in the previous photo. This may in fact have been 6 • 55, but the color segments on the wings appear to be different than those in the previous photo. It may also have been one of the Bf 109 Bs in the modified RLM 70/71/65 scheme. *Private Collection*

Members of *Gruppe Drohne*, the Legion Condor's armored battalion, pose for a photo in front of Bf 109 B 6 • 44. By this time the aircraft had been repainted in the ultimate camouflage scheme of RLM 63 gray upper surfaces and RLM 65 pale-blue undersurfaces. The machine also has the more vertical windscreen. *Private Collection*

RLM 63/65 (GRAY, PALE BLUE)

This camouflage scheme appears to have been introduced in the summer of 1938 and remained in use until the end of the war.[4] Aircraft already in Spain were repainted during overhaul or major repairs, while others appear to have been repainted after arriving in Spain (Bf 109 A, B, D, and E).

2.J/88 prepares for an operation from La Senia. In the foreground is 6 • 60, the Bf 109 D which was flown by *Uffz*. Werner Schob. On the left is 6 • 6, an upgraded Bf 109 A. For a time it was the aircraft of Herbert Ihlefeld, who scored a total of nine victories in Spain. There are five victory bars on the aircraft's tail. Beyond 6 • 60 can be seen 6 • 64, another Bf 109 D. Further in the background is 6 • 10, another of the three upgraded Bf 109 As still in service at that time, the other being 6 • 16. All of these aircraft appear to be finished in the RLM 63/65 color scheme.
Private Collection

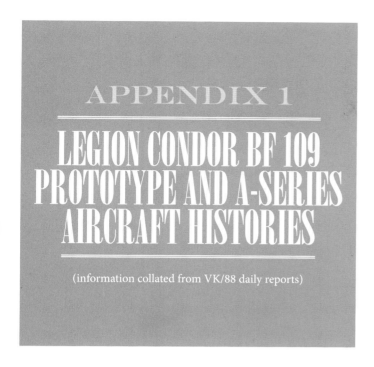

LEGION CONDOR BF 109 PROTOTYPE AND A-SERIES AIRCRAFT HISTORIES

(information collated from VK/88 daily reports)

PROTOTYPES

V3 (6 ● 2)

December 1936

15/12	arrives in Seville
17/12	unpacked
18/12	coolant pump found defective, replaced; assembly completed
19/12	undergoes checks
20/12	calibration; *Oberleutnant* Winterer arrives as pilot
21/12	engine test run, readjustment necessary
22/12	propeller damaged by stones
28/12	practice flights
30/12	machine guns recalibrated

January 1937

01/01	propeller pitch changed to 29 degrees
02/01	cocking cable starboard machine gun broken
03/01	scramble to intercept reported raid; no contact
04/01	engine removed
05/01	installation of Jumo 210 B
06/01	installation completed
08/01	engine installation checked, followed by test run
09/01	undercarriage pump damaged, replaced
10/01	test flight with new engine
11/01	check flight, engine trouble, forced landing near Palacios
12/01	recovered after forced landing
13/01	began engine change
14/01	engine removed
15/01	installation of new engine
18/01	installation of new engine complete
20/01	engine checks
21/01	engine boost pressure adjusted, defective fuel pump replaced
22/01	ground run, coolant thermometer replaced, bulge in barrel of MG C 30
23/01	test flight, engine run satisfactory; Bosch horn not working
24/01	Bosch horn repaired, carburetor drain line broken
28/01	canopy center section failed to close properly, torn loose during attempted takeoff; subsequently repaired
29/01	canopy center section repaired

February 1937

01/02	canopy center section repair completed
02/02	ground run and adjustment of engine
03/02	Test flights, carburetor preheat corrected, shock struts rechecked. Aileron and wingtip damaged during takeoff; being repaired.
04/02	repair of wingtip and aileron
05/02	practice flights
09/02	practice flights
10/02	practice flights, preparations for transfer to Villa del Prado
11/02	Took off for Villa del Prado. En route stop in Caceres. Aircraft destroyed in crash after taking off from Caceres.

V4 (6 ● 1)

December 1936

04/12	horizontal stab badly damaged, engine cowling slightly damaged in bombing raid on 4/12
05/12	arrives crated in Tablada
10/12	undergoes checks
12/12	engine runs
14/12	successful test flight
15/12	radiator leak
17/12	cleared to fly as escort
28/12	engine set to weaker mixture; broken fuel pump lever replaced with lever from the [Bf 109] V6

January 1937

03/01	scramble to intercept reported raid; no contact
04/01	practice flights
05/01	practice flights
06/01	practice flights
07/01	practice flights

08/01   practice flights
09/01   practice flights
10/01   fuel feed problem
11/01   carb preheat reduced
12/01   Three-hour patrol near Cadiz. Landed with tailwheel retracted, damage to rudder.
13/01   rudder repaired
23/01   new tail section fitted
28/01   horizontal stab and elevator sent to Villa del Prado

February 1937
19/02   flown from Villa del Prado to Seville (relief of *Oberleutnant* Trautloft)
23/02   practice flights
26/02   practice flights
27/02   practice flights
28/02   practice flights

March 1937
01/03   practice flights; undercarriage stuck in retracted position because of dented panel; is being repaired
02/03   Undercarriage retraction cylinder fork head replaced. Undercarriage fairings fitted.
03/03   Practice flights. Undercarriage failed to retract properly during test flight; piston too tight; is being remedied.
04/03   repairs to undercarriage
05/03   undercarriage repairs complete, test flight, formation practice
08/03   practice flight; operational sortie to Cordoba
09/03   practice flight
12/03   practice flights and formation exercises
14/03   first *Kette* of Bf 109s (6 ● 1, 6 ● 3, and 6 ● 4) flew to Almorox
16/03   Return flight from Almorox to Seville. Canopy jettison lever pulled during engine run-up; canopy center section blown away. Repairs are being carried out in Seville.
18/03   Test flights. Mechanical undercarriage position indicator not working; is being checked.
19/03   practice flights
20/03   flown to Almorox

April 1937
15/04   flown from Vitoria to Seville for partial overhaul
16/04   Airframe and engine partial overhaul. Installation of new oil tank.
Aircraft subsequently operated by 2nd *Staffel* of J/88 and later 1st *Staffel*. The aircraft was ultimately wrecked in forced landing.

V6

December 1936
5/12/   arrives crated in Tablada
6/12   assembly begins
8/12   calibration and checks
9/12   written off in crash on December 9, 1936; retained at Tablada for cannibalization for parts

BF 109 A

6 ● 3

17/02/1937   unloaded and shipped to Tablada
18/02   uncrated
19/02   assembly work begins
20/02   mounting of wings and tail section
21/02   undercarriage checks and installation of MG C 30; propeller fitted
22/02   fuselage bottom panel fitted, instruments removed, cannon firing mechanism put in order
23/02   Propeller mounting complete; cannon installation complete. F.T. (radio) removed.
24/02   F.T. (radio) removed. Aircraft assembly complete except for undercarriage checks.
25/02   Installation of fuselage bottom panel complete; in order. First ground run satisfactory.
26/02   undercarriage checks with engine running; found to be in order by inspector
27/02   test flights, satisfactory
28/02   engine retuned and throttle control rod lengthened
01/03   practice flights; carburetor preheat clearance hole reduced to 2 mm for improved engine running
02/03   practice flights
03/03   Practice flights. Engine test flight; bumpers must be fitted to supercharger pushrods.
04/03   installation of a shiftable linkage for the two-speed supercharger
05/03   Shiftable linkage for the two-speed supercharger installed. Test flight with no complaints. Formation practice.
06/03   Test flight. Ignition reset to 37 degrees; test run faultless.
07/03   operational sortie to Cordoba
08/03   operational sortie to Cordoba
09/03   return from Cordoba
12/03   practice flights and formation exercises
13/03   installation of oil tank complete
14/03   first *Kette* of Bf 109s (6 ● 1, 6 ● 3, and 6 ● 4) flew to Almorox
Operated by 2.J/88, and later 1.J/88. Aircraft written off in crash later in 1937.

19/02/1937   uncrating
20/02   uncrating and fitting of undercarriage
21/02   tail section installed, attachment of wings completed
22/02   propeller installed, instruments removed
23/02   Undercarriage check; not in order. Radio equipment removed.
24/02   undercarriage checks; radio equipment removed
25/02   undercarriage switch replaced
26/02   New undercarriage switch installed. Undercarriage check with engine running.
27/02   test flights; ground run and test flight satisfactory
28/02   water leak; engine replaced
01/03   engine change
02/03   engine change
04/03   engine change
05/03   Engine change complete. Test flight satisfactory.
07/03   guns calibrated and test-fired
08/03   practice flight; operational sortie to Cordoba
09/03   practice flight
12/03   practice flights and formation exercises
14/03   first *Kette* of Bf 109s (6 ● 1, 6 ● 3, and 6 ● 4) flew to Almorox

Operated by 2.J/88. Summer 1937: forced landing in northern Spain with 2.J/88. New oil tank installed by time of forced landing. Subsequent fate not known.

15/03/1937   uncrated and undercarriage installed
16/03   preparations for fitting of wings
18/03   installation of tail section
19/03   installation of tail section; oil tank removed
20/03   installation of propeller; brake fluid filled
21/03   Installation of propeller and tail section complete. Undercarriage checks; in order.
22/03   port wing fitted and lines connected
23/03   Connection of lines complete; shock struts filled with fluid. Ready for checks.
24/03   acceptance test flights
25/03   test flight complaints remedied
26/03   Practice flights. Guns calibrated and test-fired. Undercarriage failed to lock during test flight; is being repaired.
27/03   practice flights; undercarriage latch repaired
29/03   practice flights and *Kette* formation exercises; fuselage fairing panels put in order
30/03   Practice flights. Blanking plug lost from engine. Tailwheel cover changed.
31/03   flown to Vitoria

Operated by 2.J/88. Summer 1937: undercarriage failure; aircraft written off and used as source of spares.

16/03/1937   uncrated and undercarriage installed
18/03   leading edge slats removed and preparations made for modification as per directive from Berlin
19/03   Magdeburg engine removed, since the Magdeburg engines are said to be more susceptible to the problems discovered in Germany
20/03   engine change and modification of leading-edge slats as per directive from Berlin
21/03   engine change
22/03   engine change
23/03   engine change; leading-edge slat modification
24/03   Ground test run satisfactory. Bosch horn sounded during test flight and the ??? is not in order; are being checked.
25/03   engine change and trim mechanism leading-edge slat modification
26/03   engine installation; oil intake fitting on oil tank modified; installation of tail section
27/03   engine and oil tank installation
29/03   radiator fairing sealed with rubber; brakes checked
30/03   canopy replaced and adjusted; installation of port wing root complete
31/03   modification of correction rod; wing, fuselage, and tail fairings installed
01/04   shock struts filled with fluid, idle set, tailwheel locking pump repaired
02/04   radiator flap repaired; boost pressure adjusted
03/04   calibration and test firing of guns; radiator flap hinge repaired
04/04   engine adjusted, leading-edge slats made usable
05/04   Practice flights. Complaints resulting from flight tests remedied.
06/04   port wing removed, two new strengthened nuts for shock struts fitted
07/04   test flight and flown to Vitoria

Operated by 2.J/88. Wrecked in crash in summer 1938 while being flown by 3.J/88.

29/03/1937   uncrated and undercarriage fitted; engine replaced (Magdeburg engine)
30/03   engine change
31/03   engine change and tail section assembly
01/04   engine change, oil tank removed, tail section installation complete
02/04   wing installation, engine installation complete, mounting of propeller

03/04   installation of new oil tank, lines connected, brake and undercarriage fluid filled
04/04   installation of new oil tank
04/04   installation of new oil tank
05/04   installation of the new oil tank; control box installed
06/04   Installation of new oil tank complete. Supercharger control rod adjusted.
07/04   complaints resulting from check of oil tank rectified
08/04   complaints resulting from check of oil tank rectified
09/04   Shock strut nuts replaced. Complaints resulting from check of oil tank rectified.
10/04   shock strut nuts replaced; oil tank complaints remedied
12/04   check complaints remedied
13/07   assembly complete; engine test run satisfactory
14/07   test firing and calibration of guns
15/04   ready for flight testing
16/04   undercarriage checks; repair of radiator flap actuator rod
17/04   undercarriage complaint addressed; ready for flight testing
18/04   flown to Vitoria

September 1937: forced landing at Santander due to contaminated fuel. Subsequent fate is not known.

6 ● 8

06/03/1937   Crate unloaded from ship, transported to Tablada for uncrating
09/03   uncrated; undercarriage installed
10/03   installation of wings, tail section, and propeller
11/03   assembly complete; preparations for engine ground run
12/03   ready for engine run
13/03   ready for engine run
14/03   checks; ready for ground run
15/03   control complaints addressed; preparations for test run
16/03   repair of coolant indicator device
18/03   High-altitude throttle-actuating rod modified; machine guns calibrated and test-fired. Engine ground run, ready for acceptance flight trials.
19/03   practice flights
20/03   Practice flights. Water pump not in order, is being replaced with new one.
21/03   water pump installed
22/03   practice flights
23/03   Practice flights. Boost pressure gauge removed, new fuel trap installed.

24/03   Practice flights. During air raid alert, took off and flew toward Cordoba; no enemy contact. Engine change and wing modification.
25/03   starboard machine gun fired continuously; breech block replaced
26/03   practice flights
29/03   Practice flights and *Kette* formation exercises. Oil tank cap modified.
30/03   Practice flights. Flown to Vitoria.

Operated by 2.J/88. Summer 1937: written off in crash in northern Spain.

6 ● 9

22/03   uncrated and undercarriage installed
24/03   starboard wing installed, oil tank removed, and oil tank mount modified
25/03   oil intake fitting modified, oil tank installed, and tail section installed
26/03   port wing installed and lines connected
27/03   assembly complete; clear for ground test run
29/03   tailwheel changed, radiator fairing sealed with rubber, and control complaints remedied
30/03   Port undercarriage leg put in order. Undercarriage position indicator repaired.
31/03   complaints resulting from test flight remedied
01/04   threaded caps for cannon connection made
02/04   spark plug change, oil pressure adjusted
03/04   Practice flight and scramble in direction of Malaga with no enemy contact. Fuel pump sealed, oil outlet thermometer replaced.
04/04   flown to Vitoria

Operated by 2.J/88, subsequent fate not known.

6 ● 10

29/03/1937   uncrated and undercarriage fitted; engine replaced (Magdeburg engine)
30/03   engine change
31/03   engine change and installation of tail section
01/04   engine change, oil tank removed, starboard wing fitted
02/04   starboard wing mounted, oil tank installation (new model)
03/04   installation of new oil tank, tail section adjusted, rubber seal fitted to radiator flap
04/04   installation of new oil tank
05/04   installation of new oil tank
06/04   installation of the new oil tank; control box installed
07/04   oil tank installation
08/04   oil tank installation

09/04	oil tank installation
10/04	oil tank installation
12/04	oil tank installation
13/04	oil tank installation
14/04	oil tank installation
15/04	oil tank installation complete; ready for test flight
16/04	ready for ground test run
17/04	guns adjusted and tested
18/04	preparations for installation of canopy
19/04	Assembly of pilot's canopy. Shock strut nuts replaced with nuts of a new type.
20/04	complaints resulting from checks addressed
21/04	undercarriage checks; ready for test flight
22/04	ready for test flight
23/04	preflight complaints addressed; ready to fly
24/04	ready to fly
25/04	ready to fly
26/04	ready to fly
27/04	ready to fly
28/04	ready to fly
29/04	flown to Vitoria

Delivered to 2.J/88 and flown by Lützow. Fifteen victory bars on tail by summer 1938. Aircraft brought up to Bf 109 B standard with updated cowling, windscreen, wings, and oil cooler. Transferred to Spanish air force in late 1938.

6 ● 11

23/03/1937	uncrated and undercarriage installed
24/03	starboard wing installed, oil tank removed, and oil tank mount modified
27/03	Oil tank and port wing fitted; lines connected. Assembly complete; clear for ground test run.
29/03	test flight
30/03	Practice flights. Idle adjusted, guns calibrated and test-fired. Flown to Vitoria.

Operated by 2.J/88. Summer 1937: overturned on landing. Subsequent fate not known.

6 ● 12 (*Werknummer* 1005)

06/03/1937	Crate unloaded from ship, transported to Tablada for uncrating
07/03	uncrated; undercarriage installed
09/03	wing installation complete; preparations for test run
10/13	checks
11/03	checks
12/03	ready for engine run
13/03	insufficient oil pressure

14/03	checks; check valve in the oil pump pressure line widened because spring loading is too high, resulting in insufficient oil pressure
15/03	ground run, calibration of guns, ready for acceptance flight testing
16/03	Test flights. No power to electrical system during acceptance flights. Is being investigated and repaired.
19/03	practice flights
20/03	Practice flights. Flown to Almorox.

Operated by 2.J/88; fate not known.

6 ● 13 (*Werknummer* 1006)

06/03/1937	crate unloaded from ship, transported to Tablada for uncrating
07/03	uncrated; undercarriage installed
09/03	Assembly complete. Test run; satisfactory.
10/03	machine guns cleaned, ready for test flight
11/03	ready for test flight
12/03	ready for test flight
13/03	test firing of gun.
14/03	undercarriage safety switch not in order; is being seen to
15/03	flown to Almorox

Operated by 2.J/88; fate not known

6 ● 14

15/03/1937	uncrated and undercarriage installed
16/03	preparations for fitting of wings
18/03	canopy installed
19/03	installation of tail section
20/03	oil tank removed, installation of tail section complete, brake fluid filled
21/03	installation of oil tank complete; wings being mounted
22/03	lines connected and control complaints addressed
23/03	Ground run, satisfactory. Undercarriage switch being examined.
24/03	Acceptance test flights. Assembly complete. Ground run in order. Calibration and test firing; test flight satisfactory.
25/03	Practice flights. Jam in starboard machine gun remedied.
26/03	filler cap modified, fuselage fairing repaired
27/03	undercarriage and fuselage fairings put in order
29/03	practice flights and *Kette* formation exercises

30/03   Practice flights. Port undercarriage leg collapsed on landing; aileron, flap, and wingtip damaged (port wing); under repair. Eye of the undercarriage retraction cylinder's piston rod sheared off.

31/03   aileron, flap, and wingtip on port wing repaired and undercarriage cylinder piston rod replaced

01/04   aileron, flap, and wingtip on port wing repaired

02/04   undercarriage cylinder, landing flaps, and ailerons repaired; airspeed indicator nozzle replaced

03/04   landing flap, aileron, wingtip, and piston rod on undercarriage cylinder repaired

04/04   installation of new oil tank

05/04   installation of new oil tank; repair of wingtip, aileron, landing flap, and undercarriage cylinder fork head

06/04   port wing aileron, landing flap, wingtip, and undercarriage cylinder fork piece repaired

07/04   installation of new oil tank and replacement of shock strut nuts

08/04   oil tank installation and aileron repair

09/04   landing flap repair complete; oil tank installation

10/04   ready for engine ground run

12/04   check complaints remedied

13/04   check complaints remedied; ready for flight tests

14/04   test flight satisfactory

15/04   cracked weld on oil suction stub; being repaired

16/04   Defective new oil tank replaced. Flown to Vitoria.

Operated by 2.J/88; fate not known

6 ● 15 (*Werknummer* 1000)

06/03/1937   crate unloaded from ship, transported to Tablada for uncrating

08/03   uncrated; undercarriage installed

09/03   installation of undercarriage and wings

10/03   installation of tail section and propeller

12/03   complete except for installation of propeller

13/03   ready for engine ground run

14/03   modification of the oil tank connection piece

15/03   modification of the oil tank

16/03   installation of oil tank

17/03   Oil tank installation complete; oil hold pressure valve removed and brake fluid filled. Ready for ground test run.

18/03   pump is not drawing any oil from tank; is being repaired

19/03   ground run satisfactory; calibration and test firing

20/03   Test flight. No indication from port undercarriage position indicator during test flight; being checked.

21/03   undercarriage checks; in order

22/03   practice flights

23/03   practice flights

24/03   flown to Almorox

04/12   Operated by 2.J/88 and later by 1.J/88. On December 4, 1937, aircraft made a forced landing while being flown by Polenz. Captured by Republicans and sent to France and then the Soviet Union.

6 ● 16

23/03/1937   uncrated and undercarriage fitted

30/03   starboard wing root and tail section installation complete

31/03   oil tank removed (new model installed)

01/04   left wing installed; oil tank installation (new model)

02/04   oil tank installation (new model)

03/04   installation of new oil tank; engine control complaints remedied

04/04   installation of new oil tank

05/04   installation of new oil tank

06/04   installation of new oil tank complete

07/04   Installation of new oil tank complete. Fuselage fairing panels installed.

08/04   Test flight. Complaints resulting from test flight remedied.

09/04   complaints from test flights remedied; calibration and test firing of guns

10/04   Test flight. Test flight satisfactory; cleared to fly.

12/04   engine checks

13/04   test flight; satisfactory

14/04   cleared to fly

15/04   cleared to fly

16/04   flown to Vitoria

Served with all three *Staffeln* of J/88 at various times; survived to be handed over to Spanish air force.

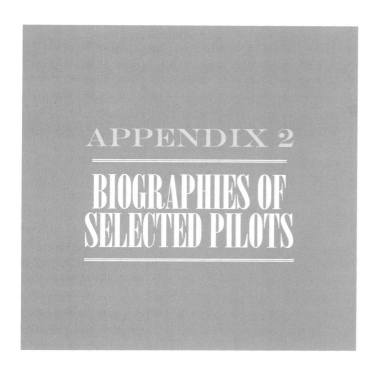

Balthasar, Wilhelm: Born in Bochum on July 19, 1912, Balthasar joined the *Luftwaffe* in 1935. In November 1936, he was sent to Spain, where he took over K/88's reconnaissance flight. Balthasar was an observer (aircraft commander) with limited flying experience, but despite this he bluffed his way into becoming the pilot of the He 112 V4 and ultimately was assigned to J/88. Balthasar shot down seven enemy aircraft in Spain and returned to Germany on March 23, 1938. He became *Staffelkapitän* of 1./JG 1 (later 7./JG 27) and emerged from the battle against France as the campaign's leading scorer, with twenty-three enemy aircraft destroyed in the air and fourteen on the ground. He was the second German fighter pilot after Werner Mölders to be awarded the Knight's Cross. Balthasar became *Kommandeur* of III./JG 3 on August 26, 1940, and on September 4, he was seriously wounded. He was flying again fourteen days later, before his wounds had completely healed, and he scored five more victories before returning to hospital in November. After his wounds had finally healed, on February 16, 1941, he assumed command of JG 2 *Richthofen*. Balthasar increased his victory total to forty by June 27, 1941, and was awarded the Knight's Cross with Oak Leaves. He was killed on July 3, 1941 near Aire, France. While diving away from a Spitfire, a wing came off his Bf 109 F and he died in the ensuing crash. Balthasar was buried in a World War I cemetery in Flanders next to his father, who had been killed in action in the First World War.

Bertram, Otto: Born in Wilhelmshaven on April 30, 1916, Bertram joined the *Luftwaffe* in 1935, and subsequently served with the Legion Condor in Spain. He scored nine victories there, making him one of the J/88's most successful pilots. He was shot down and captured on October 4, 1938. On October 26, 1939, he became *Staffelkapitän* of 1./JG 2 and ended the campaign against France with four victories. Bertram was named *Kommandeur* of III./JG 2 on September 24, 1940, but on October 28 he was taken out of action as the last surviving son, his brothers Hans and Kurt, both fighter pilots, having been killed over England. He subsequently held staff positions and commanded training units. When the war ended Betram was *Kommandeur* of I./JG 6. He died in Freiburg on February 8, 1987.

Fözö, Josef: Born in Vienna on November 7, 1912, "Joschko" was one of the Austrian fighter pilots who joined the *Luftwaffe* in 1938. He flew 138 combat sorties in Spain, scoring three victories. Fözö took over 2./JG 71 (later 4./JG 51) on July 16, 1939. On February 21, 1941, he became *Kommandeur* of II./JG 51 and by the time the war against the Soviet Union began he had claimed fifteen victories. He was awarded the Knight's Cross after his twenty-second victory. He claimed his twenty-fourth on July 11, 1941, but that same day he crashed while taking off from Stary Bykov and was seriously injured. He returned to action on May 3, 1942, and became *Kommandeur* of I./JG 51. On May 31, his aircraft overturned while landing and he was again badly injured. After recovering from his injuries Fözö took over JG 108, a fighter training unit, and led it until January 10, 1945. He died in Vienna on March 4, 1979. Fözö was credited with twenty-seven victories, including three in Spain, fifteen over the Western Front, and nine over the Eastern Front.

Fleischmann, Georg: born in Wörth/Donau on January 24, 1914. Fleischmann served with the Legion Condor during the Spanish Civil War, scoring three victories with 3.J/88. After returning to Germany he joined 3./ZG 76, flying the Bf 110. Fleischmann scored five victories after the outbreak of the Second World War. On April 30, 1940, while attacking RAF Wellingtons, twelve miles west of Stavanger, Norway his Bf 110 was damaged by return fire from the bombers. The aircraft went down 1.2 miles southeast of Stavanger-Sola while attempting to land. *Oberfeldwebel* Fleischmann and his radio operator *Obergefreiter* Hans-Dietrich Mierke were both killed in the crash.

Grabmann, Walter: Born in Bad Reichenhall on September 20, 1905. Grabmann received flight training while a member of the police, and in 1934, he joined the new *Luftwaffe*. He commanded I.(*schw.Jagd*)/LG 1 during the Polish Campaign. He was named *Kommodore* of ZG 76 on May 1, 1940. On May 18, during the Battle of France, he was shot down and captured; however, Grabmann spend just a week as a POW before he was freed by German troops. He subsequently led his *Geschwader* in operations against Great Britain and on September 2, 1940, he shot down two Spitfires, his last two victories. In spring 1941, he and his *Geschwaderstab* went to Norway, where he simultaneously filled the post of Commander of Fighters. Grabmann ultimately held commands in the Defense of the Reich, which caused some controversy. Initially, he was the Commander of Fighters Holland, then from November 7, 1943, commander of the 3rd Fighter Division, and in April 1945, he was made commander of the 1st Fighter Division. Taken prisoner at the end of the war, *Generalmajor* Grabmann was repatriated to Germany in May 1948. Walter Grabmann died in Munich on August 20, 1992.

Handrick, Gotthard: Born October 25, 1908, Handrick joined the *Reichswehr* in 1929. He won a gold medal in the Modern Pentathlon at the 1936 Olympic Games in Berlin. He joined the *Luftwaffe* and became a fighter pilot, subsequently serving with the Legion Condor in Spain, where he shot down five Republican aircraft. He commanded *Jagdgruppe* 88 from July 18, 1937 until September 10, 1938. Handrick returned to Germany, where he took command of I./JG 26 (May 1, 1939 to June 21, 1940). He became *Geschwaderkommodore* on June 26, 1940, a post he held until August 22, when he was replaced by *Major* Adolf Galland. Subsequent commands included *Ergänzungsjagd-gruppe* 2, I./JG 28 and, in June 1941, JG 77. In May 1942, he was transferred to Norway to command JG 5. Then from June 1943 to June 1944, he was *Jagdfliegerführer Ostmark*, holding the rank of *Oberst*. He then became commanding officer of 8. *Jagddivision* in Austria, a post he held until the end of the war. After the war he worked as a representative of Daimler-Benz in Hamburg. Handrick died on May 30, 1978.

Harder, Harro: Born in Freiburg on November 28, 1912. Harder saw his first action in Spain with 1.J/88 and eventually scored eleven kills there, making him the Legion's top scorer at that time. He led 1.(J)/LG 2 in the campaign against Poland, scoring one victory. On July 13, 1940, Harder was appointed *Gruppenkommandeur* of III./JG 53, replacing *Major* Werner Mölders. On August 12, 1940, he shot down two Spitfires to raise his victory total to twenty-two, however he failed to return from this combat and his body was washed ashore near Dieppe on September 13.

Lützow, Günther: Born in the Donauwörth area of Swabia on September 4, 1912. Oesau joined the German School for Commercial Aviation Schleißheim (DVS) in 1931, and received fighter training at Lipetsk in the Soviet Union. He served in Spain with 2.J/88 and scored five victories there, including the first by the pilot of a Bf 109. On November 5, 1939, he was named *Kommandeur* of I./JG 3 and on August 21, 1940, he became *Kommodore* of JG 3. Lützow's unit took part in the fighting in Russia and he quickly added to his victory total, becoming the second German fighter pilot to reach 100 victories. He gave up command of the *Geschwader* on August 11, 1942, and became Inspector of Day Fighters West in the staff of the *General der Jagdflieger*. His outspoken criticism of the *Luftwaffe*'s leadership resulted in Lützow being sent to northern Italy. In March 1945, Galland convinced him to join JV 44, his Me 262 unit. Lützow shot down two enemy aircraft flying the Me 262, but on April 24, 1945, he failed to return from a mission and has been listed as missing since.

Mölders, Werner: Born March 18, 1913, in Gelsenkirchen, Mölders joined the still-secret *Luftwaffe* in 1934. On May 24, 1938, he succeeded Adolf Galland as commander of 3.J/88 in Spain. Mölders rose to become the Legion's leading scorer with fourteen victories. After returning to Germany, on March 15, 1939, he became *Staffelkapitän* of 1./JG 53. On September 26, he took over the newly-formed III./JG 53. Mölders was shot down and captured on June 5, 1940, by which time he had twenty-five victories. He was released on June 30, and on July 20, was named *Kommodore* of JG 51. Leading his unit against the Soviet Union, Mölders raised his victory total to 101, becoming the first German fighter pilot to pass the 100 victory mark. On August 7, 1941, he was named Inspector of Fighters. Despite a ban on operational flying, while visiting fighter units on the Eastern Front he flew combat missions, and scored additional victories, which of course he could not submit for confirmation. Mölders was killed on November 22, 1941, when the He 111 flying him home to attend the funeral of Ernst Udet crashed in bad weather. JG 51 was subsequently awarded the honorary name *Jagdgeschwader Mölders*.

Oesau, Walter: Born June 28, 1913, in Farnewinkel. Oesau began his military service in the artillery but in 1934 he reported to the German School for Commercial Aviation in Schleißheim. He subsequently attended officer school and in October 1936 joined the *Jagdgeschwader Richthofen* as an *Oberfähnrich*. In April 1938, by then a *Leutnant*, Oesau went to Spain, where he flew with 3.J/88 under Werner Mölders. With ten victories he was one of the most successful German fighter pilots during the Spanish Civil War. On March 1, 1939, he joined *Stab* I./JG 2, and on July 15, 1939, by then an *Oberleutnant*, he became *Staffelkapitän* of I./JG 20 (later 7./JG 51). By the end of the campaign against France, Oesau had scored five victories. His victory tally rose steadily during the fierce fighting over Great Britain in the summer of 1940, and on August 18, he became the fifth German fighter pilot to reach twenty victories. On August 25, he was named *Kommandeur* of III./JG 51. On November 11, he became *Kommandeur* of III./JG 3 and on February 5, 1941, he shot down his fortieth enemy aircraft. His unit was part of the fighter force that took part in "Operation Barbarossa" and Oesau quickly added to his total. After his eightieth victory he was awarded the Knight's Cross with Oak Leaves and Swords, becoming its third recipient after Mölders and Galland. He returned from Russia at the end of July 1941, and became *Kommodore* of JG 2 *Richthofen*. On October 26, 1941, he became the third German fighter pilot to reach 100 victories and was grounded, however, the ban on flying was lifted in autumn 1942. On July 1, 1943, Oesau became *Jagdfliegerführer 4* Brittany and on October 10, 1943, *Kommodore* of JG 1 in the Defense of the Reich. Walter Oesau was shot down and killed southwest of St. Vith on May 11, 1944. His score at the time of his death was 127 victories, including ten in Spain, forty-four in the east, and fourteen heavy bombers.

Pingel, Rolf: Born in Kiel on October 1, 1913, Pingel joined the *Luftwaffe* in 1937 and was posted to I./JG 134. He served with the Legion Condor in Spain, scoring a total of six victories. He became *Staffelkapitän* of 2./JG 334 in October 1937, and in March 1939, the unit was renamed 2./JG 53. In August 1940, Pingel became *Gruppenkommandeur* of I./JG 26 and in September, was awarded the Knight's Cross. On September 28, he shot down a Hurricane near Maidstone but his own aircraft was damaged and he was forced to ditch off the English coast and was picked up by the German air-sea rescue service. On July 10, 1941, Pingel's aircraft was hit by return fire from a Stirling bomber he was chasing and he subsequently crash-landed near St. Margaret's Bay. His Bf 109 F-2 was recovered by the British and was flight tested until October 20, 1941, when it crashed, killing its pilot. Pingel became a POW and was released in 1947. He was credited with a total of twenty-eight victories, six in Spain, and twenty-two during the Second World War. Pingel died in Lollar on April 4, 2000, at the age of eighty-six.

Schellmann, Wolfgang: Born in Kassel on March 2, 1911. He became a fighter pilot, and in December 1937, was named *Staffelkapitän* of 1.J/88 in Spain, where he became the second highest scoring fighter pilot after Mölders. When the Second World War broke out he was attached to *Stab* I./JG 77, with which he took part in the fighting in Poland. He subsequently served in the staff of *Luftflotte 2* until December 15, 1939, when he was appointed *Kommandeur* of II./JG 2. Schellmann shot down seven enemy aircraft during the Battle of France, and on September 3, he was named *Kommodore* of JG 11 *Richthofen*. On October 20, he was transferred to KG 27 as *Kommodore*. On June 22, 1941, the first day of the war against the Soviet Union, Schellmann collided with wreckage of an I-16 he had just shot down and baled out over enemy territory. He attempted to reach the German lines but was captured and was most likely shot by the GPU on June 24. Schellmann was promoted to *Oberstleutnant* posthumously.

Schob, Herbert: Born in Leipzig on May 12, 1915, Schob became a fighter pilot in 1936, and in September 1938, joined 2.J/88 in Spain. In March 1939, he joined 1.(Z)/LG 1 flying the Bf 110 *Zerstörer* and took part in the fighting in Poland, scoring two victories. On April 17, 1940, he was transferred to 3./ZG 76 as an *Oberfeldwebel*. He was transferred to 2./ZG 26 on April 1, 1941, and subsequently took part in the Balkan and Crete campaigns. In Russia Schob was very successful, especially in attacking ground targets. On June 18, 1942, he was transferred to the *Zerstörer* Replacement Training *Gruppe* at Deblin and in October began training to become an officer. *Leutnant* Schob was placed in charge of training Bf 110 reconnaissance crews to fly in the Defense of the Reich. He joined 1./ZG 76 on August 28, 1943, and became *Staffelkapitän* in December. He scored nine victories against the American 8th Air Force, then on March 6, 1944, he was shot down and wounded by a P-51 after destroying two B-17s. He and his gunner baled out. In May 1944, he joined *Stab* ZG 76 as operations officer. Schob later spent time with the *Zerstörer* Replacement *Gruppe*, and in November 1944, was appointed operations officer with *Stab* JG 300. He died in Frankfurt/Main on April 5, 1981.

Scholz, Günther: Born on December 8, 1911, Scholz served under Werner Mölders in 3.J/88 during the Spanish Civil War. Scholz took part in the war against Poland and the Battle of France as a member of 1./JG 21. He became *Staffelkapitän* on May 20, 1940. On July 15, 1940, 1./JG 21 became 7./JG 54. Scholz remained with the unit as *Staffelkapitän*, seeing action in Russia after the start of "Operation Barbarossa." From January to March 1941, Scholz was *Gruppenkommandeur* of IV./JG 1. On March 21, 1942, IV./JG 1 was renamed III./JG 5 and attached to JG 5 in Norway as its third *Gruppe*. Scholz was made *Kommandeur* of III./JG 5 and held that position until June of 1943, when he was made *Geschwaderkommodore* of JG 5. From February until May 8, 1945, he held the post of *Jagdfliegerführer Norwegen*. Scholz scored a total of thirty-three victories and was never awarded the Knight's Cross. He died on October 24, 2014, and was the last surviving fighter pilot to have served in Spain with the *Legion Condor*.

Seiler, Reinhard: Born August 30, 1909, in Rawitsch, Seiler joined the *Reichswehr* as a career soldier in 1929. In 1935 he moved to the *Luftwaffe* and was trained as a fighter pilot. He went to Spain, where he shot down nine enemy aircraft. On September 13, 1939, Seiler became *Staffelkapitän* of 1./JG 54. He was wounded in combat over the Channel on August 5, 1940, after shooting down a Spitfire, and it was not until June 28, 1941, that he again took command of his unit. Seiler was very successful in Russia, raising his victory total to eighty-two by the end of 1942. In 1943, his unit was transferred to the Defense of the Reich, and in April he shot down a B-17. In May, he was sent back to the Eastern Front, where he took over I./JG 54. On July 6, 1943, Seiler scored his ninety-eighth to one-hundredth victories, but that same day he was himself wounded and forced to abandon his Fw 190. He was found to be unfit for combat duty, and in April 1944, he joined JG 104, and on August 8, became the unit's commander. Seiler was credited with 109 victories, including nine in Spain. He died on October 6, 1989.

Tietzen, Horst: Born on July 19, 1912, in Neu-Ostwalter. "Jakob" Tietzen flew with 1.J/88 in Spain until March 1939, scoring seven victories there. In mid-August 1939, he became *Staffelkapitän* of of 5./JG 51. He was one of the leading aces during the German air offensive against Britain, on August 18, 1940, becoming the fourth German pilot to reach twenty victories. That same day, however, he was shot down by RAF fighters over the Thames Estuary. His body was later found near Calais. Tietzen scored a total of twenty-seven victories, including seven in Spain.

Trautloft, Hannes: Born in Groß-Obringen near Weimar on March 3, 1912. Trautloft trained at the German School for Commercial Aviation Schleißheim (DVS) and spent four months at the secret training base at Lipetsk in the Soviet Union in 1932. He subsequently joined the army and in 1934, arrived at the fighter school in Schleißheim as a *Leutnant*. Trautloft went to Spain in July 1936, and scored five victories there [flying the He 51] before returning to Germany. He held a number of commands, finally taking over 2./JG 77 just before war broke out. Trautloft led the unit during the war with Poland, scoring one victory. On September 22, 1939, he assumed command of I./JG 20 (later III./JG 51) and led it through the fighting in France and over Great Britain until, on August 25, 1940, he was named *Kommodore* of JG 54. He led the *Geschwader* over England, the Balkans, and against Russia until July 6, 1943. Trautloft subsequently became the Inspector of Fighters in the east, and later was named Inspector of Day Fighters. On January 27, 1945, he was named commander of the 4. *Flieger-(Schul)-Division*, however he was relieved on April 10. Trautloft was credited with a total of fifty-eight victories. He died on January 11, 1995.

APPENDIX 3

J/88 VICTORY LIST

(FROM THE ESTATE OF GEORG FLEISCHMANN)

Via Axel Urbanke

Note: This victory list differs in some respects from the one published by Ries and Ring.

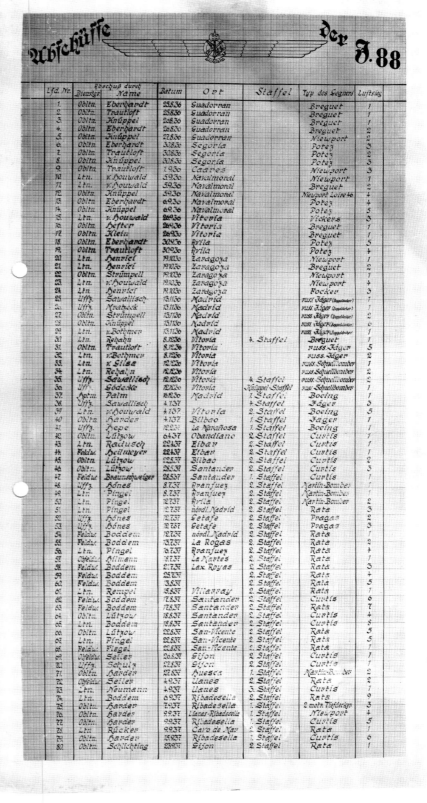

Abschüsse der J. 88

Lfd. Nr.	Abschuß durch Dienstgr.	Name	Datum	Ort	Staffel	Typ des Gegners	Luftsieg
81.	Ltn.	Woltke	27.9.37	Gijon	1. Staffel	Rata	7
82.	Obltn.	Harder	27.9.37	Gijon	1. Staffel	Rata	8
83.	Obltn.	Harder	27.9.37	Gijon	1. Staffel	Rata	0
84.	Obltn.	Harder	28.9.37	Gijon	1. Staffel	Rata	9
85.	Ltn.	Woltke	30.9.37	Gijon	1. Staffel	Rata	2
86.	Obltn.	Harder	7.10.37	Gijon-Aviles	1. Staffel	Curtis	10
87.	Obfeldw.	Stegmund	7.10.37	Aviles	1. Staffel	Curtis	1
88.	Obltn.	Schlichting	29.11.37	Alcala de Henares	2. Staffel	Rata	2
89.	Uffz.	Rochel	29.11.37	Alcala de Henares	2. Staffel	Rata	1
90.	Obfeldw.	Seiler	29.11.37	Alcala de Henares	2. Staffel	Rata	3
91.	Ltn.	Gneisert	30.11.37	Alcala de Henares	2. Staffel	Rata	1
92.	Uffz.	Stange	30.11.37	Alcala de Henares	2. Staffel	Rata	1
93.	Uffz.	Staege	30.11.37	Alcala de Henares	2. Staffel	Rata	1
94.	Hptm.	Harder	5.12.37	Bujaraloz	1. Staffel	Curtis	11
95.	Ltn.	Adolph	30.12.37	Teruel	1. Staffel	Curtis	1
96.	Obfeldw.	Prestele	30.12.37	Teruel	1. Staffel	Rata	1
97.	Uffz.	Terry	30.12.37	Rubiales	1. Staffel	Curtis	1
98.	Obfeldw.	Prestele	5.1.38	Teruel	1. Staffel	Rata	2
99.	Obfeldw.	Seiler	7.2.38	Teruel	2. Staffel	Martin-Bomber	4
100.	Uffz.	Staege	7.2.38	Rubielos de la Cerida	2. Staffel	Martin-Bomber	2
101.	Obltn.	Schellmann	18.1.38	Teruel	1. Staffel	Rata	1
102.	Ltn.	Woltke	18.1.38	Teruel	1. Staffel	Rata	3
103.	Obltn.	Balthasar	20.1.38	La Puebla de Valverde	1. Staffel	Rata	1
104.	Uffz.	Rochel	20.1.38	Cordaian	2. Staffel	Curtis	2
105.	Obfeldw.	Seiler	22.1.38	Rio de Va	2. Staffel	Rata	5
106.	Uffz.	Lohner	5.2.38	Alfambra	2. Staffel	Rata	1
107.	Uffz.	Staege	6.2.38	Vilalba	2. Staffel	Rata	2
108.	Ltn.	Mayer	7.2.38	Sarrion	1. Staffel	Martin-Bomber	1
109.	Ltn.	Mayer	7.2.38	Sarrion	1. Staffel	Rata	2
110.	Obfeldw.	Prestele	7.2.38	Sarrion	1. Staffel	Martin-Bomber	3
111.	Obfeldw.	Seiler	7.2.38	Teruel	2. Staffel	Martin-Bomber	0
112.	Obfeldw.	Seiler	7.2.38	Teruel	1. Staffel	Martin-Bomber	7
113.	Uffz.	Quasinowski	7.2.38	Teruel	1. Staffel	Martin-Bomber	2
114.	Uffz.	Terry	7.2.38	Sarrion	1. Staffel	Martin-Bomber	2
115.	Obltn.	Schlichting	7.2.38	Pueblo de Castrelo	2. Staffel	Rata	3
116.	Obltn.	Balthasar	7.2.38	Teruel	2. Staffel	Martin-Bomber	2
117.	Obltn.	Balthasar	7.2.38	Teruel	2. Staffel	Martin-Bomber	3
118.	Obltn.	Balthasar	7.2.38	Teruel	2. Staffel	Martin-Bomber	4
119.	Obltn.	Balthasar	7.2.38	Terua	2. Staffel	Martin-Bomber	5
120.	Uffz.	Staege	19.2.38	Sarrion	1. Staffel	Curtis	3
121.	Ltn.	Rue	21.2.38	La Puebla	1. Staffel	Rata	1
122.	Ltn.	Mayen	21.2.38	La Puebla	1. Staffel	Rata	3
123.	Ltn.	Woltke	21.2.38	La Puebla	1. Staffel	Rata	4
124.	Obltn.	Schlichting	21.2.38	Sarrion	2. Staffel	Rata	4
125.	Ltn.	Rempel	21.2.38	Sarrion	2. Staffel	Rata	2
126.	Uffz.	Ihlefeld	21.2.38	La Puebla-Sarrion	2. Staffel	Rata	1
127.	Uffz.	Rochel	21.2.38	Teruel	2. Staffel	Rata	3
128.	Ltn.	Seilen	22.2.38	Sarrion	2. Staffel	Curtis	8
129.	Ltn.	Seiler	22.2.38	Teruel	2. Staffel	Curtis	9
130.	Obltn.	Schellmann	8.3.38	Hijar	1. Staffel	Curtis	2
131.	Ltn.	Rue	8.3.38	Hijar	1. Staffel	Curtis	2
132.	Obfeldw.	Prestele	10.3.38	Jattel	1. Staffel	Curtis	4
133.	Uffz.	Rochel	10.3.38	Caspe	2. Staffel	Rata	4
134.	Obltn.	Schlichting	10.3.38	Alcaniz	2. Staffel	Rata	5
135.	Ltn.	Ettling	13.3.38	Caspe	2. Staffel	Curtis	1
136.	Uffz.	Ihlefeld	13.3.38	Caspe	2. Staffel	Curtis	2
137.	Ltn.	Rue	24.3.38	la Almoda	1. Staffel	Curtis	3
138.	Obltn.	Schellmann	24.3.38	Quinto	1. Staffel	Curtis	3
139.	Uffz.	Stark	24.3.38	Gelsa	1. Staffel	Curtis	1
140.	Ltn.	Mayen	29.3.38	Lerida	1. Staffel	Curtis	4
141.	Uffz.	Ihlefeld	11.5.38	Sagunto	2. Staffel	Rata	3
142.	Ltn.	Priebe	14.5.38	Sagunto	2. Staffel	Rata	1
143.	Uffz.	Rochel	18.5.38	Castellon	2. Staffel	Rata	5
144.	Hptm.	Hermann	18.5.38		St. J. 88		1
145.	Ltn.	Heinrich	2.6.38	Engarcenan	2. Staffel	Martin-Bomber	1
146.	Ltn.	Heinrich	2.6.38	Villafamés	2. Staffel	Martin-Bomber	2
147.	Ltn.	Heinrich	2.6.38	Costur	2. Staffel	Martin-Bomber	3
148.	Uffz.	Meyer	2.6.38	Riboccacen	2. Staffel	Martin-Bomber	1
149.	Uffz.	Ihlefeld	2.6.38	Cati-Tinig	2. Staffel	Martin-Bomber	1
150.	Uffz.	Seufert	10.6.38	Oropesa	2. Staffel	Rata	1
151.	Uffz.	Rochel	10.6.38	Villar de Canes	2. Staffel	Rata	6
152.	Ltn.	Mayen	10.6.38	Tales	2. Staffel	Martin-Bomber	5
153.	Ltn.	Neumann	11.6.38		St. J. 88		2
154.	Uffz.	Staege	13.6.38	Sagunto	2. Staffel	Curtis	3
155.	Uffz.	Seufert	13.6.38	Coult de Berenques	2. Staffel	Curtis	2
156.	Ltn.	Ewald	13.6.38	Sagunto	2. Staffel	Rata	1
157.	Ltn.	Keller	13.6.38	Sagunto	1. Staffel	Curtis	4
158.	Obltn.	Schellmann	30.6.38	Castellon	1. Staffel	Rata	5
159.	Obltn.	Schellmann	25.6.38	Vall de Uxo	1. Staffel	Rata	5
160.							

Abſchüſſe der J. 88

Lfd. Nr.	Abschuß durch Dienstgr.	Name	Datum	Ort	Staffel	Typ des Gegners	Luftsieg
161	Uffz.	Kuhlmann	13.6.38	Sagunto	1.Staffel	Curtis	1
162	Feldw.	Kuhlmann	14.6.38	Sagunto	1.Staffel	Curtis	2
163	Ltn.	Keidel	12.7.38	Sagunto	2.Staffel	Curtis	1
164	Feldw.	Ihlefeld	12.7.38	Sagunto-Valencia	2.Staffel	Curtis	5
165	Ltn.	Oesau	13.7.38	Sagunto-Valencia	St.J.88	Curtis	1
166	Feldw.	Ihlefeld	13.7.38	Navajas	2.Staffel	Curtis	6
167	Feldw.	Ihlefeld	13.7.38	Navajas	2.Staffel	Curtis	7
168	Ltn.	Lippert	13.7.38	Viver	3.Staffel	Curtis	1
169	Obltn.	Müller	13.7.38	Segorbe	1.Staffel	Curtis	1
170	Ltn.	Keller	15.7.38	Segorbe	1.Staffel	Curtis	2
171	Feldw.	Kuhlmann	15.7.38	Segorbe	1.Staffel	Curtis	3
172	Uffz.	Quasinowsky	15.7.38	Segorbe	1.Staffel	Curtis	2
173	Obltn.	Nöldens	15.7.38	Rigau	3.Staffel	Curtis	1
174	Obltn.	Nöldens	17.7.38	Liria	3.Staffel	Curtis	2
175	Uffz.	Bauer	17.7.38	Segorbe	3.Staffel	Curtis	1
176	Uffz.	Bauer	17.7.38	Nardines	3.Staffel	Curtis	2
177	Ltn.	Resch	17.7.38	Segorbe	2.Staffel	Curtis	1
178	Ltn.	Oesau	17.7.38	Segorbe	St.J.88	Curtis	2
179	Uffz.	Quasinowsky	17.7.38	Segorbe	1.Staffel	Curtis	3
180	Ltn.	Oesau	18.7.38	Segorbe	St.J.88	Rata	3
181	Uffz.	Quasinowsky	18.7.38	Segorbe	1.Staffel	Rata	4
182	Obltn.	Schellmann	18.7.38	Segorbe	1.Staffel	Rata	6
183	Ltn.	Tietzen	19.7.38	Milan del Republico	3.Staffel	Rata	1
184	Obltn.	Nöldens	19.7.38	Milan del Republico	3.Staffel	Rata	3
185	Obgefr.	Hien	19.7.38	Liria	3.Staffel	Rata	1
186	Ltn.	Ebbighausen	19.7.38	Andilla	3.Staffel	Rata	1
187	Obltn.	Schellmann	20.7.38	Segorbe	1.Staffel	Rata	7
188	Obltn.	Schellmann	20.7.38	Segorbe	1.Staffel	Rata	8
189	Uffz.	Brucks	20.7.38	Segorbe	1.Staffel	Rata	1
190	Feldw.	Menge	23.7.38	Liria	1.Staffel	Rata	2
191	Ltn.	Lippert	23.7.38	Liria	3.Staffel	Rata	1
192	Uffz.	Jaenisch	1.8.38	Flix	3.Staffel	Curtis	1
193	Uffz.	Bauer	1.8.38	Ribarroja	3.Staffel	Curtis	3
194	Obltn.	Ebbighausen	1.8.38	Flix	3.Staffel	Curtis	2
195	Obltn.	Knoeck	2.8.38	Ginestar	2.Staffel	Rata	1
196	Uffz.	Brucks	12.8.38	Vinebre	1.Staffel	Martin-Bomber	2
197	Hptm.	Schellmann	12.8.38	Vinebre	1.Staffel	Martin-Bomber	9
198	Ltn.	Bertram	12.8.38	Vinebre	1.Staffel	Rata	1
199	Ltn.	Lippert	14.8.38	Tivissa	3.Staffel	Rata	3
200	Ltn.	Bertram	14.8.38	Falset	1.Staffel	Rata	2
201	Hptm.	Schellmann	14.8.38	Falset-Tivissa	1.Staffel	Rata	10
202	Ltn.	Bertram	15.8.38	Vinebre	1.Staffel	Rata	3
203	Uffz.	Kuell	15.8.38	Einbruchsraum	2.Staffel	Curtis	1
204	Uffz.	Kuell	19.8.38	Einbruchsraum	2.Staffel	Rata	2
205	Obltn.	Keller	19.8.38	Flix	1.Staffel	Rata	3
206	Obltn.	Nöldens	19.8.38	Flix	3.Staffel	Rata	1
207	Ltn.	Scholz	19.8.38	Flix	3.Staffel	Rata	11
208	Hptm.	Schellmann	20.8.38	Venta de Camposines	1.Staffel	Rata	11
209	Ltn.	Oesau	20.8.38	Venta de Camposines	St.J.88	Rata	4
210	Ltn.	Bertram	23.8.38	Flix	1.Staffel	Rata	4
211	Obltn.	Müller	23.8.38	Flix	1.Staffel	Rata	5
212	Obltn.	Nöldens	9.9.38	Villalba	3.Staffel	Rata	3
213	Obltn.	Nöldens	13.9.38	Flix	3.Staffel	Rata	1
214	Uffz.	Szuggar	14.8.38	Falset	1.Staffel	Rata	1
215	Uffz.	Hien	14.8.38	Falset	3.Staffel	Rata	2
216	Ltn.	Ensslen	5.9.38	Falset	2.Staffel	Curtis	1
217	Ltn.	Ensslen	20.9.38	Flix	2.Staffel	Rata	1
218	Hptm.	Grabmann	22.9.38	Flix-Fayon	Kdr.J.88	Martin-Bomber	1
219	Obltn.	Nöldens	23.9.38	Sierra de Balaguer	3.Staffel	Rata	7
220	Uffz.	Menz	23.9.38	Sierra de Balaguer	3.Staffel	Rata	1
221	Uffz.	Schob	24.9.38	Gandesa	2.Staffel	Rata	1
222	Ltn.	Bertram	22.9.38	Nora de Ebro	1.Staffel	Rata	5
223	Obltn.	Unger	22.9.38	Nora de Ebro	1.Staffel	Rata	1
224	Ltn.	Tietzen	22.9.38	Nora de Ebro	1.Staffel	Rata	2
225	Ltn.	Tietzen	1.9.38	Nora de Ebro	1.Staffel	Curtis	3
226	Ltn.	Bertam	4.10.38	Falset	1.Staffel	Curtis	6
227	Ltn.	Lippert	4.10.38	Ninaret	1.Staffel	Rata	4
228	Uffz.	Szuggar	4.10.38	Falset	1.Staffel	Curtis	1
229	Ltn.	Ehrig	7.10.38	Nora de Ebro	1.Staffel	Rata	1
230	Feldw.	Menge	7.10.38	Nora de Ebro	1.Staffel	Rata	2
231	Hptm.	Grabmann	10.10.38	Gandesa	Kdr.J.88	Martin-Bomber	2
232	Obltn.	Nöldens	10.10.38	Flix	3.Staffel	Rata	8
233	Obltn.	Semmingen	10.10.38	Corbera	3.Staffel	Martin-Bomber	1
234	Hptm.	Grabmann	15.10.38	Nola	Kdr.J.88	Rata	3
235	Obltn.	Nöldens	13.10.38	Nola	3.Staffel	Rata	9
236	Obltn.	Nöldens	13.10.38	Nola	3.Staffel	Rata	10
237	Ltn.	Oesau	13.10.38	Nola	St.J.88	Rata	5
238	Hptm.	Nöldens	31.10.38	Ribarroja	3.Staffel	Rata	11
239	Hptm.	Nöldens	31.10.38	Flix	3.Staffel	Rata	12
240	Ltn.	Főző	31.10.38	Ginestar	3.Staffel	Rata	1

Abſchüſſe der J. 88

Lfd. Nr.	Abſchuß durch Dienſtgr.	Name	Datum	Ort	Staffel	Typ des Gegners	Luft/weg
241	Hptm.	Schellmann	12.8.38	Vinebre	1. Staffel	Martin-Bomber	12
242	Uffz.	Hier	14.8.38	Falset	3. Staffel	Rata	3
243	Uffz.	Sauggar	14.8.38	Falset	1. Staffel	Rata	3
244	Ltn.	Oesau	13.8.38	Tivisa	Sn.St.J. 88	Curtiss	3
245	Ltn.	Ensslen	23.8.38	Balaguer	2. Staffel	Curtiss	3
246	Hptm.	Nölders	23.8.38	Ribi	3. Staffel	Martin-Bomber	13
247	Hptm.	Grabmann	23.9.38	Mora de Ebro	Sn.St.J. 88	Curtiss	1
248	Hptm.	Grabmann	23.9.38	Falset	Sn.St.J. 88	Rata	4
249	Uffz.	Braunshirn	23.9.38	Mora de Ebro	2. Staffel	Martin-Bomber	1
250	Uffz.	Schob	13.10.38	Garcia	2. Staffel	Rata	2
251	Feldw.	Fleischmann	3.10.38	Perello	3. Staffel	Rata	1
252	Feldw.	Fleischmann	3.10.38	Vinebre-Mola	3. Staffel	Rata	2
253	Ltn.	Ihrig	3.10.38	Falset	2. Staffel	Rata	1
254	Ltn.	Schumann	3.10.38	Rasquera	2. Staffel	Curtiss	1
255	Uffz.	Braunshirn	3.10.38	Miravet	2. Staffel	Curtiss	2
256	Uffz.	Kerting	3.10.38	Ribroro	3. Staffel	Rata	1
257	Feldw.	Menge	3.11.38	Falset	1. Staffel	Curtiss	1
258	Hptm.	Nölders	3.11.38	Mola	3. Staffel	Rata	14
259	Ltn.	Oesau	3.11.38	Capsanus	Sn.St.J. 88	Rata	6
260	Uffz.	Braunshirn	3.11.38	Tivisa	2. Staffel	Curtiss	3
261	Oberg'r	Freund	3.11.38	Tivisa	2. Staffel	Curtiss	1
262	Uffz.	Schob	3.11.38	Balaguer	2. Staffel	Rata	3
263	Uffz.	Närz	4.11.38	Garcia	3. Staffel	Rata	3
264	Oberfw.	Menge	5.11.38	Vals	1. Staffel	Rata	2
265	Ltn.	Bretnütz	6.11.38	Cambrils	2. Staffel	Curtiss	1
266	Uffz.	Braunshirn	6.11.38	Salou	2. Staffel	Curtiss	1
267	Uffz.	Kob	12.11.38	Granadella	1. Staffel	Rata	1
268	Feldw.	Fleischmann	12.11.38	El Mont-Sant	3. Staffel	Curtiss	3
269	Uffz.	Fischer	12.11.38	Flix	1. Staffel	Rata	1
270	Uffz.	Sauggar	12.11.38	Flix	1. Staffel	Rata	4
271	Uffz.	Schob	16.11.38	Guiamets	2. Staffel	Martin-Bomber	1
272	Ltn.	Rossiwall	2.12.38	Vals-Reus	3. Staffel	Rata	1
273	Ltn.	Tietzen	21.12.38	Vals	1. Staffel	Rata	2
274	Ltn.	Schumann	28.12.38	Nanresa	2. Staffel	Rata	1
275	Ltn.	Ensslen	28.12.38	Cervera	2. Staffel	Martin-Bomber	2
276	Feldw.	Schott	28.12.38	Cervera	2. Staffel	Rata	1
277	Ltn.	Bretnütz	28.12.38	Igualada	2. Staffel	Martin-Bomber	2
278	Ltn.	Redlich	28.12.38	Cervera	2. Staffel	Martin-Bomber	1
279	Ltn.	Ensslen	29.12.38	Cervera	2. Staffel	Rata	5
280	Ltn.	Lippert	29.12.38	Lerida	3. Staffel	Curtiss	5
281	Obltn.	v. Bonin	29.12.38	Lerida	3. Staffel	Rata	1
282	Uffz.	Freund	29.12.38	Lerida	3. Staffel	Rata	2
283	Ltn.	Tietzen	9.12.38	Lerida	1. Staffel	Rata	3
284	Obltn.	Lojewski	30.12.38	Borjas-Blancas	2. Staffel	Curtiss	1
285	Uffz.	Schob	30.12.38	Cervera	2. Staffel	Rata	5
286	Ltn.	Hörmann	30.12.38	Lerida	Stabskomp.	Rata	1
287	Ltn.	Ensslen	30.12.38	Borjas-Blancas	2. Staffel	Rata	6
288	Feldw.	Schott	30.12.38	Borjas-Blancas	2. Staffel	Curtiss	2
289	Ltn.	Schumann	31.12.38	Borjas-Blancas	2. Staffel	Rata	3
290	Feldw.	Schott	31.12.38	Borjas-Blancas	2. Staffel	Rata	3
291	Ltn.	Ensslen	1.1.39	Vals	2. Staffel	Rata	7
292	Hptm.	Grabmann	4.1.39	Mollerosa	Sn.St.J. 88	Curtiss	6
293	Ltn.	Goy	23.1.39	Balaguer	3. Staffel	Rata	1
294	Ltn.	Goy	23.9.38	Balaguer	3. Staffel	Rata	2
295	Obltn.	Ebbighausen	5.1.39	Vendrell	Stabskomp.	Rata	3
296	Obltn.	Ensslen	9.1.39	Vals	2. Staffel	Rata	8
297	Obltn.	v. Bonin	17.1.39	Sabadell	3. Staffel	Rata	1
298	Fhn.	Tonnow	17.1.39	Barcelona	3. Staffel	Rata	2
299	Ltn.	Föds	17.1.39	Sabadell	3. Staffel	Rata	1
300	Oberltn	Müller	17.1.39	Barcelona	3. Staffel	Rata	1
301	Obltn.	Boly	21.1.39	Barcelona	3. Staffel	Curtiss	1
302	Oberltn.	Müller	21.1.39	Barcelona	3. Staffel	Curtiss	2
303	Obltn.	v. Bonin	3.2.39	Figueras	3. Staffel	Curtiss	3
304	Fhn.	Tonnow	3.2.39	Figueras	3. Staffel	Curtiss	2
305	Obltn.	Ensslen	5.2.39	Figueras	2. Staffel	Curtiss	9
306	Hptm.	Reents	6.2.39	Vilajuiga	1. Staffel	Curtiss	1
307	Uffz.	Plemnlnger	6.2.39	Vilajuiga	1. Staffel	Rufkl.	1
308	Uffz.	Halupczok	6.2.39	Vilajuiga	1. Staffel	Curtiss	1

ENDNOTES

PART I

OPERATIONAL HISTORY

1. Winterübung Hansa, Rügen VS 88. *Tagenbericht Nr. 1* (Daily report number 1).

2. Winterübung Hansa, Rügen VS 88. *Bericht über den Unfall des Flugzeuges Bf 109, Werknummer 880 am 9.12.1936* (Report on Accident Involving Bf 109 *Werknummer* 880 on December 9, 1936).

3. Ibid.

4. Ibid.

5. Trautloft, Hannes. *Als Jagdflieger in Spanien*, Albert Nauck & Co., Berlin 1940, pp 164–165.

6. Ibid., p. 167.

7. Winterübung Hansa, Rügen VS 88. *Tagenbericht Nr. 11*.

8. Trautloft. *Als Jagdflieger in Spanien*, pp. 167–169.

9. Ibid., pp. 174–175.

10. Ibid., p. 182.

11. Ibid., pp. 183–184.

12. Ibid., p. 186.

13. Ibid., pp. 186–187.

14. Ibid., p. 227.

15. Versuchskommando VK/88, February 23, 1937: *Bericht über den Absturz der Bf 109 V3 mit Leutnant Rehahn am 11.2.37 in Caceres.*

16. Trautloft. *Als Jagdflieger in Spanien*, pp. 231–233.

17. *Legion Condor S/88: Technischer Erfahrungsbericht an der Bf 109 Nr. 3 in der Zeit vom 16. Februar bis 30. April 1937*, p. 2. The V6 was obviously not assigned an aircraft number before its crash. Thus, while the V3 and V4 were assigned the numbers 6 • 1 and 6 • 2, the number 6 • 3 was given to the first Bf 109 A to be assembled at Seville.

18. The daily reports submitted by VK/88 and VJ/88 reveal the dates on which the Bf 109 V4 and the fourteen Bf 109 A fighters were sent to 2.J/88 at the front:

6 • 1 (Bf 109 V4)	March 14	(to Almorox)
6 • 3 (Bf 109 A)	March 14	(to Almorox)
6 • 4	" March 14	(to Almorox)
6 • 5	" March 31	(to Vitoria)
6 • 6	" April 7	(to Vitoria)
6 • 7	" April 7	(to Vitoria)
6 • 8	" March 30	(to Vitoria)
6 • 9	" April 4	(to Vitoria)
6 • 10	" April 29	(to Vitoria)
6 • 11	" March 30	(to Vitoria)
6 • 12	" March 20	(to Almorox)
6 • 13	" March 15	(to Almorox)
6 • 14	" April 16	(to Vitoria)
6 • 15	" March 23	(to Almorox)
6 • 16	" April 16	(to Vitoria)

19. Braatz, Kurt: *Gott oder ein Flugzeug: Leben und Sterben des Jagdfliegers Günther Lützow*, p. 145.

20. Ibid., p. 145.

21. Ries, Karl, and Ring, Hans. *The Legion Condor: A History of the Luftwaffe in the Spanish Civil War, 1936–1939*, translated by David Johnston, Schiffer Military History, 1992, pp. 61–62. Special markings to commemorate this victory were subsequently applied to Bf 109 A 6 • 10, but this aircraft was still at Seville on April 6 and did not go to the front until the 29th of that month. One can only surmise that 6 • 10 was Lützow's aircraft

when the decision was made to apply the special markings, the aircraft in which he actually scored the historic first victory possibly having been lost or removed from service by then.

22. Three aircraft in a vee formation.

23. Braatz. *Gott oder ein Flugzeug. Leben*, p. 157.

24. Ibid., p 157.

25. Ibid., p 157.

26. Ibid., pp. 157–158.

27. Ibid., p. 158.

28. Ibid., p. 162.

29. Ibid., p. 163.

30. Ibid., p. 163.

31. Ries and Ring. *The Legion Condor*, p. 83.

32. Ibid., p. 89.

33. Ibid., pp. 91–92.

34. Beevor, Anthony. *The Battle for Spain*. London: Weidenfeld & Nicolson, 2006, pp. 297–299.

35. Ries and Ring. *The Legion Condor,* pp. 97–98.

36. Bley, Wulf. *Das Buch der Spanienflieger*. Leipzig: Hafe & Koehler Verlag, 1939, pp. 149–150.

37. Ries and Ring. *The Legion Condor*, p. 113.

38. Beevor. *The Battle for Spain*, pp. 315–322.

39. Bley, Wulf. *Das Buch der Spanienflieger*, Leipzig: Hafe & Koehler Verlag, 1939, pp. 151–152.

40. Ries and Ring. *The Legion Condor*, p. 115.

41. Ibid., p. 116.

42. Bley. *Das Buch der Spanienflieger*, p. 240.

43. Ibid., pp. 152–155.

44. Ibid., pp. 241–244.

45. Möbius, Ingo. *Am Himmel Europas: Der Jagdflieger Günther Scholz erinnert sich*. Chemnitz, Germany: Eigenverlag Ingo Möbius, 2009, pp. 68–73.

46. Beevor. *The Battle for Spain*, p. 344.

47. Ries and Ring. *The Legion Condor*, p. 130.

48. Ibid., p. 136.

49. Möbius, Ingo. *Am Himmel Europas*, p. 84.

50. Ries and Ring. *The Legion Condor*, p. 128.

51. Beevor. *The Battle for Spain*, p. 327.

52. Bley. *Das Buch der Spanienflieger*, pp. 156–157.

53. According to Legion Condor situation report 541 of July 20, 1938, twenty-two Bf 109s arrived from Germany.

54. Forell, Fritz von. *Mölders und seine Männer*. Graz, Austria: Steirische Verlagsanstalt Graz, 1941, p. 39.

55. Bley. *Das Buch der Spanienflieger*, pp. 97–101.

56. Forell. *Mölders und seine Männer*, pp. 40–41.

57. Ibid., pp. 43–44.

58. Ibid., p. 44.

59. Ibid., pp. 45–46.

60. Beevor. *The Battle for Spain*, p. 349.

61. Forell. *Mölders und seine Männer*, pp. 49–50.

62. Ibid., p. 49.

63. Ibid., p. 51.

64. Ries and Ring. *The Legion Condor*, p. 181.

65. Ibid., p. 183.

66. Ibid., p. 185.

67. Möbius, Ingo. *Am Himmel Europas*, pp. 103–107.

68. Forell, Fritz von. *Mölders und seine Männer*. Berlin: Verlag Scherl, 1941, pp. 32–33.

69. Forell. *Mölders und seine Männer*. Graz, Austria: Steirische Verlagsanstalt Graz, 1941, pp. 52–54.

70. Forell. *Mölders und seine Männer*. Berlin: Verlag Scherl, 1941, p. 33.

71. Ries and Ring. *The Legion Condor*, p. 188.

72. Forell. *Mölders und seine Männer*. Graz, Austria: Steirische Verlagsanstalt Graz, 1941, pp. 66–67.

73. Fözö, Josef. *Freie Jagd von Madrid bis Moskau: Ein Fliegerleben mit Mölders*. Berlin: Verlag Wehrfront Alfred Becker, 1943, pp. 55–59.

74. Forell. *Mölders und seine Männer*. Graz, Austria: Steirische Verlagsanstalt Graz, 1941, pp. 67–68.

75. Ibid., pp. 68–69.

76. Ries and Ring. *The Legion Condor*, p. 196.

77. Fözö. *Freie Jagd von Madrid*, pp. 74–78.

78. Forell. *Mölders und seine Männer*. Graz, Austria: Steirische Verlagsanstalt Graz, 1941, pp. 71–72.

79. Möbius, Ingo. *Am Himmel Europas*, pp. 108–109.

80. Mölders scored his last victory on November 3 but did not in fact leave Spain until early December. He was relieved as *Kapitän* of 3rd *Staffel* on December 5, 1938.

81. Fözö. *Freie Jagd von Madrid*, pp. 74–78.

82. Ries and Ring claim that Fözö scored his first victory on September 18, but since Fözö himself writes that it took place on October 31, the latter seems more likely. Interestingly, unlike the victory list in Ries and Ring, the one from the estate of Georg Fleischmann (see appendix 3) also lists Fözö's first victory as having taken place on October 31.

83. Fözö. *Freie Jagd von Madrid*, pp. 83–84.

84. Fleischmann combat reports for October 31, 1938.

85. Forell. *Mölders und seine Männer*. Graz, Austria: Steirische Verlagsanstalt Graz, 1941, pp. 76–77.

86. The Republicans received thirty-one examples of the I-15bis (I-152) "Super Chato" in December 1938, too late to have been the aircraft described by Mölders. Josef Fözö described the unidentified type as "neither a Rata nor a Curtiss. It is a new type, fast and sleek, fast, much faster than the Rata." There has been speculation that the Soviets sent prototypes of the Polikarpov I-153 to Spain and that these may have been the aircraft met by Mölders and his pilots, but as of yet there is no conclusive evidence of this (see online article by James B. Haycraft at www.axishistory.com/axis-nations/141-germany-legion-condor/legion-condor/4323-on-the-polikarpov-i-153-in-spain).

87. Fözö. *Freie Jagd von Madrid*, pp. 79–82.

88. Ibid., pp. 94–97.

89. Forell. *Mölders und seine Männer*. Graz, Austria: Steirische Verlagsanstalt Graz, 1941, pp. 79–80.

90. Fözö. *Freie Jagd von Madrid*, pp. 106–107.

91. Beevor. *The Battle for Spain*, p. 368.

92. Fözö. *Freie Jagd von Madrid*, pp. 108–109.

93. Ibid., pp. 110–111.

94. Ibid., pp. 116–117.

95. Ibid., pp. 120–122.

96. Ibid., pp. 124–126.

97. Ibid., pp. 142–144.

98. Cerda, Juan Arraez. *L'aviation de chasse de la République espagnol, 1936–1939*. Boulogne-sur-Mer, France: Éditions Lela Presse, 1995, pp. 72–73.

99. Ibid., p. 73.

PART II

MESSERSCHMITT BF 109 VARIANTS IN SPAIN

1. Radinger, Willy, and Walter Schick. *Messerschmitt Bf 109 A-E: Development, Testing, Production*. Translated by David Johnston. Atglen, PA: Schiffer, 1999, pp. 31–34.

2. *Versuchskommando VK/88: Technischer Erfahrungsbericht an Fluggerät VK/88 in der Zeit von 1.12.36 bis 15.1.37*, p. 4. The author of the report wrote that the V3 was fitted with a "Schwarz three-blade variable-pitch propeller," but photographs show that it was in fact a two-blade unit.

3. *Versuchskommando VK/88: Bericht über den Absturz der Bf 109 V3 mit Leutnant Rehahn am 11.2.1937 in Caceres*, February 23, 1937.

4. The Spanish-Moroccan Transport Company (in Spanish: Companía Hispano-Marroquí de Transporte, or HISMA). It was set up by the Germans soon after the July 1936 decision to send aid to Franco. Based in Spanish Morocco, it served as a cover for Germany to give arms to Spain in exchange for Spanish goods and raw materials.

5. Radinger and Schick. *Messerschmitt Bf 109 A-E*, p. 35.

6. Ibid., p. 44.

7. Winterübung Hansa Rügen VS 88. *Bericht über den Unfall des Flugzeuges Bf 109 Werknummer 880 am 9.12.1936*, December 19, 1936.

8. Radinger and Schick. *Messerschmitt Bf 109 A-E*, p. 34. The daily reports submitted by VK/88 identify the *Werknummer* of three of the Bf 109 As delivered to Spain:
   1005: aircraft 6 ● 12, delivered March 6, 1937.
   1006: aircraft 6 ● 13, delivered March 6, 1937.
   1000: aircraft 6 ● 15, delivered March 6, 1937.
   All three of these *Werknummer* can be found in the Messerschmitt Bf 109 A production list in the above title.

9. See appendix 1.

10. Revi 3a Handbook.

11. Prien, Jochen, Gerhard Stemmer, Peter Rodeike, and Winfried Bock. *Die Jagdfliegerverbände der Deutschen Luftwaffe 1934 bis 1945: Teil I Vorkriegszeit und Einsatz über Polen; 1934 bis 1939*. Eutin, Germany: Struve's Buchdruckerei und Verlag, 2000, p. 34.

12. The Bf 109 B, C, and D (and presumably the A) all could be fitted with a wooden or a metal propeller. Installation of the wooden propeller required the removal of a ballast weight in the tail.

13. Prien, Stemmer, Rodeike, and Bock. *Die Jagdfliegerverbände der Deutschen Luftwaffe*, p. 37.

14. Prien, Stemmer, Rodeike, and Bock. *Die Jagdfliegerverbände der Deutschen Luftwaffe*, p. 41.

PART III
CAMOUFLAGE SCHEMES APPLIED TO BF 109S OF THE LEGION CONDOR

1. *Legion Condor S/88: Technischer Erfahrungsbericht an der Bf 109 Nr. 3 in der Zeit vom 16. Februar bis 30. April 1937*, p 1.
   General: Fourteen new Bf 109 aircraft arrived during this reporting period. With the three aircraft delivered the previous November, a total of seventeen have now been received; one aircraft (V6) was destroyed in December while being test-flown and was cannibalized here. Another (V3) crashed near Caceres on February 11, 1937, while being flown by *Leutnant* Rehahn and was scrapped.

2. *Legion Condor S/88: Erfahrungsbericht über Bf 109*, January 1938, p. 8.
   Camouflage: Both the silver-white (*silberweiss*) and dark-green camouflage colors have proved effective. Since one Bf 109 *Staffel* has only just begun flying with the dark-green camouflage and the other with *silberweiss* base color, further conclusions will not be possible until later.

3. Fözö. *Freie Jagd von Madrid*, p. 47: "The indicator moves to 0740. For a long time I have been sitting in my silver-gray bird, which trembles as if keeping pace with the beating of my heart."

4. Ritger, Lynn. *The Messerschmitt Bf 109: A Comprehensive Guide for the Modeller*. Part 1, *Prototype to "E" Variants*. Bedford, UK: SAM Publications, 2005, pp. 79–80.

BIBLIOGRAPHY

BOOKS

Beevor, Antony. *The Battle for Spain*. London: Weidenfeld & Nicholson, 2006.

Bley, Hauptmann Wulf. *Das Buch der Spanienflieger*. Leipzig: Hafe & Koehler Verlag.

Cerda, Juan Arraez. *L'aviation de chasse de la République espagnole, 1936–1939*. Boulogne-sur-Mer, France: Éditions Lela Presse, 1995.

Forrell, *Major* Fritz von. *Mölders und seine Männer*. Graz, Austria: Steierische Verlagsanstalt, 1941a.

Forrell, *Major* Fritz von. *Mölders und seine Männer*. Berlin: Verlag Scherl, 1941b.

Fözö, *Major* Josef. *Freie Jagd von Madrid bis Moskau: Ein Fliegerleben mit Mölders*. Berlin: Verlag Wehrfront Alfred Becker, 1943.

Howson, Gerald. *Aircraft of the Spanish Civil War, 1936–1939*. London: Putnam Aeronautical Books, 1990.

Möbius, Ingo. *Am Himmel Europas: Der Jagdflieger Günther Scholz erinnert sich*. Chemnitz, Germany: Eigenverlag Ingo Möbius, 2009.

Mombeek, Eric, J. Richard Smith, and Eddie J. Creek. *Jagdwaffe*. Vol., 1, Section 2, *The Spanish Civil War*. East Sussex, UK: Classic Publications, 1999.

Obermaier, Ernst. *Die Ritterkreuzträger der Luftwaffe 1939–1945*. Vol. I, *Jagdflieger*. Mainz, Germany: Verlag Dieter Hoffmann, 1989.

Ries, Karl, and Hans Ring. *Legion Condor, 1936–1939: Eine illustrierte Dokumentation*. Mainz, Germany: Verlag Dieter Hoffmann, 1980.

Ritger, Lynn. *The Messerschmitt Bf 109: A Comprehensive Guide for the Modeller*. Part 1, *Prototype to "E" Variants*. Bedford, UK: SAM Publications, 2005.

Traufloft, Hannes. *Als Jagdflieger in Spanien*. Berlin: Albert Nauch, 1940.

DOCUMENTS

Daily Reports No. 1 to No. 160/61 submitted by Winterübung Hansa Rügen VS 88, Versuchskommando VK/88, and Versuchskommando VJ/88, December 5, 1936, to May 14, 1937.

Fleischmann, Georg. *Combat Reports, Victory Confirmation, J/88 Victory List*.

Legion Condor Ia Memorandum. *Triebwerksstörungen an Bf 109*, March 20, 1937.

Legion Condor S/88, Abt. Ia. *Erfahrungsbericht über Bf 109*, December 1937.

Legion Condor S/88, Abt. Ia. *Technischer Erfahrungsbericht an der Bf 109 Nr. 3 in der Zeit von 16. Februar bis 30. April 1937*, May 1, 1937.

Memorandum from Joachim von Richthofen 2, Dipl. Ing., to S/88, Abt. Ia. *Störungen an der Bf 109*, May 31, 1937.

Telex to S/88 Ia, *Betrag: Bf 109*, March 8, 1937.

Versuchskommando VK/88. *Bericht über den Absturz der Bf 109 V3 mit Leutnant Rehahn am 11.2.1937 in Caceres*, February 23, 1937.

Versuchskommando VK/88. *Technischer Erfahrungsbericht an Fluggerät VK/88 in der Zeit von 1.12.36 bis 15.1.37*.

Winterübung Hansa Rügen VS 88. *Tätigkeitsbericht von 1. bis 4.12.1936*, December 5, 1936.

Winterübung Hansa Rügen VS 88. *Berichtswesen VS 88*, December 8, 1936.

Winterübung Hansa Rügen VS 88. *Wochenbericht Nr. 2 von 5. bis 12.12.1936*, December 13, 1936.

Winterübung Hansa Rügen VS 88. *Bericht über den Unfall des Flugzeuges Bf 109 Werknummer 880 am 9.12.1936*, December 19, 1936.

GERMAN EAGLES IN SPANISH SKIES